GODDESS SITES: *Europe*

Also by Anneli S. Rufus and Kristan Lawson

America Off The Wall: The West Coast

Europe Off The Wall

Discover Places

Where the Goddess Has

Been Celebrated and Worshipped Throughout Time

GODDESS SITES: Europe

Anneli S. Rufus and
Kristan Lawson

HarperSanFrancisco
A Division of HarperCollins*Publishers*

FIRST EDITION

Library of Congress Cataloging-in-Publication Data

Rufus, Anneli S.
Goddess sites, Europe : discover places where the Goddess has been celebrated and worshipped throughout time / Anneli S. Rufus and Kristan Lawson. — 1st ed.
p. cm.
Includes bibliographical references and index.
ISBN 0–06–250747–8 (alk. paper)
1. Sacred space—Europe. 2. Goddesses—Europe. 3. Religion, Prehistoric—Europe. 4. Religion, Primitive—Europe. 5. Cults—Europe. 6. Shrines—Europe
I. Lawson, Kristan. II. Title.

BL581.E85R84 1991 90-55308
291.3′5′094—dc20 CIP

---

91 92 93 94 95 RRD(H) 10 9 8 7 6 5 4 3 2 1

This edition is printed on acid-free paper that meets the American National Standards Institute Z39.48 Standard.

Contents

Acknowledgments

The authors are deeply grateful to the Austrian National Tourist Office; the Belgian Office of Tourism; the Consulate General of the Republic of Malta; the Netherlands National Tourist Board (VVV); KLM Royal Dutch Airlines; National Express; Mr. D. Hudson Frew; Ms. Mara Keller; Mr. Barry Drees; the Barbarae: Moulton and Archer . . . and Her.

General Introduction

The sultry Seine, along whose banks you saunter, a shower of croissant crumbs gilding your chest, was once the domain of a goddess. That traffic-choked Roman intersection had its goddess, too. So did that mountain, that bay, that cliff, that grotto, that well, that grove, that country lane, and oh yes, that cathedral. Goddesses, goddesses, everywhere: For thousands of years, Europe was utterly theirs. In temples and wayside shrines, hearths and naked hillsides, the peoples of Europe worshipped goddesses.

Where are they now? Some, like Athena of the Parthenon, are well remembered. Yet legions of their sisters, though less familiar, still swirl and roar along the byways of Europe. They tug at your sleeve as you cross their paths. They lean close and whisper their names in your ear. These are names that once made mortals tremble and sigh, great names that could raise thunder, win wars, and save sinking ships.

This book remembers their names, all those goddesses of love, poetry, forest, fortune; of the moon, milk, the sea, and death; of bread and blood, sewers and sex. By putting the goddesses into context and telling exactly how to find them, we put them and their worship sites back on the map. These sites, now as ever, are places of wonder, reverence, joy, reunion, revelation, mystery. Each site is a sharp and bright sliver of our own spiritual heritage.

Goddesses were here from the very beginning. No sooner did women and men begin to savor the blush on the pear, the gleam on the wheat, the phases of the year, the moon, the sea, and women's bellies, than they recognized their Mother. Europe's oldest shrines are hers. The first sculptures crafted by human hands are unmistakable portraits of her.

Each culture interpreted her in its own way. Stone Age people drew their goddess huge and nurturing. The sensuous Minoans put snakes into her hands. The hotheaded Celts set their goddesses on horseback and into deep rivers and told tales of them stalking the countryside in search of lovers. The classical Greeks made theirs intellectuals; Rome's goddesses were versatile and easily bribed. Goddesses from distant lands wandered in and settled down, bringing new incense, exotic rites, and richly brown complexions.

We have left some goddesses' stories unwritten, some shrines unmapped. Space does not permit us to include every one, so gingerly we chose the 150 most compelling, most powerful, most diverse, and most accessible sites from among a wealth of possibilities. The Scandinavian countries are absent from this volume because, after much research and deliberation, we had to bow to the prerogative of the Vikings and other ancient Scandinavians, who preferred not to build the kind of permanent temple structures whose ruins might survive to this day, and whose climate and culture, more than those of the rest of Europe, lent themselves to a notably masculine pantheon.

The goddesses of Europe are key characters in European history, as real and colorful as any heroes or monarchs, far more influential than some. Goddess sites, along with goddess legends, goddess lore, and goddess rituals, are a world unto themselves, a world half hidden but always lingering, waiting, patient. As long as Europeans continue to venerate, in whatever form, the female-as-sacred; as long as the shrines and temples still stand, beckoning us inside, moving us perhaps in spite of ourselves to startled reverent tears and strange dreams, then the goddesses of Europe will remain as radiant as ever, as immanent, as close.

Austria

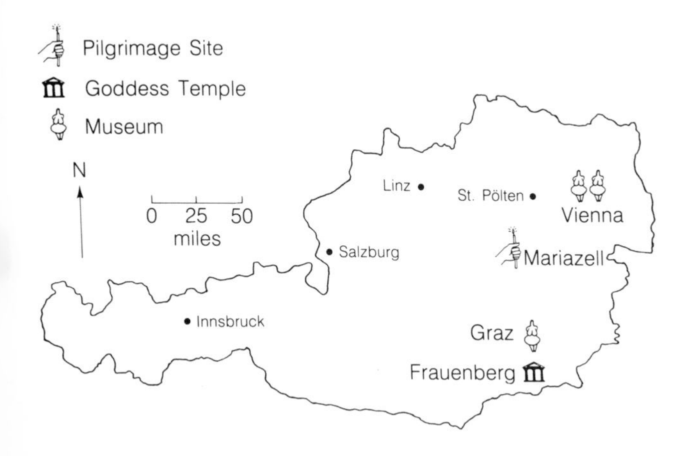

Even if Austria were not beautiful, even if its crystalline air were not laced with the perfumes of mountain pine and *kaffee mocha*, even if Vienna had no opera, no Lippizan stallions, and no Sachertorte, you'd still be duty-bound to go there.

It's a matter of seniority. Twenty-five thousand years ago, some ancient Austrian, in a moment of inspiration, carved a tiny statue of a robust woman. Rediscovered in 1908, the figure was dubbed "The Venus of Willendorf" and gained instant fame as the world's oldest image of a goddess. As if this were not enough to clinch Austria's position as the *Mutterland* for all modern goddess-seekers, an even more ancient stone carving, believed by archaeologists to represent a "dancing goddess," was found here in 1988.

Wandering tribes, dictators, yodelers, and emperors have all traipsed across Austria in the 30 millennia since those statues were carved. Some of the finest known examples of Bronze Age Celtic artwork were unearthed near Hallstatt, a lakeside dream of a village where folk traditions are still going strong and where the decorated skulls of the dead—the *recent* dead—are prominently displayed in the chapel.

But before all of this came the Old Ones, the *oldest* ones. For their sake, go to Austria. And *go ahead*: They won't mind if you taste that Sachertorte.

Frauenberg

Temple of Isis-Noreia

Finding Isis in Austria is like running into your mother at the dragstrip. Her calm eyes meet your surprised ones. One cool hand smooths your forehead and another one proffers a glass of water.

Well, you could hardly expect Isis to stay put in Egypt, could you? In her native land she was called The Great Virgin, the Mother of God, Exceeding Queen. Her followers, to whom Isis was mother, doctor, navigator, inventor, magician, and inspiration, carried her rites and legends with them wherever they wandered. Egyptian traders introduced Isis to Rome, and from there she traveled along with the expanding empire to many far-flung places, where she became as natural a fixture as if she had been born there—in this case, among chilly mountain peaks—instead of in the humid, crocodile-ridden Nile valley. A sea and river goddess, she was as readily adaptable as water. A moon goddess, she could show many different faces.

At her temple here on Frauenberg, the tantalizingly named "women's mountain," the goddess was worshipped under the title Isis-Noreia. When the Romans arrived here in the first century C.E., with Isis in tow, they found that the local Celtic tribe, the Noriker, had long revered their own tutelary goddess, Noreia. Noreia's popularity has been proven over and over by archaeological finds in this region. She was a mother goddess and much more. Her blessing safeguarded farming, metalsmithing, handicrafts, and all kinds of art; she represented fertility, fruitfulness, the earth, life, and death. She was supreme, all-embracing. However, with the arrival of the Romans, the Celts lost much of their independence and thus their cultural vitality. As their star faded, so did Noreia's. But the Romans were enthralled with her nevertheless. To bolster her sagging powers, they quickly merged her—as was their habit—with their own supreme, all-embracing adopted goddess, Isis. Thus Isis-Noreia was formed.

While the Celts had always celebrated Noreia's rites outdoors on the mountainside, the Romans were only happy worshipping among stone walls, so they built a temple to Isis-Noreia. (They built a second one nearby, on the hill called Ulrichsberg, near present-day Klagenfurt.) There she dwelt, in all her double-barreled glory, for several hundred years, enjoying the delirious praise and adoration that were unique to her religion.

Zealous Christians methodically demolished the temple sometime in late antiquity. Isis's followers had long ago credited their goddess with claiming to be "the one true and living god," that "whatever deities the nations worship are but manifestations" of her. So perhaps she smiled a little when, over her ruined shrine, a baroque convent and school were summarily erected. It is this baroque edifice that houses the Tempelmuseum today, displaying the artifacts of Isis-Noreia. Outside, you can wander among the temple's foundations, the sacrificial basins, the fountains, and the shell-shaped apsis that once held a statue of the goddess.

Isis in Austria? Isis in dirndl? Why not?

Getting there: Museum open April to October, daily, 10 A.M. to noon and 3 to 5 P.M. Admission: AS 10; children AS 5. The temple ruins outside the museum are always open and free to explore. Frauenberg is 1 mile southwest of Leibnitz, which is 20 miles south of Graz. The temple is at Seggauberg 17. Frauenberg is a very small village, and because the temple is on a hill, it isn't hard to find. The museum is in the school building on the temple grounds.

Mariazell

Black Madonna of Mariazell

Austria, for all its charm, is a many-headed hydra. Everybody knows it as a pristine, Alpine land, where rosy-cheeked hikers burst suddenly into choruses of "The hills are alive. . . ." And yet everybody knows Austria, too, as a bastion of urbane refinement, in whose rococo parlors Mozart performed for royalty. Austria is also a land of paprika and violins: a bridge between East and West.

Reigning over Austria's virtual goulash of intermingled identitites is Our Lady of Mariazell. Like Peter Pan's capable Wendy, she has quite a job: to be mother to all the different Austrias, and of course all the different Austrians.

She is called Great Mother of Austria, Great Lady of the Hungarians, *and* Mother of the Slav People. Over 1 million people visit her every year. Middle-class Tyroleans in lederhosen and knee socks kneel at her shining altar alongside shy Czechs in plaid nylon blazers.

This madonna matured along with Austria itself. At the height of the Hapsburg Empire, affairs of state were laid humbly at her feet, and kings and emperors quailed before her, begging for favors. (What's a mother to do?) Yet she began life as a simple country girl, a rustic forest dweller, a bumpkin to whom emperors would probably not vouchsafe so much as the time of day. According to the legend, Magnus, a Benedictine monk, decided to retire from urban life and establish a church in the Austrian wilderness. In 1157, he carried this limewood statue of Mary with him as he wandered through the trackless mountains in search of a suitable spot for his ministry. During his roamings, whenever the way was blocked by natural obstacles such as fallen logs or boulders, he asked the Virgin to clear them away, and (according to the legend) she quickly complied. So Our Lady of Mariazell was, early on, a powerful mistress of nature and wild things. Rocks and trees did her bidding.

Magnus found a place he liked and ceremoniously placed the wooden statue in the branches of a linden tree. The statue had already gained a word-of-mouth reputation and was soon an object of pilgrimage for shepherds and hunters and other denizens of the forest. A chapel was respectfully erected around the tree, and then a church, and then a monastic abbey.

Everyone has heard about how Lana Turner was "discovered" by a talent scout one day in Schwab's. Our Lady of Mariazell had a similar windfall, except that her talent scout was a monarch. One night in 1366, during a dream in which he was battling his erstwhile enemies, the Turks, King Louis the Great of Hungary saw Our Lady of Mariazell, who carefully instructed him how to win. Later, following her advice, he won the real-life war against the Turks, and in gratitude he erected a golden chapel in the madonna's honor. (By now the place was called Mariazell, "Maria's cell.") From that day on, she became the darling of Hapsburg rulers, and she is credited with saving their empire from France in 1673, among other political miracles. Austria's beloved Empress Maria Theresa is among the nobles who donated rich adornments to the chapel.

When doling out miracles, however, Our Lady of Mariazell is no snob. Throughout the centuries, humble pilgrims and country folk as well as nobles flocked to the chapel in huge numbers. Indulgences were dispensed here from 1330 onward. Town records from 1390 reveal the existence of no less than 23 religious souvenir shops, at a time when the number of houses in Mariazell was only 71. On a single day in 1599, the records show, 23,000 pilgrims converged on the town. Even in those days, the madonna's multicultural brood encompassed pilgrims from Switzerland, Italy, Bavaria, Bohemia, Moravia, Poland, Prussia, Silesia, Croatia, Hungary, France, and of course all parts of what is now Austria.

Today's crop of pilgrims, still international, kneels in rapt silence before an altar ablaze with gold and silver. This madonna's many friends in high places have left their mark, and the result is an intimidating blizzard of shiny cupids, columns, clouds, stars, hearts, and aggressively jagged solar rays. In the heart of it all stands the statue, just 19 inches tall. Her brown features, blunted by the centuries, look endearingly homely amid these blazing surroundings. A brocade and lace gown, one of 18 in the madonna's wardrobe, billows about her tiny form. One is not sure whether the madonna looks more like Old Mother Hubbard suddenly made queen-for-a-day, or like an adolescent princess at her own birthday party. Certainly this church, with its waves and waves of bright white frosting-like architectural details, looks like a huge birthday cake.

She is tiny, but those brown hands, that brown face, mean a million things to a million people. Austria will always need its mother.

Getting there: Open daily, 6 A.M. to 10 P.M. Admission free. Mariazell is 85 miles southwest of Vienna and 45 miles south of St. Pölten, from which it is serviced by train. The church is in the center of town on Hauptplatz. The black madonna is in the Chapel of Grace in the center of the church.

Goddesses in Captivity: Museums

Graz: Schloss Eggenberg Museum "Where's that goddess going?" That's what all the archaeologists have been wondering ever since a certain bronze artifact was discovered in a 2600-year-old grave near Strettweg, Austria. The artifact, which has since become famous as "the Strettweg Wagon," depicts a group of people and animals gathered around a tall goddess (everyone acknowledges her as such) on board a flat bargelike vehicle whose huge wheels bear them—somewhere, for some goddess-y purpose. The Strettweg Wagon fascinates scholars because its slender goddess strongly resembles contemporary Greek sculpture, yet its horses, deer, and stags (are they meant as symbols or sacrifices?) are clearly Celtic in style. It's got everybody theorizing about who lived in Austria in the seventh century B.C.E. and whom they worshipped. And, scholarship aside, art lovers croon over the wagon's beautiful craftsmanship.

Getting there: Open February through November, daily, 9 A.M. to 1 P.M. and 2 to 5 P.M. Admission: AS 25; students free. The museum is in Schloss Eggenberg, which is at Eggenberger Allee 90, at the far western side of town.

Vienna: Ephesus Museum Ephesus was a community on the shores of what is now Turkey, where the goddess Artemis reigned supreme. But the divinity so well loved in Ephesus bore little resemblance to the athletic Artemis known in Greece and elsewhere in the Mediterranean world. With 17 breasts (count 'em!) ranging down her front like so many wasps' nests, Artemis of Ephesus was a nurturing mother as well as a mistress of the beasts. Seagoing Ephesians introduced her to towns as far away as Marseille and beyond. St. Paul, on his proselytizing journey westward, had one heck of a hard time in Ephesus. Suave international types are always turning up in Vienna; Artemis of Ephesus is one of them. While one of the most famous statues of her is now in Naples (see the Naples discussion in the Italy chapter), many smaller terracotta versions can be found here in Vienna, as can various other artifacts of her temple and sanctuary in Ephesus and a diverse collection of mother-goddess figures from Asia Minor.

Getting there: Open Monday and Wednesday to Friday, 10 A.M. to 4 P.M.; Saturday and Sunday, 9 A.M. to 4 P.M.; closed Tuesday. Admission: AS 30. The museum is at 1, Neue Burg, behind the Prince Eugene statue on Heldenplatz.

Vienna: Naturhistorisches Museum (Museum of Natural History) Of those many Stone Age figurines that depict full, rounded female bodies, the most famous of all is the so-called Venus of Willendorf (mentioned earlier). Found at Willendorf, near Krems, Austria (a large replica of the Venus now marks the site, though nothing remains of the dig), this statuette now lives in Vienna's Museum of Natural History. The 25,000-year-old statuette, with tiny, slim arms tucked neatly over lush breasts and a round belly, is a 6-inch miracle of symmetry and detail. Check out her winsomely dimpled back.

Over a dozen more primitive female figurines are also on display at this museum. Our nominee for first runner-up in the Stone Age beauty pageant is the graceful

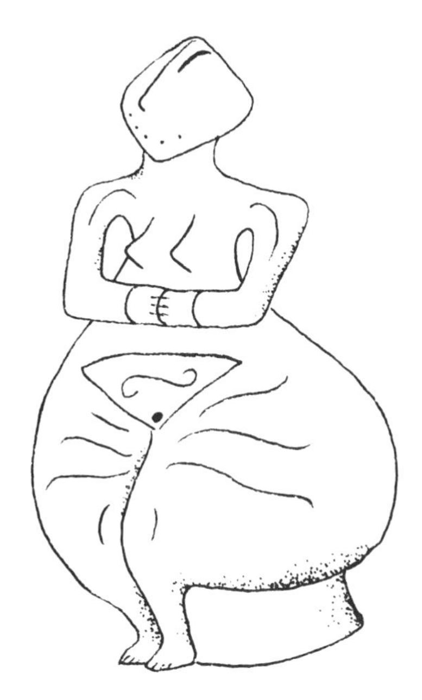

The Seated Lady of Pazardzik, Vienna's Naturhistorisches Museum

Seated Lady of Pazardzik, an almost whimsical figure found in Bulgarian Thrace, whose very interesting head makes her look as if she has just eaten a violin.

The museum is proud of its recent acquisition of a 2.8-inch carving, also found near Krems. Dubbed "the Dancing Venus of Galgenberg," it is hailed as the world's oldest female figurine, clocking in at 32,000 years old. But the slender figure, while possessing legs and what might pass for a head, has an otherwise somewhat vague physique that led at least one archaeological intern, whom we met in the museum, to blurt, "What is this thing growing out of its back? Where are its breasts? I think it's a man." Decide for yourself.

Getting there: Open Wednesday to Monday, 9 A.M. to 6 P.M.; closed Tuesday. Admission: AS 30; students AS 15. The museum is at 1, Maria-Theresien-Platz, in the building on your right when entering the plaza from the Burg-Ring. Most of the goddess figurines are in Room 11.

Belgium

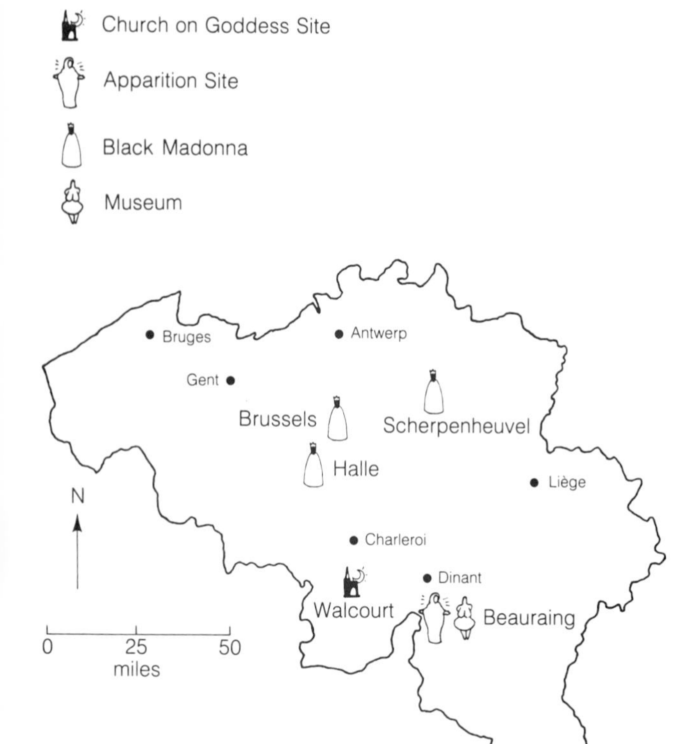

Belgium has a capacity for spirituality that puts all of its neighbors to shame. Oceans of faith sweep across this country. In Belgium, radiant ladies have materialized out of thin air and whispered secrets—not once, not twice, but dozens of times, in Beauraing and in Banneux. In Belgium we find the town of Gheel, whose inhabitants take insane lodgers into their homes, out of devotion to the obscure St. Dympna, patroness of mental illness. The people have faith in the healing powers of prayer and family life, and the result is a town entirely populated by the mad and the hopeful. Also in Belgium we find no fewer than 10 black madonnas. Their anomalous dusky faces peer out of a time and place that are far, far away, yet they offer a solace and a wisdom and a power that sustains thousands of modern Belgians.

This was once a pagan, Celtic land, whose reigning deities were those of the natural places, like the goddess Arduina, who ruled the Ardennes forest. The early Belgians, true to ancient northern European form, preferred to worship outdoors. Later, after the advent of Christianity, Belgium was the scene of terrible witch-hunts. This dark chapter of the country's history is remembered in annual events called "witch festivals" (*heksenfeest*), in which villagers stream down the streets in wigs and beak-nosed masks, howling all the way. The average Belgian schoolchild today is less concerned about what the Catholics did to the witches than about what the Protestants did, some time later, to the Catholics. The "Calvinist fury of 1566" found mobs of heresy-hating Protestants streaming into Catholic churches, smashing up furniture and artworks. This holy civil war lasted 80 years, during which time cities were burned to the ground and thousands were slaughtered. (Tales are still told about savagely mutilated monks.) The result is the divided Belgium of today, with Dutch-speaking Protestant Flanders in the north and French-speaking Catholic Wallonia in the south.

Belgian pastures and beaches were the killing fields of World Wars I and II. And so modern times have brought blood, blood, and more blood, and so faith and more faith. The goddesses of field and forest were long ago transformed into other mother-figures, who linger on in their stead. To take on this beleaguered country, they must be made of strong stuff indeed.

Beauraing

Marian Apparitions and Museum

On December 8, 1932 (the Feast of the Immaculate Conception), five children were startled to see a white-gowned woman, softly glowing, floating in the air above Beauraing's railroad bridge. "It's the Virgin!" the Catholic children all thought in unison, dropping in ecstasy to the ground. As soon as they were able, the children ran and told the convent nuns what—or whom—they had seen. They believed that they would see her again, and they did. By December 12, some 12,000 spectators had gathered in Beauraing to watch them watching her. Over the next several weeks, the lady appeared some 30 times, no longer over the bridge but poised in a hawthorn tree on the convent grounds. Of all the assembled people, only the five children could see the lady, and of these, only the four youngest could see and hear her with regularity. With each visit, she spoke more and more tenderly to the children. She told them "ordinary things," the children reported—the children who, rather than become nuns and priests, lived on to become "ordinary" homemakers in Beauraing. "Be brave," she advised them in French. "Be good. Be sage." By January 3, 1933, there were 30,000 spectators. "Do you love me?" the lady asked the children. Assured that they did, she said goodbye—forever.

And what did this do to Beauraing? Village of the sweet clear air, languishing among the sparsely peopled southern forests, Beauraing had been a minor pilgrimage spot even before the apparitions. (An old statue of Mary was venerated there.) Now, after the visions, the pilgrimages grew. But Beauraing never became a Belgian Lourdes. Today, only two souvenir shops, decorous and tasteful, are enough to meet the needs of the small but steady trickle of pilgrims who come to see the simple outdoor shrine. A statue stands at the foot of the hawthorn tree in which the children saw the lady. The statue's face wears the unfortunate simper of which early twentieth century religious sculptors were so fond. The arms are held apart to reveal Mary's golden heart, which is the way the children claimed to have seen her on her final visit.

The children's adventure in Beauraing, and the lasting aura of piety that it created, left another, quite tangible result that will delight anyone who goes in search of sacredness-as-female. Beauraing's Marian Museum, a by-product of the great events of 1932–1933, is home to hundreds of statues of the Virgin Mary, made in every corner of the world, out of every imaginable material. Though each statue was crafted by Catholic hands, they tell us a lot about how the world envisions holy women, miracle workers, and mothers of god.

Some of the statues are rough-hewn; others, like the French porcelain ones, would not be out of place in the Louvre. One particularly curious specimen has a statue of Mary (made from a child's doll) presiding over a toy wagon and, towering over the wagon, a stuffed hedgehog; it was made by devout Belgian gypsies.

Hundreds of pairs of eyes follow you around the room—ivory eyes, wooden eyes, china, leather, and plastic eyes. They were made in Africa, Japan, Portugal . . . and yet the eyes speak a common language, which is no language at all. The eyes and the hands, which are gentle, compassionate, fierce, protective, laughing, sad, warning, and mourning, tell us all we need to know, all we had suspected all along: a mother of god by any other name is still a mother of god.

Getting there: The shrine and hawthorn tree are always open and visible. Admission free. The opening hours and admission of the museum are not yet set because it was undergoing renovation at the time of writing. Beauraing is 12 miles south of Dinant (from which it can be reached by train), next to the French border, in southern Belgium. The shrine is on rue de l'Eglise, between rue de la Gendarmerie and the railroad bridge. The Musée Marial is across the street from the shrine.

Walcourt

Church on Pagan Goddess Site

Materne is a funny name for a man, even a saintly man. So one can't help but wonder about the St. Materne, bishop of Tongres, who carved this statue out of dark, rich, earth-colored wood and placed it on the altar here at the end of the tenth century. The statue's brown hue, its motherly mien, no doubt echoed those of the pagan deity whose sanctuary had long stood on the site of what is now the Basilica St. Materne. Materne did his job well. He is famous in the local history books as the one who single-handedly Christianized this region, for establishing a Marian shrine on the ruins of some goddess's shrine. Sure enough, that goddess is absolutely unknown today. (Some speculate that St. Materne is totally apocryphal and that "his" name springs from that of the Matronae, a trio of Celtic mother goddesses who were known in this region and beloved throughout the Rhineland, farther south.)

The goddess's wild woods and fertile fields still beckon at the edge of town. The church sponsors nature walks—"*13 kilometres avec Marie*." People come here, as ever, in search of a dark mystical mother who will reach out her healing hands from another world to soothe their pain, mend their bones, cool their fevers. The goddess has gone underground. But her brown successor, Our Lady of Walcourt, has been anything but idle these past thousand years. Countless are the instant healings and other miracles attributed to her. Not the least among these is the story of her escape from an inferno that consumed the shrine in 1220. According to legend, the statue leaped from the flames and came to rest (panting, one assumes) in the branches of a nearby tree. She refused to be taken down until a local nobleman, the Seigneur de Walcourt, crawled to the tree on his hands and knees and vowed to build an abbey on the spot. An annual procession commemorates that event, and the tree scene is duly reenacted.

Some say the smoke from that fire darkened the statue. But she was dark to begin with. On top of that, she was given a silver-plate coating in 1626, which tarnished to a dusky shade and was allowed to stay that way. A silver mask covered the statue's original features, as carved by St. Materne, and it is impossible to say whether the mask is a faithful replica of the original face or whether the features have been altered in some way.

But what features they are! Our Lady of Walcourt looks like no other European madonna, dark or light. A wide, shiny forehead (the silver is dented on the right side, so she looks bruised) beetles like a bluff over a pair of dazed bug eyes, a wide nose with splayed nostrils, a sharply cleft upper lip and a drooping lower one—and a mere suggestion of a chin, as if the craftsperson had become exhausted molding the rest of the face and could do no more. Unbeautiful, she is yet unforgettable.

The distinctive tower of Walcourt's Basilica St. Materne

That weird upper lip is almost simian. She's a veritable slap in the face to every sweet-faced, smiling madonna. Besides the fact that she resembles primitive Celtic deity images—the big head, straight prominent nose, and staring eyes—Our Lady of Walcourt wears a look of unshakable concentration. This is a serious face, a face in which to place your trust. Thousands of Belgians have done so. Ex-voto plaques, artificial legs, and crutches hang on the walls around the statue today, as well as heavy chains and leg irons, left there by former prisoners who credit this madonna with their speedy releases from jail.

The church's eclectic decor doesn't stop there. The floor tiles have a mazelike design. Carved wooden choir stalls depict a startling array of non-ecclesiastical scenes, the kind whose presence in churches can usually be taken as evidence of some craftsperson's pagan roots. Depicted here, among other things, are a bare-buttocked person being pecked by a goose, an androgyne with legs widely spread, and a pair of people companionably sharing a chamber pot. Even from the outside, the church has many odd architectural features, including a bulbous tower.

Who was the goddess who dwelt here before? Whoever she was, she should not blame Our Lady of Walcourt for her extinction. She should, in fact, be proud of the continued good works of this madonna. In the cool, deserted church, you can almost see the sweat popping out on her shiny brow.

Getting there: Open regular church hours, generally Monday through Saturday around 8:00 A.M. to 7:00 P.M., and whenever services are not being held on Sunday. Admission free. Walcourt is 12 miles south of Charleroi (from which it can be reached by train) and 8 miles northwest of Philippeville. The Basilica St. Materne dominates the Grand'Place in the center of town. Notre Dame de Walcourt is on the left side of the interior.

Black Madonnas

Surely they didn't achieve their fine skin color by basking in the North Sea climate. Their blackness is a sharp contrast, a surprise, in these chilly Belgian landscapes of gray, white, buff, and green, this broad, pallid watercolor of a country. And yet black madonnas are so numerous and popular in Belgium as to form a persistent thread in the country's spiritual fabric. They're dark, far darker than the thousands who worship them and who firmly believe in the statues' powers to heal.

Black madonnas are venerated all over Europe. Many scholars see a clear correlation between them and ancient fertility goddesses, believing that wherever there is now a church housing a black madonna, there was once a shrine to a goddess, whose dark, earthy powers made people visualize her as dark-skinned—truly *of* the earth. They're an enigma, as much a mystery here as everywhere else. But rather a slumbering, benign mystery, as Belgians seem far less anxious than other people—their French neighbors, say—to explain away the blackness of their black madonnas, to construct apologies. The Belgians, instead, are content just to pray to them, to ask for the occasional miracle; to count them as members of that sisterhood of Belgian madonnas—unquestioned, like so many black Belgian sheep in a field of white ones. (For more information, see the Black Madonnas discussion in the France chapter.)

Brussels: A band of rioting Protestants, railing against the church's glamorous trappings and its affection for the Virgin Mary, seized the city's lovely fifteenth century black madonna one day in 1744 and toppled the statue into the River Senne. Satisfied with their deed, the mob departed, apparently unaware of the well-known fact that you can't keep a good black madonna down. She was found floating down the river a few days later. Her escape from doom was hailed as miraculous because the statue was found floating on "a piece of turf"—as if the very earth had given a piece of itself in order to save her—and also because the statue had so boldly flouted the law of gravity. It was, after all, made of solid stone.

The madonna was placed in St. Catherine's Church and has been venerated there ever since. Her glossy black face gives out a sort of forthright, challenging gaze, as if asking you whether or not you believe in her miracle. The statue's willowy pose and the locks of hair waving gently away from its face suggest ancient Greek or Roman statues—as of Diana or Aphrodite.

This statue has seen many changes. But what must she think of the church's latest innovation? The high altar of St. Catherine's sports a huge ultramodern wooden cross. Set into its horizontal bar is an electronic display screen, across which play the words of prayers, in red dot-matrix letters. In a constant, angular, crimson stream they flow past. Will the madonna rise up one night, draw her cloak around her shoulders, and stalk out of the church in shame?

Getting there: Open in summer Monday through Saturday, 7:30 A.M. to 7:00 P.M., Sunday, 7:30 A.M. to noon. In winter, Monday through Saturday, 7:30 A.M. to 5:00 P.M.; Sunday 7:30 A.M. to noon. Admission free. The Church of St. Catherine is on Place Ste-Catherine, about five blocks northwest of the Grand'Place. The black madonna (De Zwerte Lieve Vrouw, or La Vierge Noire) is in a glass case in the church's left-hand side chapel.

Halle: You can't look this Virgin in the eye. The black-faced former babydoll of saints and royalty, Our Lady of Halle occupies a skyscrapery position so high above the church's main altar that you can barely see her. Perhaps she was placed so high to reassure her that even in these dull days of democracy, her noble connections have not been forgotten. (Surely her outsize golden crown, bigger than her head, serves this purpose.) More likely it was because the church wants to "protect her modesty": as she suckles the child in her lap, Our Lady draws aside her robe and bares her breast. (Isis was depicted in a similar pose, suckling her son, the god Horus, in countless ancient statues.)

The 3-foot wooden statue, embellished with silver and waxed linen, was made before 1231. Its original owner was St. Elizabeth of Hungary, and then it was handed down among female family members, all of whom held noble titles. Aleydis, Countess of Hainaut, brought the statue to Halle in 1267. Three hundred years later, Halle was being bombarded by Calvinists. The statue, then positioned on the town wall, "caught" 33 of the attackers' cannonballs in her skirt and thus saved the town. Some apologists say it was the cannonsmoke that turned the statue's features black. The cannonballs are still on exhibit at the church, as are ex-votos attesting to Our Lady of Halle's smaller, more personal acts of salvation. (Also in the church crypt is possible evidence that a tree deity was worshipped here in pre-Christian times, and at least one researcher has pointed out the connection between the name of Halle and that of Hel, a Norse underworld goddess.)

The Virgin is nicknamed *La Siege de la Sagesse* ("the

Seat of Wisdom"). Surely, hers is one of the most capable and accomplished laps in all of Belgium.

Getting there: Open daily, 9:00 A.M. to 6:00 P.M. Admission free. Halle is 10 miles southwest of Brussels. Basilica St. Martin (also called the Basilica of Notre Dame de Halle) is on Grote Markt, in the center of town. The black madonna is above the high altar, atop a 20-foot column.

Scherpenheuvel (Montaigu): As early as the eleventh century, pilgrims were already flocking to this hilltop shrine to ask the Virgin Mary for healings. A small chapel was attached to an oak tree; in the tree was perched a statue of the Virgin. Her healing powers were so renowned that, according to one probably spurious legend, the shrine's Flemish name, Scherpenheuvel, comes from the words for hill (*heuvel*) and bandage (*scerpen*).

Such devotion was not quite enough for the lady in the oak tree. One day in 1514, the story goes, a local herdsman, passing the chapel, was shocked to see the statue of Mary lying on the ground. It had somehow fallen from the tree. The herdsman's first thought was to carry the statue to his master's house, where it would be safe. But no sooner did he gather the statue into his arms than the man was suddenly paralyzed, glued to the spot where he stood. (He fell into a *stupeur*, says the legend.) In this condition he stayed all day, until his master finally appeared on the scene and instantly sized it up for the miracle it was: The Virgin, he declared, was trying to tell the people that she wanted a bigger, better shrine on this spot. So they built her one.

Today, Scherpenheuvel (its French name is Montaigu) is one of those few towns that Belgians refer to as a "holy city." The octagonal church with its huge dome rests on the very summit of the hill, and all roads lead to it. In the church resides the statue. Its placid toffee-colored face with its pursed lips belies a strange and wilful nature. Twenty-six years after the herdsman's misadventure, a gang of heretics sacked the chapel, seizing the statue. This time, for some reason, she allowed herself to be carried away. No trace was seen of her for 6 years. At last she was discovered, inexplicably, in the home of a local woman and then was brought back to the church, where she picked up the thread of her miracle-working career, which continues to this day. The madonna's halting of a local epidemic in 1629 is still celebrated with an annual candlelight procession held on the first Sunday after All Saints' Day. It is a Belgian custom to save the candle stubs from this procession and to relight them, later, in times of personal crisis.

Getting there: Open daily 8:00 A.M. to 7:00 P.M. Admission free. Scherpenheuvel is 30 miles northeast of Brussels and 4 miles west of Diest. The black madonna is on the altar in the Basilica of Onze Lieve Vrouw, in the exact center of town.

Czechoslovakia

Hluboke-Masuvky, Ostrava Petrkovice, and Dolni Vestonice are not names that dance easily on the tongue or linger lastingly in the ear. But they should, because thousands upon thousands of years B.C.E., these were places where goddesses were worshipped, where priestesses were active, and where women, just by being women, were magical creatures. Czechoslovakia, like most of Eastern Europe, is the home of a dazzling array of ancient statues attesting to this fact: handsome traces of a fascination, a matriarchy, an earth-centered way of life that reverberates in Czechosolvakia to this day.

The last of those names, Dolni Vestonice, should actually be the first. This former mammoth-hunting community in the Pavlov Hills near the Austrian border, active around 24,000 B.C.E., has yielded some of the world's very first ceramic sculptures. Naturally, these sculptures, fired in primitive hearths, depicted the most important subjects of all: women and mammoths.

Czechoslovakia, neither Romanized nor developed, remains deeply rural. There in the freshly ploughed furrows awaiting onions, in the unpeopled woods and ponds, in villages so still at midday, as if baked in custard, pulses the heartbeat, heavy and slow, of the Mother.

Dolni Vestonice

The Venus of Vestonice

The mammoth hunters of 26,000 years ago never knew the cool, unyielding touch of iron. Not very easily could you have explained to them the whimsical concept of an Iron Curtain, which would close around their legacy and their goddess, keeping it all hidden. And then—for no reason that mammoth hunters could ever understand—the curtain would hissingly melt away almost overnight. And standing there in the clear light would be the mammoth hunters' legacy, a small clay statue of a Stone Age goddess as beautiful and wise as the Venus of Willendorf, as cryptic and universal as the question mark she resembles. But who, until now, ever heard of the Venus of Vestonice? On how many modern hearts did she have the chance to etch her silhouette? Outside of scholarly circles, just a few, just a few. Like the Martian woman who dreamed wistfully of becoming Miss World, the Venus of Vestonice was a victim of geography.

Near the site of the present-day village of Dolni Vestonice, at a time when the chilled, tundra-like earth still remembered the last ice age, a community of about 100 people made their homes. For security they dug the floors of their huts below the surface of the ground. For light and warmth, they created hearths. For tent posts they used the bones of the mammoth, whose flesh they craved and in whose fierce power lay the mysteries of life and death.

In their fire-and-ice, hungry-and-full world, the hunters clearly saw what was real and what was holy.

When they discovered—by accident, it is thought—that fire-baked clay becomes hard and keeps its shape, when they taught themselves to carve stone, bone, and wood, *what* became the subject of the world's oldest art? Mammoths, yes, but mostly women—women's bodies, bursting with life.

It is known that these people traced their ancestries matrilineally. Mothers were goddesses, and goddesses mothers, and at the root of everything was one great mother: she who had spawned the race between her thighs, she whose reassuring bulk lingered always nearby.

The Vestonice Venus created a sensation when it was found. Smooth and brown, small enough to fit in the palm of the hand, the statuette offered proof that religion was no more and no less than human nature, that it was older than politics. What's more, this was a faith that modern people could comprehend, whether or not they admitted it. It was woman worship, breast worship, belly worship.

The mammoth hunters' encampment, where the statuette was found, still has a raw look about it. Excavations have left the site exposed, but it is still a primal place, a place of sounds and impulses rather than words. None of the prehistoric people's creations remain on this spot, nor do the gigantic beasts for whom the people lay in wait. But still here are the elements from which they made a life and a religion: the earth, the water, the air that once carried the cries of the mammoth and the smoke from the nourishing hearths.

Today you can see a replica of the Vestonice Venus (the original resides in Prague) at Dolni Vestonice's archaeological museum. Next to it is a map of Europe showing places where Stone Age goddess statuettes have been found. The map labels this site—the intersection of two westward- and eastward-sweeping cultures—as the center of a singular prehistoric culture that has been named Pavlovian, after the neighboring village of Pavlov.

The chocolate-brown statue stands beside replicas of its Eastern European sisters, a surprising number of them: the so-called Venuses of Jelizejevici, Kostenki, Pekarna, Petrkovica, Avdejevo. You can immediately

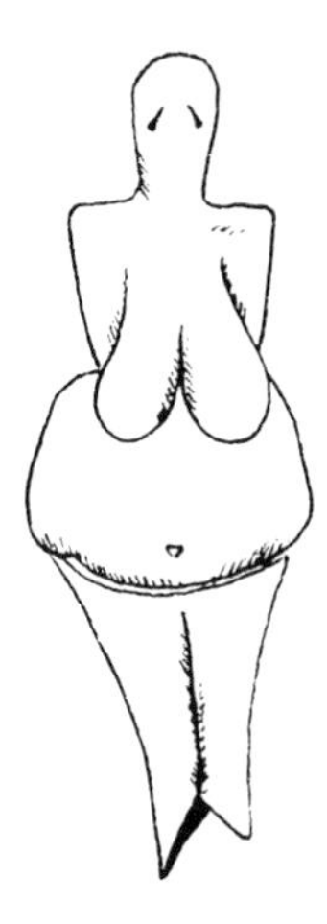

The Venus of Vestonice, Dolni Vestonice

see the striking family resemblance between them all and between them and other Stone Age goddess images, including the Venus of Willendorf, which was discovered just across the border in Austria.

Their little heads hang low, as if deep in thought, meditation, trance, or sleep, above massive mountains of body. They are faceless. Careful Stone Age hands molded the curve of knees, the tapering arms. Careful hands carved the breasts, the bellies, and the hips that hang like baggage, like symbols of the material world, which the goddess carries with her.

Down deep, you look a little like those statues, and so does every woman in the museum, every woman you meet in the village and on the bus. Take this with you, this lesson from the Venuses, this family resemblance, this comforting sameness of woman's body. Take it with you across borders; it's as good as a passport.

Getting there: The archaeological site is always open and free to visit. The museum open Tuesday through Sunday, 8:00 A.M. to noon and 1:00 to 4:00 P.M. Admission: 4 Kcs; students 2 Kcs. Dolni Vestonice is 20 miles south of Brno and 6 miles north of Mikulov, on the southern shore of a small lake near the Austrian border in central Czechoslovakia. The nearest large city is actually Vienna, Austria, from which you can visit Dolni Vestonice as a daytrip: take a train to Breclav, just across the Czechoslovakian border. From there take a train or bus 15 miles to Mikulov, and from there take a bus to Dolni Vestonice. The museum, called Archeologicke Muzeum Dolni Vestonice, is just a few steps from the bus stop, one block west of the church tower. The archaeological site is difficult to find, about 2 miles east of town toward the village of Pavlov, in an agricultural area right next to the shore of the lake. There are no signs, so you may need to ask for directions.

France

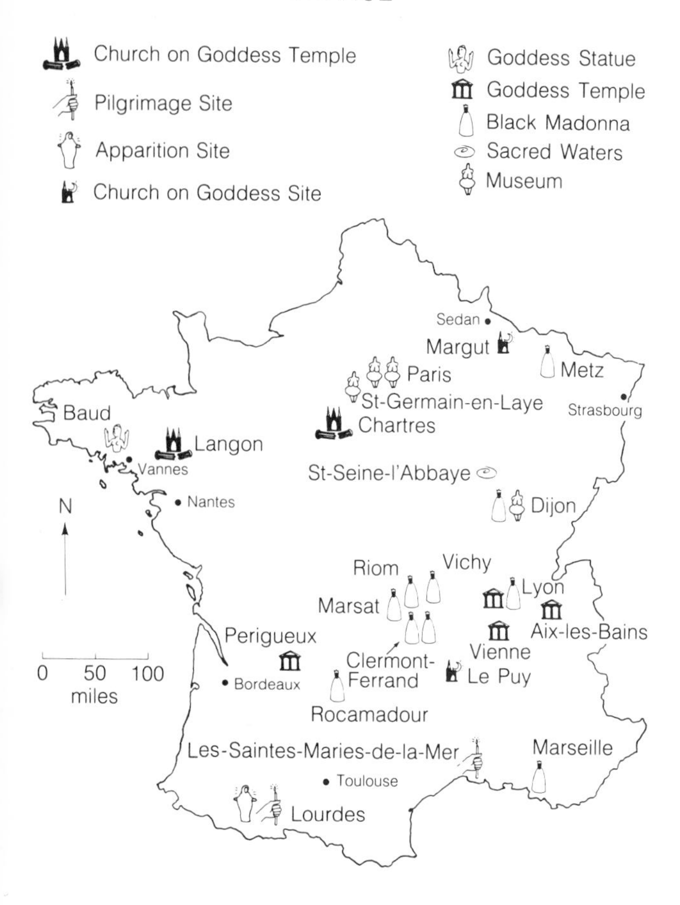

France is a country of consummate talents. Everything France touches turns to gold, or at least—and this is really no hardship—to meringue. What is this country's secret? Who was her teacher? Capable, inventive Isis? Impassioned Cybele? Lovely Venus, feminist Bona Dea? It could have been any or all of them, for all were worshipped in France at one time or another. So, too, were many others, whose less familiar names sprang fresh from the French soil: the strong, maternal goddesses whom the Celtic Gauls worshipped on mountaintops, at springs, and in the "great and sacred forests" that one Roman writer, arriving in Gaul, found so awesome.

And France's first goddesses, whose tiny chiseled images tell us, in the eloquent silence of full breasts and ripe bellies, how well they were loved in caverns and campsites 20,000 years ago: What were *their* names, or did they, born of earth, even need names? Those smooth curves were the first triumphs of French art, early testaments to the holiness of breasts and belly. This is a holiness that the French, enraptured to this day, have never, ever forgotten.

Aix-les-Bains

Temple of Diana

To walk outdoors in the Savoie is to know that an athletic goddess strides just one step ahead of you. Every gust of air, high-altitude thin and cold, but delicious, is the jetstream off her long smooth thigh as she rushes past you. Savoie's muscular charm, now lapped up by skiers and eaters of triple-cream Gruyère, was by no means lost on its ancient inhabitants, who in turn explained all this bounty by peopling it with deities.

For as long as anyone can remember, and longer, people have been coming to Aix-les-Bains to "take the cure." The oldest town in Savoie, Aix-les-Bains was built around a spring, a *source*, whose healing powers were already celebrated before the arrival of the Romans. Inscriptions reveal that the spring was ruled by a Gallic divinity or divinities, identity unknown. The Romans, arriving over two thousand years ago, named the city Vicus Aquensis, "place of the waters," and forthrightly dedicated the spring to their own goddess, Diana.

The Romans had a stubborn habit of doing that, rededicating colonial waterholes to Diana. She doesn't spring immediately to mind as a water goddess. (Venus, born of the sea foam, seems more appropriate.) But at least one famous bath story revolves around Diana.

One day the goddess was savoring a bath with her best friends, the water nymphs. A young hunter, Actaeon, burst suddenly upon the scene. Transfixed by surprise, curiosity, and lust, he stood staring. He stood too long. Diana spotted him and, outraged, turned Actaeon into a stag. Instantly his own hunting hounds were upon him and ripped him to shreds. No man would rend Diana's virgin privacy and live to tell the tale.

Under Diana's watchful eye, the Romans embellished the baths at Vicus Aquensis so that, from the second century onward, they were renowned as not merely health-inducing but also miraculous, even divine.

The spa's eighteenth century heyday is what most people think of today when they think of Aix-les-Bains. It is that period that inspires the gooiest nostalgia. But Aix's Roman years, *avec* Diana, are still in evidence. Diana's temple, whose entrance faced east, toward the sacred spring, has been incorporated into a series of increasingly modern buildings over the centuries. Finally, it was subsumed by Aix's *hôtel de ville*, the town hall. Now every visitor who wanders through the town hall and its tourist office pays inadvertent homage to the goddess. The Roman-built wall peeps here and there through the modern masonry. A handful of ancient artifacts is now on display at one end of the building, and the temple wall looms over these treasures as it did of yore. Among the artifacts is a large marble goddess: No one is quite sure *which* goddess.

In the baths, the steam is as thick and warm as an all-over poultice. Outside, the air is sharp and rare, fit for mountain goats. Could this place be anything else but what the nineteenth century bathers called "tonic?" "Salubrious?" Hearty, hard-muscled Diana is behind all this. She doesn't cosset or cuddle; she slaps the hopeful back into good health and then bounds up the mountain, sure that you will follow.

Getting there: Open Monday through Saturday, 9 A.M. to noon and 2 to 7 P.M.; Sunday, 9 to noon and 3 to 7 P.M. Admission free. Aix-les-Bains is in the Alps, 8 miles north of Chambery and 65 miles east of Lyon. The remaining wall of the temple is now incorporated into one of the walls of the Musée Lapidaire, which is right next to the tourist office inside the *hôtel de ville*, in the center of town on Place des Thermes.

Baud

The Venus of Quinipily

The authorities were worried. Peasants along the Blavet River in southern Brittany, the reports claimed, were worshipping a goddess. They called her Groa-houarn, Breton for "old woman" or "sorceress." Her statue stood next to the river on a peninsula called Castennec. The sick and the lame claimed to have received miraculous cures after touching the statue. Country folk made pilgrimages to the goddess and gave her generous offerings. Young women, seeking the goddess's aid in attracting lovers and husbands, performed rites shocking and bizarre.

A thriving enclave of paganism in the seventeenth century? It was practically beyond belief.

In 1661, the Bishop of Vannes sent an ecclesiastical mission to Castennec to investigate the "problem." It was even worse than he had feared. The statue of the goddess showed her naked, and her exaggerated sexual features were in plain view. That was the final straw. The bishop ordered that the statue be thrown in the river. His minions, over the peasants' heated protests, did just that.

Needless to say, the goddess was not pleased. Torrential storms battered the countryside shortly thereafter, severely damaging crops and fields. The peasants knew who was responsible. Still, it took 3 years for someone to get up the nerve to dredge the river. In 1664, the statue was retrieved and again set up near the bank. Word eventually filtered back to the bishop, and in 1668 (news traveled slowly in those days) he ordered the local Count de Lannion to have the statue irrevocably destroyed. The count sent a small army to Castennec: professional stonemasons armed with special hammers, accompanied by an entourage of servants. The masons stepped up to the statue, took a couple of swings—and panicked. No one is quite sure why; perhaps they feared reprisals from the peasantry, or perhaps they too felt some reverence for the goddess. Either way, they decided on a compromise. They toppled poor Groa-houarn, now missing an arm and a breast, back into the river.

Not long after, the Bishop of Vannes died, and Count de Lannion was thrown from a horse and spent some time in a coma. Again, the country folk were not surprised—you can't go tossing goddesses into rivers without expecting some kind of retribution.

She remained at the bottom of the Blavet for 30 years, until the new Count de Lannion, son of the mean old one, got the inspiration to spruce up his castle grounds. He bought a bulky fountain at a nearby town, but it lacked that special something. A statue, perhaps, to set on top . . . ?

The folks at Castennec went wild with gratitude when they heard of the count's plans to resurrect the goddess. Their glee did not last long. When they learned that the count was going to install the statue on the grounds of his castle at Quinipily several miles to the south and that he would keep the gates firmly locked, they were heartbroken. In desperation they took the count to court in an attempt to stop the move. The count won.

He brought the goddess home, but she was in sorry shape. Thirty years underwater had not been kind, nor had the hammerblows. Besides, she was a bit lewd for proper castle decoration. So the count told his mason to give her a little reworking.

The fractured stone crumbled under the chisel, and poor Groa-houarn fell to pieces. The count was not fazed. He ordered a whole new statue, made to his specifications. He dragged the fountain home, put the new statue on top, and faded from history.

The peasants were not fazed either. A new statue, miles away, on private property—they still came. In 1779, an historian recorded that the goddess was still receiving offerings.

In her new guise at the castle in Quinipily, Groa-houarn took on a new name: the Venus of Quinipily. The count had chiseled a phony Latin inscription on her pedestal, which stated that she was a Venus erected by soldiers in Julius Caesar's army. This inscription has fooled many naive travelers and journalists over the last two centuries. It seems plausible enough. There *had* been a Roman settlement, called Sulim, at Castennec, and the Romans were uncommonly fond of leaving their statues lying about.

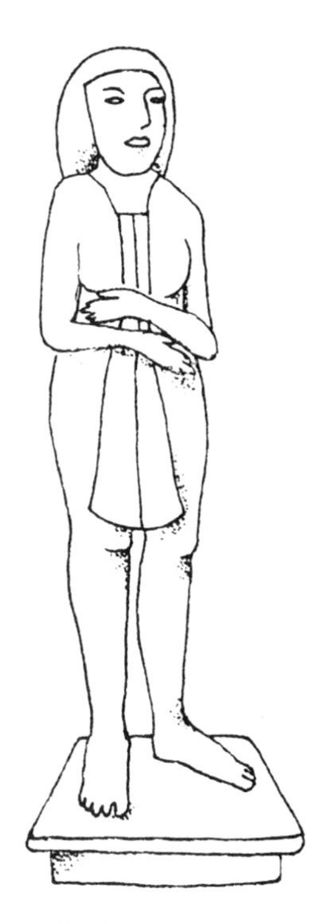

The Venus of Quinipily, Baud

On the other hand, Sulim wasn't established until centuries after Caesar had passed through, and the statue looked nothing like Venus. In fact, she looks a little like a chunky Isis, with an Egyptianesque head and a stiff, formal pose. It is said that the soldiers at Sulim had been recruited in North Africa and brought the Isis cult with them.

Other writers claim that she is a Gaulish goddess, or even Cybele. However, all these arguments are based on the assumption that the statue at Quinipily is the original one, only slightly altered. We know now that it is only a facsimile, even though this replacement was also venerated as an image of a goddess.

The Venus of Quinipily still surveys the countryside from atop her fountain near the now-ruined Quinipily Castle. Her arms are folded across her mottled gray stomach. She stands straight upright, larger than life-size, legs close together. A stole or scarf hangs down to her knees. An Egyptian-style headdress frames a placid, square-jawed face. If anything, she resembles a sarcophagus from a Nile Valley tomb. She may not be the original Groa-houarn, but her followers treated her as a worthy successor.

She seems lonesome, but she is actually the youngest sister in a very large family: a divine family. The Venus of Quinipily may very well be the last goddess to have been openly worshipped anywhere in Europe.

Getting there: Open daily, 9 A.M. to 7 P.M. Admission: 6F; children 2F50. Baud is 20 miles northeast of Lorient and 20 miles northwest of Vannes, in the Morbihan department of Brittany. From Baud, head west on the road that goes toward Hennebont. After 1 mile, turn left, heading toward Quinipily Castle. After another quarter-mile you'll come to a fork; keep to the left. Keep going. After a short way the gates to the castle grounds and the Venus will be on your left.

Chartres

Cathedral on Druidic Goddess Site

"At a certain time every year the Druids have a gathering on sacred ground in the territory of the Carnutes, whose land is considered to be in the middle of Gaul. People with disputes that need resolving come to this gathering from all over Gaul and accept the decisions and verdicts which the Druids give to them."

So wrote Caesar in a famous passage from his *Gallic Wars*, in which he described the social customs of the natives of France. The territory of the tribe called the Carnutes is actually a little northwest of the center of ancient Gaul, in the area around the modern city of Chartres. The name Chartres is itself probably a modern descendant of the name Carnutes. Archaeological evidence, and the total absence of any competing sites, has convinced most historians—at least, the few historians who care about this sort of thing—that the city of Chartres is the very place to which Caesar was referring.

Later writers, describing the Christianization of the region and the founding of Chartres Cathedral, recount the almost comical exploits of the early evangelizers.

They arrived at Chartres to find the Gallic tribespeople worshipping a mother goddess whose statue represented her in the process of giving birth. Unable to tempt the natives away from the old religion, the evangelizers resorted to desperate tactics. Don't you realize, they cried out to the stubborn Gauls, that the statue you worship represents the Virgin Mary? You're Christians already and you don't even know it! Why, we'll build a new church on your holy shrine, put your statue in the church, and, heck, we'll even worship it ourselves!

That did the trick. The Gauls didn't have to change their behavior or beliefs in the slightest. They continued to venerate the same statue on the same sacred site, and probably even with the same rites. What did it matter that these foreigners wanted to call her by a different name?

Later Catholic officials devised a handy term for images of Mary that had already been made or seen (as in visions) before Mary was even born. They called them "prefigurations of the Virgin," a concept that calls for quite a suspension of rational thought. Many non-Catholics find it downright laughable. Still, it has helped the Church explain away some otherwise sticky theological contradictions (see the discussion of Rome's Church of Santa Maria in Ara Coeli in the Italy chapter for another example).

This mother goddess statue was placed in each succeeding church built on the ancient sanctuary, including the one built in the 1100s, the cathedral that stands today. Somewhere along the way her name was changed to Our Lady Underground (Notre-Dame de Sous-terre) because she was kept as close as possible to the site of the original pagan shrine, which, as the surrounding ground level rose over the centuries, became part of the cathedral's crypt.

Chartres became a major center for Marian pilgrimage as the hopeful came from all over France to fall to their knees before Our Lady Underground. The tables were turned: Now the Christians were worshipping a pagan goddess without even knowing it. During the anti-Church frenzy of the French Revolution, Our Lady Underground was destroyed and lost forever. A modern replacement of the original was installed in the crypt, where it is venerated to this day.

This ancient mother goddess shrine still hums with mystical power, and pilgrims of every sort are inexorably drawn here. Architects spend years analyzing the magic numbers and sacred geometry used in the cathedral's design. Art lovers stand transfixed before the radiant stained glass windows, whose blood reds and sapphire blues seem to vibrate with a life of their own. New Age enthusiasts and dowsers excitedly trace the "telluric currents" that converge on Chartres. Pious Catholics pay their respects to Notre-Dame de Sous-terre and her aboveground counterpart, Notre-Dame du Pilier. Uninformed travelers convene here because, well, just because it's one of those places in Europe that you "must visit."

The crypt beneath the cathedral is one of the largest in the world, practically as spacious as the cathedral that looms above it. The guided tour of the crypt makes a quick stop at a well called Saints-Forts, directly below the central nave of the cathedral. The guide usually glosses over the early history of the well, concentrating on its later history, such as how ninth century Viking invaders used it as a convenient receptacle for the bodies of unfortunate locals. A church information sheet is a little more to the point, explaining that Saints-Forts "has been venerated for a very long time." In fact, the well is of Gallo-Roman construction and was, in all probability, one of the focal points of the Druidic sanctuary even before the Romans arrived. Wait until the tour group has moved on, and then linger beside the well. Peer into its depths: your face will practically glow with a strange warmth.

A few yards away is Our Lady Underground, on the high altar of the Chapel of Our Lady of the Crypt (one of her other names). This new statue, carved in a pseudo-Romanesque style and seated in front of a weirdly inappropriate modern tapestry, does not exude the same primitive power as her venerable ancestor. Unpainted and naturally nut-brown, this young would-be goddess has many years to mature before she can slip comfortably into her ancient sister's cloak of mystery.

Chartres has yet another black madonna: Notre-Dame du Pilier, placed in the main part of the cathedral, directly above Notre-Dame de Sous-terre. The *pilier* is the 10-foot pillar upon which she perches. There is some connection between the two madonnas, one elevated on a pillar, the other down below her, under the floor. Are they two aspects of the same power? Is Notre-Dame du Pilier an attempt to bring Our Lady Underground up to a respectable higher realm? The pilgrims who come to Chartres for religious reasons rush past the cathedral's famous artwork and head straight for Notre-Dame du Pilier. She is surrounded by flowers and flickering candles.

The feminine power of this spot has never dimmed, and perhaps it never will. Druidic mother goddess became Catholic mother-of-god; holy well grew into cathedral. But the spiritual energy remains unchanging, unchangeable.

Getting there: Cathedral open daily in summer, 7:30 A.M. to 7:30 P.M.; in winter, 7:30 A.M. to 7 P.M. Admission free. Tours of the crypt given daily at 11 A.M., 2:15 P.M., 3:30 P.M., 4:30 P.M., and 5:15 P.M. Admission to tour: 7F. Chartres is 50 miles southwest of Paris, from which there is frequent public transportation. The cathedral is in the center of town, visible for miles around. Notre-Dame du Pilier is in the left-side ambulatory, on top of a pillar in a small open chapel. The only way to visit Notre-Dame de Sous-terre, in the crypt, is by guided tour; buy tickets at the shop called Maison des Clercs de Notre-Dame (also called simply La Crypte) at 18 Cloitre Notre-Dame, just on the right side of the cathedral. The tour departs from the store, takes a little over half an hour, and leads you to the holy well and the underground chapel.

Langon

Church on Venus Temple

Venus didn't have a mother, and it's a lucky thing, for if Venus's mother had ever come to Langon, a fiery scene would surely have ensued.

"Venus!" the mother would have shouted in horror. "Get out of there!" Grabbing her daughter's satiny smooth and ever so erotic wrist, she would have hauled her roughly down the aisle, past crucifix, past priest, past a startled congregation. Out in the street, Venus's mother would have boxed her daughter's shell-like and irresistible ears. "How many times have I told you to stay away from churches?"

"But, Mama, it wasn't my fault. I didn't know. . . ."

And she would have been telling the truth. To this day, no one, Venus included, knows exactly what a fresco of Venus-emerging-from-the-waves is doing on a wall of Langon's Catholic Chapel of St. Agatha.

In 1839, during a routine restoration, a worker inadvertently scraped away the outer layers of paint from the wall behind the main altar, to reveal, hiding underneath, a voluptuous surprise. It was a fresco depicting a pale-skinned woman rising from the frothy sea. Her full breasts just clear the surface of the water, and she brushes back her long hair with one hand. Sea creatures romp all around her. Eros, the embodiment of romantic love, cavorts nearby astride a dolphin.

Imagine the shock waves that spread through this quiet Breton community when excited scholars immediately identified the painting as a rendering of the birth of the goddess Venus. (Remember, she had no mother. She was born, fully grown, from the sea foam.) It was a scene familiar to scholars from temples and villas all over the former Roman Empire.

They quickly concluded that the Chapel of St. Agatha had once been a Gallo-Roman temple of Venus. It had not, they deduced, been simply a church erected on the debris of a demolished pagan shrine, as was the case all over Europe, but an actual intact temple, rededicated in the name of St. Agatha. The edifice was erected during the fourth or fifth century, a bittersweet "cusp" time during which Christianity was making steady inroads into previously pagan Gaul. Later embellished in the Romanesque style, the stone and brick structure has long been celebrated as both a rare example of still-extant Gallo-Roman architecture and as the most beautiful church in Brittany.

But the chapel's history has yet another rabbit to yank out of its hat. Before it was named St. Agatha, it had yet another name: Ecclesia Sancti Veneris. The French called it St. Venier. Both Veneris and Venier are masculine names, but Christian records contain not the slightest reference to a St. Veneris or St. Venier. Scholars believe the church's name was a setup, designed to make the locals remember-yet-forget that this was once a temple of *Venus*, of which Veneris and Venier are cognates. A quick sex change was one way to separate the new boss from the old.

No one knows exactly when, or under what circumstances, the Venus fresco was painted over. The chapel was renamed St. Agatha during the Middle Ages, a time of deep devotion to female saints. Agatha, a virgin martyr and the patron saint of nursing mothers, is always associated with breasts, namely, her own severed ones, displayed on a platter. Thus, there is a distinct relationship between St. Agatha and the bare-breasted bather in the fresco.

Some say Venus, as depicted and worshipped in ancient Langon, is no more and no less than a Romanization of the native water goddess Morgane. Especially popular in sea-girt Brittany, Morgane was often depicted baring her breasts and was, like Venus, the patroness of sensual pleasure.

Now carefully preserved, although part of it is irrevocably damaged, the fresco remains in plain view behind the church's main altar. We will never know whether additional images, or even words, once enriched the watery scene. Some skeptics have suggested that the chapel was never a temple at all but a mere Roman villa and that the nautical scene was a mere ornament on a secular bathroom wall. Such scenes were indeed favorites among Roman bathers. But another compelling discovery near the church's entrance should make skeptics break out in a cold sweat. It is a roughly chiseled stone statuette of a woman, obviously quite old, but its age and identity are impossible to determine. The figure's right hand covers its heart; its left hand cups a breast that is, of course, full and bare and round as the moon.

Getting there: Open normal church hours. Admission free. Langon is 8 miles west of Grand Fougeray, northeast of Redon on the River Vilaine in southern Brittany. Langon is accessible by train. The fresco of Venus is visible on the right side of the apse in the church.

Lourdes

Grotto of the Apparitions

Lourdes is ridiculous. In streets as congested as tubercular lungs, pilgrims swarm over mountains of shocking merchandise: Our Lady egg timers, Our Lady potholders, Our Lady lampshades, Our Lady toothpick caddies, Our Lady alarm clocks, Our Lady weather forecasters, Our Lady pencils, Our Lady coasters, Our Lady collapsible drinking cups, and plastic bubbles filled with water, which you can shake and make it snow all over Our Lady. Ever since a poor shepherdess named Bernadette had a series of visions here in 1858, Lourdes has grown larger and then larger than life: swollen and distended, like a cyst. All the drama of religious pilgrimage is epitomized here, with the added mania of the twentieth century. If Walt Disney had wanted to create a Religionland, he would have needed only to annex Lourdes.

And yet most of these pilgrims are in earnest. They buy egg timers, but they are also deeply in love with a merciful lady who cures the sick, who performs wonders, *who graced this town*, they say, *with her presence*. Souvenirs are a way to grasp at her shadow, to stake a claim on her grace.

Many, many people who come here are gravely ill. When the Virgin appeared to Bernadette Soubirous, she pointed out a spring whose waters are now considered the world's healingmost. Pilgrims fill cups, vials, and gallon jugs at the pumps.

All day, every day, a continuous stream of pilgrims, many of them looking quite moribund, line up for a chance to bathe in pools filled with Lourdes water. Those who can walk and bathe by themselves do so. The others are wheeled in, undressed, and lifted into the water by uniformed volunteers. This is clearly the

Wheelchair-bound pilgrims at the grotto of Our Lady of Lourdes

last resort, the last hope, for many. Every evening, the Procession of the Sick finds miles and miles of wheelchair-bound pilgrims, representing every country in the world, laboring down the Esplanade while thousands, holding candles aloft, chant "*Ave, ave, ave Maria.*" You get used to the pale sunken faces, the suppurating feet. You start to forget that other towns are not like this.

Bernadette Soubirous was 14, desperately poor, and considered a stupid child when a radiant, smiling woman appeared to her in the moist, trash-littered grotto called Massabielle. The pair shared 15 visits over the next two weeks. Bernadette called the visitor simply *Aquero*, local dialect for "that one." Churchmen pressured Bernadette to make her new friend identify herself in writing, but Aquero demurred: "It is not necessary." Finally, under more pressure, she gave her elusive reply, in fluent Bigourdan, the Pyrenees dialect: *Que soy era immaculada concepciou:* "I am the immaculate conception."

Although Bernadette was made a saint following her early death in a convent, biographers are still quick to point out that she was canonized not for her visions, but "just for her simple faith." Are they jealous? Don't they think a plain, less-than-brilliant girl deserves to meet the Virgin?

She was not the first on her block to do so. Once in the fifteenth century, and again in the sixteenth, by which time the region was already totally devoted to the Virgin, white-gowned ladies appeared to sheepherders in villages very close to Lourdes. Also, some researchers even speculate that the grotto of Massabielle was used as a worship site as long ago as the Ice Age.

Grottoes always make people think of the Mother. Today at Massabielle, a broad semicircle of pilgrims, many of them slumped in wheelchairs or prone on stretchers, gazes up rapt at the blue and white statue of the Virgin, perched high up against the dark rock. Through half-blind eyes they stare at her; through runny and cataracted eyes. Through desperate eyes, and eyes that brim over with tears.

Getting there: Open daily, 5 A.M. to midnight. Admission free. Lourdes is in the foothills of the Pyrenees, 100 miles southwest of Toulouse, and easily accessible by train. The grotto, the basilica, and the sanctuary that has grown up around it are on the west side of town, just across the River Gave. The grotto is set into the hill on the north side of the basilica. The holy water fountains are just to the left of the grotto. The Esplanade of the Processions is the area between the Pont St-Michel and the basilica. Photographs of miraculous healings attributed to Our Lady of Lourdes are in the Medical Bureau on the right (north) side of the Esplanade.

Lyon

Temple of Cybele

"We would like," we told the Tourist Bureau officer in Lyon, "some information about the ancient temple of Cybele."

"The what?" she blurted. "In *this* city?" She smoothed her lush hair back over eyes that were well-intentioned but blank. "I'm afraid I don't know of it."

"The goddess Cybele," we began again. But she was honest enough, perhaps young enough, to roll those huge eyes and whisper, as if confessing to a murder, "I am very sorry, *monsieur-dame*, but I do not know who that is."

This woman was a native of Lyon and a professional expert on the city. And yet the poor child had never heard of Cybele! A native of Lyon!

It just goes to show you how much times have changed. Had we shown up in that office, say, 1800 years ago, it would have been an entirely different story. "Ah, *oui*, right this way," the employees would have said, taking us firmly in hand. "The Great Mother's temple is right up there, *là*. You want to buy a souvenir? The gift shops are just outside the temple." They might even have laughed at us, those Gallo-Roman tourist officers, for having asked such a stupid question. After all, who in ancient Gaul didn't know the way to Lyon's great temple? What sort of bumpkin would have to *ask*?

Lyon was Cybele's city, as surely as Toto was Dorothy's dog. By the second century C.E., an international panoply of deities was duly saluted in this Gaulish capital. Among them were the native goddess, Tutela, as well as Roman Mercury, Egyptian Isis, and Celtic Lugh (for whom Lyon—ancient Lugdunum—was named). But above them all rode mighty Cybele, whose tragical religion had traveled up the Rhone in the ships of Syrian traders.

Lyon's temple of Cybele, which celebrated its grand opening on December 9, 160 C.E., was the most important in the entire Roman empire, displaying to all the world where this city's loyalties lay. We know the temple's inauguration date because of an inscription on a stone altar that was discovered on the site. It is one of several altars now on display in the nearby Museum of Gallo-Roman Civilization.

These are *taurobolium* altars, and they served a special purpose unique to the worship of Cybele. On these altars, the goddess's devotees used to sacrifice live bulls, cutting the animals' necks over the smooth white stone and then bathing themselves in the spurting blood. It was a kind of baptism, designed to unite worshipper and goddess, to cleanse and renew. It was a rite as wild and urgent as Cybele herself. An ancient writer, describing the scene at Lyon's temple, wrote of priests and priestesses standing with curved sacrificial knives in hand, poised over the bull as a haunting flute split the air. . . .

The temple had a wide central courtyard, an enormous statue of the goddess, and a regal view of the sprawling, river-fed lowlands. Religious curio shops did a flourishing business nearby. They still do, but not for Cybele. Not anymore. Spiritually sophisticated Lyon, whose people had so fervently embraced one exotic faith under the banner of Cybele, was just as quick to embrace yet another. This time, the banner was decorated with a cross. Lyon became the first Christian community in ancient Gaul. A great many converts were drawn from the legions of Cybele worshippers.

Today a basilica dominates the hill of Fourvière on which the ruined temple of Cybele now crumbles. The church, dedicated (not surprisingly) to the Virgin Mary, is as lavish, in its own way, as the great temple once was. And in fact, the church, in many ways, pays a sly laconic tribute to its spiritual forebear. Many carved bulls' heads are among the wall decorations here, just as stone bulls' heads used to decorate the taurobolium altars in Cybele's temple. And all over the church are images of lions. The lion, golden image of savage strength, was Cybele's ever-present mascot, a reminder of her eastern origins. The basilica's wall mosaics, as if content that bygones are indeed bygones, include in the background a fanciful depiction of the temple as it once probably looked.

As you stand among the temple's dull ruins, you can hear the cathedral bells ever so sharply. The temple is now reduced to mere foundations, most of its masonry having been long ago carted off to make other buildings, other walls, all over Lyon. The temple looks razed, shaven. Lumps of granite and shale, slathered with mortar, are overgrown with purple flowers whose tint recalls the free-flowing blood of sacrificial bulls. The church bells sing—too sweet and clear to be sneering, much too pretty to be pompous. Still, those bells make you stare down at your feet, at the silent rubble, and feel very sorry.

Times have changed.

Getting there: Open daily, 9:00 A.M. to sunset. Admission free. The entrance to the temple and the Roman theaters is on rue Roger Radisson, near rue Cleberg, on the hill of Fourvière on the west side of the Saône river. The temple ruins are on the terrace above the large theater. There is no identifying sign. The Museum of Gallo-Roman Civilization is open Wednesday through Sunday, 9:30 A.M. to noon and 2:00 P.M. to 6:00 P.M. Admission free. The museum is next to the entrance to the temple site, at the intersection of rue Roger Radisson and rue Cleberg. The Basilica of Fourvière is just a few blocks away. (See the *Getting there* discussion in the Lyon entry in the Black Madonnas section, pp. 67–68.)

Margut

Arduina Sanctuary

The Ardennes Forest has seen more than its share of history. In 1940, the trees shook as Nazi tanks rumbled through the Ardennes on their way to Paris. In 1918, the forest floor ran red with the blood of slaughtered infantrymen. Saint Hubert, sometime around 700, saw, deep in the woods, a stag with a glowing cross between its antlers. But the most remarkable and interesting date in the history of the Ardennes was the otherwise obscure year 565 C.E. That year, a strange man wandered into the forest. His name was Wulfiliac. He had been a barbarian Lombard, a member of a German tribe that had settled in northern Italy. Wulfiliac had been converted to Christianity, and he set off on an evangelizing mission, leaving his homeland behind. He somehow found his way to the Ardennes, a vast, wild forest that Christianity had not yet begun to penetrate. The people of the Ardennes worshipped a goddess named Arduina, the patroness of the forest. She rode a sacred boar that thundered through the wilderness. She was the goddess of natural forces, of animals and hunters, of life and death. The Celtic Trevires tribe (after whom the city of Trier, on the other side of the Ardennes, is named) first recognized Arduina's power and instituted her worship here in what they called the Forest of Arduina. When Wulfiliac arrived, he discovered the locals venerating a statue of the goddess that towered above the woods atop a hill called Mont Arduina.

Wulfiliac had found his calling. He determined to turn these people away from "idol worship." But to achieve that end, he did a very strange thing: He made himself into an idol. He erected a column near the statue of Arduina. One day he climbed to the top of the column, vowing that he would not come down until Arduina was toppled. Wulfiliac was true to his word. He stayed atop the column for years, surviving on a diet of bread, water, and prayer. He had not invented this strange form of worship: Column sitting was all the rage in the Middle East, where the ascetic, self-denying monks were called "stylites" by those down on the ground. But Wulfiliac was the only stylite in this neck of the woods. The curious gathered around his column. Day by day, the crowds grew. Suddenly, Arduina had competition.

At first, the people of the Ardennes just laughed at Wulfiliac. When, from atop his column, he urged them to destroy the statue of Arduina, they must have dismissed him as a madman. But his unrelenting patience and perseverance began to make an impression. Mockery turned to curiosity, and curiosity to respect. He reiterated his demand endlessly: *Tear down the idol.* The number of his converts swelled until the balance of faith finally tipped in his favor. One fateful day, Wulfiliac's followers converged on Arduina's statue and sent it crashing down.

Wulfiliac eventually came down from his column, finished evangelizing the area, and built a church and hermitage on the top of Mont Arduina. In the following centuries, as the French language evolved, the spellings in this story changed: Wulfiliac became Walfroy, and

Arduina became Ardennes. Walfroy was made a saint, and Mont Arduina was renamed Mont St-Walfroy. And they all lived happily, and Christianly, ever after.

At least that is the official story. But think back to St. Hubert. After his experience with the unusual stag, he too set out to Christianize the Ardennes, where he found "idol worship" continuing as firmly as ever. And this happened almost 150 years *after* St. Walfroy had supposedly uprooted paganism and Christianized the forest. Even hundreds of years after St. Hubert, the Ardennes was a wild, untamed land where "idol worship"—that is, Arduina worship—was still common.

St. Walfroy's church and hermitage were repeatedly destroyed during the many wars that raged through this region. Each time, they were rebuilt; the current buildings date from 1947. The church's modernistic stained glass window is supposed to symbolically represent "the struggle of faith against the idol Arduina." Battles and bombs long ago obliterated any trace of Arduina's statue and Wulfiliac's column, though the church is said to mark the site.

St. Walfroy's spiritual descendants continue, as he did, to call Arduina an "idol." Perhaps that is their mistake. By demoting the goddess to a mere object or symbol, they camouflage her true nature. The destruction of Arduina's image in no way meant the destruction of the goddess herself, or of her worship. The forest is still here, maybe not as wild as it used to be, but wild enough.

And as long as there is an Ardennes, there is an Arduina, for she is the forest itself.

Getting there: Always open and visible. Admission free. Margut is 7 miles southeast of Carignan on the N43 road. Carignan is 12 miles southeast of Sedan, in the Ardennes district on the Belgian border. The Hermitage of St. Walfroy is 2 miles south of Margut on the hill called Mont St-Walfroy. There is no public transportation to the site, but it is signposted.

Perigueux

Tour de Vesone (Tower of Vesuna)

The ancient Gauls, who inhabited what is now France, had lots of goddesses and gods of their own. But unlike the Greeks and Romans, the Gauls did not build lasting temples to their deities, nor did they leave behind a convenient stack of written records about those deities' adventures. Presumably the Gauls were otherwise occupied. They were perfecting the art of making omelettes, perhaps, and fragrant apricot tart.

So it happens that we know almost nothing about the Gaulish deities, the true native goddesses and gods of France. (Was there a goddess who presided over croissants? Over *couture*? A goddess whose mascot was a nasty toy poodle?) As history would have it, the Roman Empire crept steadily across Gaul ("*Gallia est omnis divisa in partes tres,*" wrote Julius Caesar), during which time the Roman colonists, meeting countless native divinities, ignored some, adopted others, and synthesized some with favorite Roman deities whom they in some way resembled. As was their wont, the conscientious Romans got right to work building temples. Thus, most of the archaeological remains in France today are classified as "Gallo-Roman." And thus we know the name of the goddess Vesone.

She was Gaulish; possibly she was the protectress of the region. Virtually all we know about her today is her name. (Names, actually—the Romans de-Gallicized it to Vesuna, which was more comfortable to Latin-speaking tongues. She is often referred to by that name today.) Once, the whole city bore her name. Before there was a Perigueux, there was a village called Vesone, which had been founded by the Petrocore tribe on the banks of the Isle River. The Romans founded a colony here, mingling with the native Gauls, and the resultant community was, according to at least one historian, "brilliant."

The vital heart of the community was its temple-complex, dedicated to Vesuna. Romans had erected it in the second century C.E. Apparently the Romans liked what they saw in Vesone, and liked her for herself, for they did not automatically merge her personality with

The scarred circular cella of Perigueux's temple of Vesuna

that of Minerva, Juno, or Diana, which was a common fate of local goddesses during the Roman occupation. Vesone's town and temple flourished for over 200 years.

There might still be a town called Vesone (or at least Vesuna), and there might be many more towns still named after goddesses, were it not for the Christianization of Europe in the decades following the conversion of the Roman emperor in the fourth century C.E. The man who was to become known as St. Front set up his diocese right next to the town of Vesone. The two communities, pagan and Christian, stood side by side, competing, for a while. Then the Christian town, called Puy-St-Front, began to prosper as the older, goddess-centered town faltered. By the time the two communities were officially merged in 1251 (under the name of Perigueux, in honor of the founding Petrocore tribe), the once mighty temple of Vesone was in near ruins. Only its central tower remained standing, and that tower was scarred from top to bottom, like a wheel of Camembert with a slice removed. "Credit" for the scar is traditionally given to St. Front, who cursed the tower "as he chased away the last demons of paganism." But history tells us that the tower was partially dismantled by the citizens of Perigueux, who used the old stones to build a defensive wall around the city during a time of barbarian invasions. (We can only hope that the goddess viewed this as a somewhat worthy cause.)

Today the marred Tour de Vesone, looming over the rooftops of Perigueux, is acknowledged as the world's most interesting extant example of Gallo-Roman architecture. To sit on a park bench beside the tower and admire its height, the solidity of its brick walls, the grand curving sides that strain toward the central scar like a pair of embracing arms, is to sense the power of this goddess—whoever she was—and to see her feet still resolutely planted on her native soil. But to imagine how the temple once looked is to be nothing less than awestruck at what people would do, what people used to do, for their goddesses. The tower, its red brick skeleton now standing alone, once formed only the *cella*, or the innermost sacred core, of a sprawling complex whose huge dimensions still amaze archaeologists. Rows of columns once echoed the vertical grace of the tower (which, to embellish its own beauty, was once covered in marble). Today, a gardener trims the cedar in the tower's shadow, as in any well-manicured city park. Across the street, an animal clinic and an apartment complex both bear Vesone's name. (Curiously, these modern buildings rest on the foundations of what was once the huge temple. Part of the temple's outer wall is still visible on the same block.)

What were her songs, her feast days? What were her eyes like? Her pretty name is still a household word here, because of the tower. But so, in these parts, is St. Front's. *But so is Vesone's. . . .*

Getting there: Open daily, April through September, 7:30 A.M. to 9:00 P.M.; October through March, 7:30 A.M. to 6:30 P.M. Admission free. The tower is in the

Jardin de Vesone, bounded by rue C. Bernard, rue de Vesone, and the railroad tracks, in the southern part of town. Part of the sanctuary wall can be seen across the tracks on rue Romaine.

Le Puy-en-Velay

Notre Dame du Puy

Of another city you might be able to say, "Its bland facade hides a mysterious past." But not Le Puy. With its otherworldly jagged volcanic outcroppings, twisting passageways, and foliage-swathed, goat-horned, carved faces leering unexpectedly from stone lintels, the town of Le Puy fairly oozes mystery. And this mystery reaches far below the surface and the not very bland facade—deep, deep, to the very essence of this sacred place.

Le Puy sits at the center of a veritable hailstorm of legends, facts, fables, truths, and half-truths. Some seem reasonable, some bizarre. Some are in agreement, others contradictory. But they all in some way or another concern goddesses and female spirituality. Le Puy, like the goddess herself, cannot be easily categorized, pinned down, or understood.

Take, for example, a single stone set into Le Puy's cathedral. You see it just as you enter; it is long, low, and dark. This huge hand-chiseled slab, called The Fever Stone, or The Apparition Stone, was supposedly once part of a "Druidic dolmen." This dolmen marked an important ritual site for goddess-worshipping Druids, and the church was built around the old sacred site. The dolmen supposedly stood intact inside the church until as late as the seventh century C.E. The stones were then disassembled and placed throughout the building. Eventually the Fever Stone was moved near the entrance, where it is today.

However, the construction of dolmens predates the arrival of Druids in France by thousands of years, so it hardly could have been a "Druidic dolmen" in the sense that it was built by Druids. They could have used it for rituals, just as modern witches still use the prehistoric stone circles of England, but the connection would be no stronger than that. In any case, the idea of a Stone Age dolmen being used as part of a cathedral is exciting enough in itself, Druids or no Druids.

The Fever Stone, however, has many other tales to tell. Another legend recounts how the Virgin Mary appeared next to the stone in 46 C.E. (other versions give a later date). She appeared again in 430 C.E. and told a woman dying of a fever to lie down on the stone. Miraculously, the woman was cured—hence the stone's two names. A bishop hurried to the site to witness the healing for himself. He arrived just in time to see a stag run out of the woods and trace the plan of a cathedral in the drifts left behind by a freak July snowstorm.The church was then built according to the stag's design, and the miraculous stone was positioned inside. People came from afar to lie on the Fever Stone and be cured. When the pilgrimage to Santiago de Compostela was popularized in the Middle Ages, Le Puy became a favorite stop on the route. The miraculous stone was one of its star attractions.

Yet the stone actually may have had little to do with the pilgrimage to Le Puy. Another tradition states that a powerful black statue of Mary drew worshippers here from all over central Europe. There was something electrifying about her, something exotic that set her apart even from the other black madonnas of the region. The standard story was that she was brought back from the Seventh Crusade by Louis IX (better known as Saint Louis) in the thirteenth century. But there are accounts of a black madonna being venerated at Le Puy long, long before St. Louis was even born. Explanations and theories abound. Here's a sampling: She was a Coptic madonna, brought here from Egypt; she was an "oriental goddess"; she was a gift from the Grand Sultan of Babylon to Louis VII, *not* Louis IX; she was brought back from the Middle East by an unnamed local crusader; she was a representation of the Celtic goddess Velauna; she was made by St. Luke himself; she was a local carving, the very first "Virgin in Majesty" upon which all other enthroned, crowned madonnas are modeled; she was a statue of Isis renamed the Virgin Mary.

None of these tidbits can be proved or disproved, alas, as the original statue was destroyed, like so many others, during the French Revolution. Yet surprisingly, almost shockingly, the most likely option is the last one: that she is Isis.

It was on June 8, 1794, that extremist revolutionaries stormed Le Puy's cathedral, seized the statue, and carried it to Place du Martouret, in the center of town. They ceremoniously burned the statue, and to prevent continued veneration of its remnants, they scattered the ashes in a nearby field. After the revolutionaries had departed, a local man sifted through the ashes and found among them a small red oval stone. On the stone was a finely carved, if tiny, image of a stately woman standing in a boat, surrounded on either side by various Egyptian-looking divinities. Her crown was a crescent moon. The stone's significance was not recognized at the time. Nowadays, anyone who sees a drawing of this carving has no hesitation identifying the moon-crowned woman in the boat as Isis.

If the statue had represented Mary, then why would it have contained an Egyptian seal of Isis? The red stone had clearly been part of the original black "madonna" statue. If we accept the story's validity, then the conclusions are inescapable. Even if we don't, there is other evidence. A drawing made of the original statue in 1777 has survived to this day. Not surprisingly, the statue shared many characteristics with well-known depictions of Isis, including the position of the child on her knees, the placement of their hands, her facial features, and of course her skin color.

Other legends and theories still swirl around Le Puy. The cathedral was built on a Roman temple to Diana, or a Roman temple to the deified Emperor Augustus and Adidon. The cathedral has "oriental influences." The Marian sanctuary at Le Puy is, along with Chartres, the oldest Marian sanctuary in France, and the cult is descended from that of the Celtic mother goddess Koridven, better known as Cerridwen. There is a healing spring, once a pagan sanctuary, behind the cathedral's main altar. And so on.

The current black madonna of Le Puy sits high on the main altar, sumptuously adorned with long robes and finery. She is like the stamen at the center of a flower, the focal point of the entire cathedral. She is even darker than her predecessor.

In the sacristy gift shop is a small reproduction of the original statue, based on the 1777 drawing. She sits calmly at one end of the room, tall and dignified, as if this were indeed a place of reverence and not a shop. We asked if there were any copies for sale here, as there were copies of many other French madonnas.

"Of *her*?" the cashier laughed, looking up at Isis. "No no no!" The very idea was absurd, tantamount to sacrilege.

Getting there: Open daily 9 A.M. to 7 P.M. Admission free. Le Puy-en-Velay is in the Auvergne, 75 miles southeast of Clermont-Ferrand. The cathedral is at the top of rue des Tables, at the foot of the Rocher Corneille, below the towering red statue of Notre Dame de France. The Pierre des Fièvres (the Fever Stone, aka Pierre de l'Apparition) is just inside the main gate of the cathedral at the top of the stairs, directly in front of you as you enter. The statue of Notre Dame du Puy is prominently displayed on the main altar inside the cathedral. Enter the sacristy shop with its copy of the original statue from the right aisle of the cathedral.

St-Seine-l'Abbaye

Source of the Seine

Modern Parisians who saunter and smooch alongside the Seine give hardly a thought to where this great river comes from, much less to who might be responsible for its timeless, romantic beauty.

Their ancient Gaulish ancestors thought deeply about such matters, however. They knew that the goddess Sequana ruled the Seine. She could work miracles with its waters. Her sanctuary straddled the river at its source, in an unassuming, peaceful forest that now lies just outside Dijon.

People still visit the source of the Seine. But the only healings modern visitors seek are the subtle ones that picnics and Frisbees have to offer. Their forebears—Gauls and eventually Romans as well—came for more palpable cures. For tumors, for goiters, for hernias, for lameness and blindness they came to Sequana's shrine, begging the goddess for miracles. Often they brought ex-votos, lifelike carved or cast replicas of their afflicted members and organs, that they offered in exchange for the goddess' blessing, or in thanks for a cure accomplished. (For more on these ex-votos, see the Dijon: Archaeological Museum entry.)

This was a sprawling complex, with many different facilities to accommodate the pilgrims who came in a steady stream, and who came in large numbers on special holy days. A spacious "welcoming hall" attests to the grand scale of the sanctuary in its heyday. In a series of rooms branching off a long hallway, pilgrims would spend the night in hopes of meeting the goddess in their dreams, at which time she might deliver a miraculous prescription. A Gallic-style temple was tended by specially trained clergy whose knowledge of herbal cures was helpful and comforting to the pilgrims.

It was the water itself, the *source captée*, that inspired the deepest devotion. Pilgrims doused themselves in it, sure that its crystal clarity, inhabited by their beloved goddess, had the power to heal. We can only conclude that many actual healings took place here. Why else would this shrine have been so popular and so well endowed? Yet the water, examined in a modern lab, has been shown to possess absolutely *no* mineral or therapeutic properties.

Today the sanctuary, picked over for some 150 years by the fine-toothed combs of French archaeologists, lies well hidden behind fences and is quite off-limits to modern would-be pilgrims. But you *can* visit the source—one of several, actually, as a number of springs conjoin to form the Seine. A sculptured stone nymph languishes above the spring, guarding the dank grotto and the burbling waters. But this is not Sequana, and even the grotto is a phony.

In 1865, France's Emperor Napoleon III commissioned the sculptor Jouffroy to create this monument, "the Nymph of the Seine," a sentimental homage to "the most illustrious river of Gaul and France." The marble

A nineteenth-century nymph guards the source of the Seine

lady, nude, grasping an enormous cluster of ripe fruits, and yet harshly, almost frighteningly listless, is no match for the vital Sequana. The water bubbles up, newborn, innocently eager to begin its long journey. And even a listless nymph, in these times, is better than no goddess at all.

Getting there: Always open. Admission free. The Source of the Seine is 5 miles northwest of St-Seine-l'Abbaye, which is 17 miles northwest of Dijon, the nearest large city. From Dijon, take a bus heading toward Chatillon-sur-Seine; tell the driver you want to get off at the Sources Seine Croisement stop. The driver will then drop you off at a crossroads, at which there are signs pointing down a side road 1½ miles to the source. Once you're there, the source emerges directly in front of the nymph statue. The remains of the Roman-era sanctuary are fenced off, near the explanatory signboard.

Les-Saintes-Maries-de-la-Mer

Saint Sara

People will go where they want to go; they will follow their hearts. When you see a procession, a caravan, a massive inrush of people all heading the same way, you have to ask, "Where are they all going?" because logic tells you that if so many hearts are drawn to a single place, then it must be important. You might not like the answer. It may not make any sense. But the place must be important; human hearts have declared it to be so.

In the case of Les-Saintes-Maries-de-la-Mer, church officials didn't like the answer. They didn't like the fact that twice each year for as long as anyone can remember, once in May and once in October, tens of thousands of gypsies had converged on this town to keep an appointment with a slender wooden statue of a woman named Sara, her shoulders draped in pink and yellow satinette. Rhinestones shine bright and glitzy against her masses of black hair. Her face, so tiny amidst hair, gown, and crown, is deepest black.

Tens of thousands of gypsies couldn't be wrong. This place was and is important. The church officials stood scratching their heads until as recently as 1933, when they officially sanctioned the pilgrimages.

In the ancient social register, the woman who was to become known as St. Sara was the least important person aboard a certain small boat that set sail, legend has it, from Palestine soon after Jesus' death. The boat foundered, struggled, and finally came to rest on the shores of southern France, disgorging an energetic crew to rival that of the SS *Minnow*. The passengers included Mary Salome (Jesus' aunt); Mary Jacob; Mary Magdalene and her sister, St. Martha; Lazarus; a few other biblical bigwigs—and Sara. She was supposedly the servant of the Maries and was nicknamed "the Egyptian." Her skin was darker than that of the other passengers. Once on land, Sara neither attempted nor accomplished the kind of feats her fellow travelers promptly undertook: Martha marched off to kill a monster in Tarascon; Mary Magdalene hiked off to find a suitably uncomfortable hermitage; the other Maries (les Saintes Maries) founded a spanking new church in their adopted homeland, in the town that would one day be named for them. Yet Sara, obscure Sara, is the reigning queen today. Sara, venerated nowhere else but here: She is the one they come to see.

The Maries' church is built of light-colored stone, rough and simple, and sparsely decorated inside. Along one wall, a carved image depicts the Maries riding in their little boat. Many paintings and photographs of shipwrecks and car accidents surround the carving, placed there by grateful Catholics who credit the Maries with saving their lives. The church floor is patterned with alternating bands of pitted, charcoal gray stone and smooth pinkish marble—as if to mirror the light skin of the Maries as contrasted with the shadowy face of Sara, who waits darkly, below, in the crypt.

Most church crypts are cool and refreshing and even more meditatively silent than the churches themselves. And yet this one in Les-Saintes-Maries-de-la-Mer pulsates hotly, like some living human organ, or the molten core of the earth. The room fairly crackles with the light and heat of votive candles. And then there is Sara, the coal at the heart of the fire, her silly raiments shimmering in the fervent, jittery glow of those countless waxen tributes. Oh, she doesn't make sense, this one. Saint Sara? Who has heard of Saint Sara? Yet her fine eyes slam you; they nail you to the wall.

Despite the passing minutes, despite the jostling parade of tourists and pilgrims passing in and out of the crypt, you and the statue stare fixedly at one another, keeping an appointment of your own—an appointment you don't really remember making, and that you never dreamed could be so important. Don't draw too close to Sara or she'll look away. Stand just the right distance away, and over blazing black cheekbones her eyes scour and search and continue to search until finally you back wrenchingly away. So—is she sad, or smiling, or both? The little chin, the pointed nose, are firmly set. What does she want; what does she want to say to you; what *doesn't* she know about you?

What's Sara's story, really? Her secret? We know the Christian legend. But history also tells us that Egyptian deities (remember her epithet, "the Egyptian") were fervently worshipped in this region as long ago as the fourth century B.C.E., their rites and religions having been carried to these shores by Egyptian sailors. The town now known as Les-Saintes-Maries-de-la-Mer was originally called Ratis, or Ra, in honor of the Egyptian sun god. Isis, too, counted this strange swampy region among the many places where she was known and loved.

The Christian legend says that the Maries established their church on the debris of an old pagan temple. The legend neglects to mention to whom that temple was dedicated.

No one really knows why the gypsies love Sara so much, or why they chose her, of all the holy personages they encountered on their travels, as such a special object of devotion. Some scholars are willing to state that the enigmatic figure today known as Saint Sara is actually a direct descendant of Isis, a not so subtle replacement, and that that dark-skinned goddess never relinquished her loving hold on this place, these wetlands that resembled her own native Nile Delta more than they did any other part of Europe. Other scholars suggest that Saint Sara represents Sara-Kali, a black-skinned mother goddess traditionally sacred to the Rom, or gypsy, people.

Today, from all corners of Europe the gypsies come, in vans and cars and campers, to keep their appointment with Sara. They convene in the crypt with the statue, they tie layer upon layer of billowing pastel capes around Sara's neck, the pinks and yellows of after-dinner mints. They carry the statue on a litter down to the seashore, just as worshippers of Isis, two thousand years ago, carried their goddess's swarthy image, swathed in festive robes, down to the fertile sea.

Getting there: Open daily, 8:00 A.M. to noon and 2:00 P.M. to 7:00 P.M.. Admission free. Les-Saintes-Maries-de-la-Mer is 20 miles southwest of Arles, on the coast. The church is in the center of town on Place de l'Eglise. The statue of Saint Sara is in the crypt. The pilgrimages take place every year on May 24 (with the procession of Saint Sara at 4:00 P.M.), May 25 (with the procession of the Saintes Maries at 11:00 A.M.), and on the Sunday closest to October 22.

Vienne

Temple of Cybele and Theater of the Mysteries

You'd scarcely find a more humdrum public park than this one if you searched the entire length and breadth of France. Polyester-clad citizens chat amiably as their terriers root in the scrubgrass; teenagers talk of cheeseburgers and teach each other to smoke among the old stone walls.

Who would dream, to look at them, that those walls once bore the bloody traces of yet another kind of initiation? For this was a temple of Cybele. The men and women who loved that goddess felt a passion as intense as the hot blood in which they bathed, ever striving to know her more closely. Theirs was an eastern-flavored mystery, a religion of life and death. Theirs was a world of lions and bulls—never terriers.

Cybele's native territory was Phrygia, in the Near East. Her religion found countless enthusiastic converts as it spread westward to Rome and throughout the Roman Empire. By the first century C.E., the Roman Emperor Claudius was a devotee of Cybele, and worship of the goddess was sweeping through Gaul.

The Gaulish people of Vienne had plenty of their own native goddesses. But there was something about Cybele, foreign as she was, that touched a deep nerve. She was *strong*. An earth goddess, she was both lover and grandmother to the handsome boy Attis. That love would have been enough, but then Attis, with his roving eye, made Cybele jealous. The goddess's ensuing rage drove Attis crazy, and in crazy shame he castrated himself and died. His bloody death and subsequent rebirth—and Cybele's sorrow and joy—formed the crux of the religion's mystery, which was celebrated en masse at spring equinox festivals. It was also celebrated in private with the *taurobolium* ritual, in which a devotee would bathe in the blood of a freshly sacrificed bull (see the Lyon entry earlier in this chapter).

Both public and private kinds of ritual took place in Vienne. A temple and its attendant Theater of Mysteries was discovered here in 1963. The theater was distinguished by impressive semicircular tiers. The temple, which was probably destroyed when Vienne was invaded in 275 C.E., was a complicated structure with many rooms, as well as sacred basins in which initiates could wash the blood off their bodies. These ancient structures were excavated and finally integrated into a public park—a humdrum one by most standards, but especially humdrum, *obscenely* humdrum when you think of the furious bloody faith these old stones once saw, the gasps of pain and revelation that the old stones heard.

They were anything but callow, the people who worshipped here. Nor was their goddess a frail thing, she who held the secrets of death and transcendence. So do not step so lightly as you cross this park, nor so lightheartedly. And dare not think of cheeseburgers.

Getting there: Open during daylight hours. Admission free. Vienne is on the River Rhone, on the train line, 17 miles south of Lyon. The temple and the theater are in the Jardin Archeologique de Cybele; the entrance is on rue Victor Hugo at the intersection of rue Henri Jacquier. The Theater of Mysteries is the upper part of the park, consisting primarily of grassy terraces with a few ruins on the right side. The washing basins are at the bottom of the theater to the right as you look down, and the temple is the area between the basins and the large portico arches.

Black Madonnas

Black madonnas are France's great riddle. In a country where the Virgin Mary could easily clinch every political election, popularity contest, or beauty pageant, literally hundreds of the venerated statues representing her have black faces. Or dark brown ones. Or charcoal gray, tarnished silver, russet, tawny, chestnut: rich mineral hues that resound deep in the primitive parts of the soul.

From the chic hurlyburly of Paris's Left Bank to the loneliest reaches of the high Alps, black madonnas hold the French in thrall. Kings, queens, and emperors have knelt humbly at the black madonnas' feet and crowned their dark heads with gold and diamonds. Peasants, lacking diamonds, cover the altars with wheat, butter, flowers, and spring lambs.

Some of France's most celebrated Maries are black: the ones at Chartres, for example. But the famous ones have no monopolies on either beauty or miracles. One obscure black madonna specializes in resuscitating dead children; another in freeing unjustly held prisoners from jail. Some of them save sinking ships. Others banish plagues, stave off epidemics, repel enemy invasions. Some weep. Many heal.

No one, scholar or otherwise, can begin to explain how so many French madonnas came to be black. Theories are rife. The Church, for its part, tends to downplay and even hide the dark statues. Some say their darkness is the result of accumulated candlesmoke. But if that is true, then why would their faces and hands be dark while their dresses and shoes remain bright and colorful? Some maintain that the statues were brought home to France by returning Crusaders and were made in the Holy Land, where of course women were naturally darker skinned. The leading book on the subject, *Étude sur l'Origine des Vierges Noires* (Marie Durand-Lefebvre, 1937), explores at length the connections between the black madonnas and pagan goddesses who were worshipped on French soil before Christianity took hold. Scholars today are continuing to pursue those exciting connections. They note that we find the heaviest concentration of black madonnas in rural and/or geologically unusual parts of France where people were known to have once worshipped earth, fertility, and mother goddesses, often so stubbornly that the Church, finding the cults alive and thriving into the fourth or fifth century C.E., often simply erected its own Marian shrines directly on top of goddess shrines. They slyly left the goddess statues in place, changing only their names. Many black madonnas in France are actually direct descendants of venerable goddesses. Isis, Cybele, and Artemis were worshipped in ancient France alongside countless native divinities, and they were usually depicted as dark skinned, which isn't surprising when you consider their eastern origins. Also, Isis and

Cybele were often depicted suckling their sons. (You can see ample proof of this in museums.)

The madonnas themselves are silent on the matter. Serene in their dark skins, these queens of mystery, queens of darkness, seem to ask with their half smiles and heavy-lidded eyes, "I am beautiful and I am *here*. Do you really need to know anything else?"

Clermont-Ferrand (Notre Dame de Clermont): Black is a lucky color for the city of Clermont-Ferrand. It is the color of highways and tires, and Clermont-Ferrand is the headquarters of France's tire industry. This is also the heart of the Auvergne, a region whose devotion to statues of females startled and angered early Christians and whose present devotion to black madonnas is the strongest in France.

Not one but two of the madonnas venerated in Clermont-Ferrand are dark. The city's tutelary madonna, Notre Dame de Clermont, sits in a niche, bathed in lamplight that sets her golden gown ablaze. When she was carved in the tenth century, she was not painted black. But, curiously, she was deliberately altered during the nineteenth century. Now her face and hands are blackest black, as are those of the child she holds. Their lips are cherry red, the red-on-black of life against death, and of the volcanoes whose eruptions, countless centuries ago, contributed to the Auvergne's geology and its haunting, nippled landscape.

Getting there: Open Monday to Saturday, 8 A.M. to noon and 2 to 7 P.M.; Sunday whenever masses are not being held. The statue is in the Cathedral of Clermont-Ferrand, on Place de la Victoire in the center of the old town. The statue occupies a niche at the very back of the cathedral, behind the main altar.

Clermont-Ferrand (Notre Dame du Port): Comfortable and comforting, La Vierge de Tendresse, the Virgin of Tenderness, sits beside a sacred well in a subterranean chamber that is as dark, moist, and welcoming as a womb.

A church has stood here in the ancient *port* or warehouse district of the city since the sixth century. Even then, it was acknowledged that the church, dedicated to the Virgin, had been erected squarely on top of a former Celtic sanctuary where a water goddess, queen of the well, had been revered.

That goddess's descendant, Notre Dame du Port, whose nickname is La Vierge de Tendresse, has a calm face of glossy black. The nickname undoubtedly stems from the tender way she holds her child, her strong hands supporting his realistically carved black body. Cheek to cheek, the pair greet you with a contented look that transcends all sorrow and suffering, their own as well as yours. The statue was carved in the eighteenth century to replace a Byzantine icon that had been brought back as a souvenir of the Crusades. The icon was venerated here for centuries, but it finally became hopelessly careworn. The replacement, enthroned beside the ancient well, seems the embodiment of the water itself. The smooth curves of her body and gown, her liquid gaze, and the soothingly dark sheen of her skin instantly put you at ease. You too feel liquid, deep, at rest.

Getting there: Open daily 8 A.M. to 7 P.M. The church of Notre Dame du Port is on rue Notre Dame du Port in the old part of town, just south of rue Montlosier. The statue is in the crypt.

Dijon: While it's not polite to muse about one's mother's naked body, Notre Dame de Bon Espoir's body, with its pendulous breasts, swollen belly, and matchstick-thin legs, spread wide, is just too interesting to overlook. Jet black, this body is not exposed to the public very often. But as you look at the madonna's long nut-brown face, its lips downturned at the corners and its black button eyes nonchalant over yards and yards of concealing linen, you will know her secret.

She *is* a puzzle. For some reason, a small carving of an owl on the outside wall of the church has always been linked with her, like a pet or mascot. People have been rubbing the owl for good luck for so many centuries that its features are now worn smooth. At least one writer, describing this church, has pointed out that owls are the traditional animals of Athena.

Medieval crusaders supposedly brought this madonna back from the Holy Land. Now, 800 years later, the Virgin's chapel is the brightest corner in the church. The light from many candles dances across the warm colors of the frescoed walls. The madonna sits alone, no sign of the baby Jesus anywhere. If you really squint, you can just make out a crucifix painted on the wall behind her, but her bold conical form blocks it out completely, preempting it.

To the right of the statue hangs a huge tapestry, a feast of vivid oranges and greens. Woven in 1946 to thank Notre Dame de Bon Espoir for protecting the city throughout World War II, it depicts the humble people of Dijon gathering together, while just outside the town walls, wild beasts—a wide-eyed wolf, a raven, an owl, a boar —clamor and slather in the dark woods. Above it all towers the flower-decked figure of Our Lady, and over her head a single word: TERRIBILIS. That's "terrible," as in awesome, huge, unfathomable.

Getting there: Open daily, generally 7:30 A.M. to 7 P.M. The black madonna is in the Church of Notre Dame, at the intersection of rue de la Prefecture and rue Musette. The statue is to the right of the main altar at the back of the church. The owl is on the ouside north wall, about 100 feet back from rue de la Prefecture and about 6 feet off the ground.

Lyon: Two black madonnas, venerated under one roof, atop a hill that once was sacred to Cybele. What could be better? But wait, there's more! Across the street from the enshrined black madonnas, a Marian museum houses dozens of their disenfranchised sisters, black and otherwise, who once enjoyed devotion in churches all over Europe.

Now, put out to pasture and reduced to the status of mere artifacts, the assembled madonnas range from the thirteenth to the nineteenth centuries. They show Mary's fascinating gradual transformation from craggy-featured worldwise matron to svelte movie star, from swarthy to pale.

In the chapel, Notre Dame de Bon Conseil—Our Lady of Good Advice —has a tiny, shiny black face, surmounted by a five-pointed star. Her dusky roommate, Notre Dame de Fourvière, overlooks a large votive plaque in which the city of Lyon officially thanks her for her miraculous aid during two separate cholera epidemics.

Getting there: Both madonnas are in the "Ancient Chapel" adjacent to the Basilica of Fourvière, at the very top of the hill of Fourvière, on the west side of the Saône river. The Ancient Chapel is next to the sacristy on the right side of the basilica. Notre Dame de Bon Conseil is on a side wall facing the chapel's entrance, and Notre Dame de Fourvière is at the back of the chapel on the high altar. The Marian museum, Musée Fourvière, is open May through October, daily, 10 A.M. to noon and 2 to 6 P.M.; closed November through April. Admission free. The museum is just to the right of the Basilica of Fourvière; signs point the way.

Marsat: Our Lady of Marsat, whose church and village rise up out of fertile fields, is as black as compost. She wears a gown the color of a ripe persimmon. Looking so autumnal, like something aching to be harvested, she sits in darkness in her corner of the church. Only when a visitor comes and presses a button does she become flooded in light, and even then her features, black against black, are hard to discern. Step up very close to her, and you'll see a face sagging with unbearable misery. The chin, tense, seems to struggle against trembling; the puffy eyes tell of sorrows no mortal can fathom.

With griddlelike black hands, each one easily as big as her head, the madonna steadies the child on her knees. Oddly tall and adolescent looking, he has inherited her blackness.

Ever since the Middle Ages, Our Lady of Marsat has been one of the most beloved black madonnas in the Auvergne, a region in which there are many fine ones. Though she sorrows, she still manages to pull off miracles, the most notable being her saving the nearby town of Riom from a Norman invasion in 916 C.E. An annual procession still commemorates that event.

Getting there: Open daily, normal church hours. Marsat is 2 miles southwest of Riom, which is 10 miles north of Clermont-Ferrand. The madonna is located in the side altar of the Church of Marsat, in the center of town.

Marseille: In a crypt that is probably the coolest, most peaceful place in all of teeming Marseille, Notre Dame de la Confession holds up one exquisite nut-brown hand. Her royal blue gown with its delicate gold stars suggests the night sky over Provence.

Historians tell of a rule, enforced in this church as recently as the seventeenth century, that forbade women and animals from entering the crypt. Why would women and animals be denied access to a madonna? Unless, of course, churchmen harbored disturbing memories of a time when women gathered here to worship yet another Mother. And animals? Perhaps those disturbing memories also included animal sacrifices.

Today, all are welcome in the crypt, where the dark madonna reigns in unearthly silence. Across the street, at Marseille's oldest bakery, you can buy cookies that are traditionally associated with the Virgin. Called *navettes* (boats), the aromatic sweets are said to resemble the little boat in which Mary Magdalen and her friends rode to Provence after the crucifixion and thus spread the word of Christianity. Curiously, the cookies also look like long, fleshy *labia majora*. The formula that makes them so feathery light and elusively spicy has been, of course, a family secret for some 200 years.

Getting there: Open daily, 8 A.M. to 6:30 P.M. Admission: 5F. The madonna is in the Abbey of Saint Victor, which is on Place Saint-Victor, one block from Quai de Rive Neuve along the old port. The statue is in the crypt.

Metz: Metz doesn't sell pictures of its black madonna, Notre Dame de Bon Secours. There's not a postcard, a keychain, or a dashboard magnet with her image on it to be found anywhere in the whole town, a town where, according to one author, a statue of Isis was venerated under the guise of Mary until as recently as the sixteenth century. Today the word is that the local clergy prohibits the reproduction and distribution of the black madonna's image, though whether the prohibition is motivated by shame or by reverence is not clear.

It's a pity, anyway, because Metz's black madonna, with her filmy lace cuffs and flowing gown, is the prettiest—if not the fairest—of them all. She stands directly across from the door and instantly seizes your attention. A bank of candles in front of her altar makes this the brightest, warmest spot in the cathedral. Over her black head spreads a canopy of golden lilies, so that she looks like a May Queen, or a Jewish bride.

Getting there: Open daily, 7:30 A.M. to noon and 2 to 6 P.M. The black madonna is in the Cathedral of Saint-Etienne, on Place d'Armes in the center of town.

Riom: Riom's black madonna lives the life of an understudy. Far more celebrated is her gloom-puss neighbor, Our Lady of Marsat (discussed earlier). Even in her own church, the nameless black madonna of Riom is upstaged by another Virgin, Notre Dame à l'Oiseau, an inexplicably famous fourteenth century sculpture rendered in pale stone.

Riom's black madonna huddles like Cinderella in a dingy alcove. Yet the faithful know her. They seek her out, sweeping brusquely past Notre Dame à l'Oiseau without so much as a *Bonjour, madame*. Before the dark mother, they pray out loud, these old ladies of Riom. And she, looking younger in her vivid dress than her daughters do in their black ones, always has time to listen.

Getting there: Open daily, normal church hours. Riom is 10 miles north of Clermont-Ferrand. The black madonna is in the Eglise Notre-Dame du Marthuret, in a chapel on the right side. (*Not* to be confused with Notre Dame à l'Oiseau, which is also in a chapel on the right, but closer to the front door.) The church is at the corner of rue du Commerce and rue du Marthuret, in the old part of town.

Rocamadour: Despite or perhaps because of its precarious location, high atop a rocky promontory,

Rocamadour, with its black madonna, enjoys a reputation as *"le deuxième site de France,"* the second most popular destination in France. (The first is Mont-St-Michel.) Ever since the Middle Ages, French kings (Henri Plantagenet, Philippe le Bel, Louis XI), saints (Dominic, Bernard, Louis), and numberless waves of tour bus passengers have made their way up the rock to kneel before the golden altar of Our Lady of Rocamadour.

One of the most richly endowed madonnas in France, black or otherwise, the coal-visaged madonna of Rocamadour has inspired legendary loyalty among her followers and is credited with many wonders, including sea rescues, granting fertility to formerly infertile couples, and of course countless healings. In her chapel is a bell that is said to toll of its own accord whenever the Virgin performs a miracle.

A human skeleton found on this site in the Middle Ages was heralded as being that of St. Amadour, an apocryphal biblical-era figure who worked as the Virgin Mary's servant and was married to St. Veronica, who gained fame after wiping Jesus' face with her veil on the day of the crucifixion. Legends say that Amadour retired to France—why not? James Baldwin did—where he became a hermit. Skeptics later pointed out that St. Amadour probably never existed.

One thing everyone agrees on is that a sanctuary occupied this dizzying site long before the advent of Christianity. In its hallowed, rarefied confines, some deity enjoyed the people's worship. Perhaps she too received visits from kings.

Getting there: Open daily, generally daylight hours. Rocamadour is in the Lot department, in south-central France, 110 miles north of Toulouse and 40 miles north of Cahors. The black madonna is in the Chapelle Notre-Dame, also known as the Chapelle Miraculeuse, in the sanctuary area at the top of the cliff overlooking the town. The statue is below the main altar.

Vichy: Notre Dame des Malades—Our Lady of the Sick—watches over this spa town and all its people with a twisted smile and a woozy, crooked gaze, looking as afflicted as many of those who come to ask her for healings. She follows in the footsteps of goddesses: The Gallo-Roman town that flourished here in the first century C.E. was studded with a variety of temples, all of which are lost now. The citizens of that town revered a divine presence that inhabited the therapeutic springs. They were probably not the first to have done so. To this day, the main reason people visit Vichy is to "take the cure" in its waters.

During the French Revolution, an angry mob burned Vichy's treasured old black madonna in the public square. Legend has it that a boy managed to rescue the madonna's head from the flames. To this head a new body was subsequently attached, and this surgical miracle is venerated in the town today.

Though skillfully carved and polished, the features of the madonna's coffee-colored face are all oddly skewed, as if on purpose. Her eyes are markedly different from one another, and her mouth is downright bizarre. A pair of knee-length braids lends a whimsical touch.

Getting there: Open daily, normal church hours. Vichy is 33 miles northeast of Clermont-Ferrand. The black madonna is in the old section of the Church of St. Blaise, which is on rue d'Allier and rue de l'Eglise, on the west side of town between Parc Kennedy and Parc des Sources. The madonna is on the altar at the rear.

Goddesses in Captivity: Museums

Dijon: Archaeological Museum The Gaulish goddess Sequana ruled the River Seine and was worshipped at its source near Dijon. The French archaeologists who excavated her sanctuary were astounded by the discovery, in 1963, of over 300 ex-votos, images of pilgrims' afflicted body parts, which had been left so many years ago as tokens of faith. Now these artifacts are in this museum, and you, like the archaeologists, will be amazed at their state of preservation—some of these are made of *wood,* believe it or not—and by their strange, quirky beauty. Bronze, stone, and wooden arms,

The river goddess Sequana, Dijon's Archaeological Museum

legs, genitals, eyes; poor sick heads and lungs and stomachs, as well as full-body images, display a remarkably confident sense of style and knowledge of human anatomy. Stolid wooden faces stare beseechingly out at you from under heavy brows; sensitive lips seem about to speak. These faces haunt you for days afterward.

Among these heartfelt gifts to the goddess is an image of the goddess herself, a bronze statuette in which Sequana, arms benificently outspread, rides aboard a boat that is fancifully shaped like a duck.

Getting there: Open Wednesday through Sunday, 9:30 A.M. to noon and 2 to 6 P.M.; during July and August, Wednesday through Sunday, 9:30 A.M. to 6 P.M. Admission: 8F40. The museum is located at 5 rue Docteur Maret.

Paris: The Louvre Let the others come to see the Mona Lisa. She's as cryptic, as compelling, as any goddess. Grant her that. But for those whose taste in goddesses runs to the more traditional, the Louvre offers Europe's best and most beautiful, captured and controlled within these famed walls so that millions of art lovers might admire them in their out-of-context glory. There are so many goddess images here, so much trapped power, that with a gaggle of Athenas at the helm, a bunch of Venuses to distract the enemy, they might just decide, late one night, to form an army. Watch out!

In addition to classical statues of Demeter, Kore, Athena, Cybele, Artemis, and Diana, the Louvre also houses Aphrodite Removing Her Sandal, Aphrodite Crouching, Aphrodite the Progenitress, and many more, including, of course, the Venus de Milo.

The Egyptian section houses many renditions of Isis and Hathor. Elsewhere dwell Mesopotamian goddesses as well as Punic, Minoan, and Cypriot goddesses. Images of Ishtar stand guard over squadrons of small terracotta female figurines. Four-thousand-year-old baking implements bear bas-reliefs of goddesses, proving that ancient people ate bread with her image imprinted on it.

Getting there: Open Thursday through Sunday, 9 A.M. to 6 P.M.; Monday and Wednesday, 9 A.M. to 9:45 P.M.; closed Tuesday. Admission: 27F. The Louvre is located between Quai du Louvre and Rue de Rivoli, just north of the Seine. Metro: Palais Royale Musée du Louvre (one stop, long name).

Paris: Musée de l'Homme France's first goddesses didn't give a hoot about fashion. Dressed in nothing or nearly nothing, buttocks and breasts heaving every which way, they lived in caves and camps and the preliterate hearts of the Stone Age men and women who worshipped them. The Musée de l'Homme celebrates these early goddesses with a new permanent exhibit, "Nuits des Temps." Subtitled "the history of humanity," the exhibit features some of the world's most beautiful prehistoric female figurines. Besides good replicas of the Austrian Venus of Willendorf and the so-called "fat

The Louvre Museum's Aphrodite de Cnide, *attributed to Praxiteles*

ladies" of Malta, the museum houses an ivory carving from Laugerie-Basse, France. Called a *Venus impudique*, a "lewd Venus," the flat-chested little figure radiates a strong female energy. The 20,000-year-old ivory Venus of Lespugue wears a rudimentary skirt flap in back, which doesn't hide much. Great egg-shaped breasts, twin bolsters of thigh, round vulnerable shoulders, and a tiny head tilted, as if listening, make this a body of striking geometrical grace.

Getting there: Open Wednesday through Monday, 9:45 A.M. to 5:15 P.M.; closed Tuesdays. Admission: 16F;

students 8F. The museum is in the Palais de Chaillot on Place du Trocadero in the sixteenth arrondissement. Metro: Trocadero.

St-Germain-en-Laye: National Antiquities Museum Louis XIV was born in this chateau. In his substantial shadow, a mob of goddesses have gathered, huddling in the silent dethroned rooms like squatters. But once, their full moons shone brighter than Louis's sun.

A walk-through replica of the prehistoric painted cave at Lascaux provides a moist, pungent passage into the museum. Thereafter, you wander through several million years of human history, meeting goddesses all along the way. Arduina, the forest goddess whose name lingers on in the Ardennes, is depicted mounted on a boar. Epona, the Celtic equine goddess, is here, riding sidesaddle. Also here are Venus (dozens of renditions), Minerva (dozens), Isis, Diana, Abundantia, and a downright comforting profusion of ancient French mother goddesses who, suckling infants, look very much like the French madonnas who follow in their footsteps.

The museum's prehistory collection is the world's richest and includes the Stone Age "Venuses" of Grimaldi, Tursac, Monpazier, Pechialet, Sireuil, and Brassempouy. It's a bouquet of curved bellies and buttocks: soft contours from a hard, cold world.

Getting there: Open Wednesday through Monday, 9 A.M. to 5:15 P.M.; closed Tuesday. Admission: 16F; children under 18 free; people under 25 and over 60 8F. St-Germain-en-Laye is a suburb a few miles west of Paris. Take the RER commuter train from central Paris to the St-Germain-en-Laye station at the end of line A1. As you exit the station, you'll be facing the chateau that houses the museum, on Place du Château.

Germany

The Roman chronicler Cornelius Tacitus, writing of the Germany his compatriots encountered in 98 C.E., noted with surprise that the natives "do not . . . imprison their gods within walls. . . . Their holy places are the woods and groves."

The Roman army gritted its teeth against the cold and settled in here for 300 years, during which time the soldiers ended up falling in love with many of the local goddesses. One of their adopted favorites was Epona, the Celtic goddess of horses and riders. The cavalry especially cherished her. Perhaps her modern legacy is the sleek Porsche, galloping pell-mell down the limitless autobahn.

Most popular of all were the Matronae, a native trio of mother goddesses. Though called by many different names along the Rhineland (*Matronae* is simply their generic Latin title), they were always depicted the same way: one young, nubile mother seated on a bench between two matrons whose hair rises in bouffant clouds around their kindly faces. Bestowing earthly fertility as well as motherly protection, they hold food and full baskets. The Matronae's appeal is as obvious now as it was in the first century C.E. Wouldn't *you* want three mothers to tuck you in at night? Three birthday cakes, six shoulders to cry on? Thirty eager fingers removing that bit of lint from your eye?

Aalen

Goddess Altars

Aalen is pagan Germany's Hall of Fame. On a sunny day, you can spread your altar cloth on the grass and picnic with the goddesses.

In its Roman-era heyday, Aalen was important not as a worship site but as one of many links along the Limes, a partly physical, partly psychological frontier line. Running from the Rhine to the Danube, the 330-mile-long Limes was intended to keep eastern barbarians out of Roman Germany. Today, Aalen's Limesmuseum explores the Limes and its history. But for the goddess-seeker, Aalen has another, far more compelling attraction.

The Römisches Parkmuseum is a placid green swath—a park—studded with ancient-looking stone altars, statues, and other monuments. They are not quite real, but they are conscientious replicas of original monuments that have been found throughout this region. The monuments are dedicated to a wide range of divinities, which illustrates the tantalizing variety of choices available to the spiritually minded ancient German. Even during military occupation, when the Roman army came and stayed for centuries, the natives were still free to worship whomever and however they chose.

In some cases, the Romans took to Celtic and Germanic deities with a relish, erecting their own heartfelt monuments and temples. The best example of this practice was the Celtic goddess Epona, protectress of horses and cavalries. In Celtic tradition, Epona was sometimes personified by a mare, with whom the chief or king would have ritual intercourse, thus ensuring the fertility and sacredness of his domain.

The altar dedicated to Epona here in Aalen depicts the goddess seated between two horses. On her knees is a full basket. A common attribute of Epona's, the basket is said to contain horse fodder.

The altar dedicated to Diana is a revealing blend of Roman and Celtic styles. Though clad in her traditional short *chiton* (classical dress) and grasping a bow, this version of the goddess of hunting has the sturdy, large-featured, almost matronly bulk of most Celtic goddesses rather than the lithe look with which Roman artists usually invested her.

A cylindrical "Seven Gods' Stone" contains tributes to Venus, Vesta, and Maia/Rosmerta, a Celtic love goddess who was appropriated as a consort for the Roman god Mercury. The altar dedicated to the *Vierwegegottinnen*—the goddesses of the crossroads—depicts a quartet of female figures. And yet another, very rare indeed, honors Herecura, a local goddess of fruitfulness.

Now, surely Herecura can be persuaded to bring the salad for our picnic. And Diana can bring the venison steaks. On the other hand, can Epona be dissuaded from bringing her specialty, fodder torte?

Getting there: Always open and visible. Admission free. Aalen is 45 miles west of Stuttgart, from which it is accessible by train. The Romisches Parkmuseum is on the southwest side of town between Huttfeldstrasse and St. Johann-strasse. From the center of town, follow the signs pointing to the Limesmuseum, but continue past the museum and the Roman foundations behind it. The park with the altars is on the right side of St. Johann-strasse where the street ends.

Pesch and Nettersheim

Matronae Altars

In ancient Germany, Pesch was where you went to prove that you loved your mother.

Mothers, that is. Pesch was, for 350 years, the site of a sanctuary dedicated to the Matronae, that trio of sweet-faced mother goddesses whose worship was firmly established among the Celts, and later among the Romans, in the Rhineland.

The sanctuary was large and multipurpose, with an array of facilities rivaling those of a modern convention center. Pesch's sanctuary offered an indoor, typically Gallo-Roman-style temple to the goddesses; an open-air worship area with statues; houses for the clergy; other buildings whose purposes have as yet to be deciphered; and even a pilgrims' lounge, which was once amply adorned with images of the Mothers and tablets inscribed in their honor. A covered walkway, 100 feet long, flanked the courtyard, with a well at its midpoint.

Archaeologists, who began excavating the site in 1912, pinpointed distinct phases in the sanctuary's history. It was first used around 50 C.E., then again from 200 to 300 C.E. During this time, Gallo-Roman spirituality had evolved to the point where Cybele, the Asiatic mother goddess, was worshipped at Pesch alongside the venerable local Matronae.

The archaeologists discovered something else as well: This shrine did not merely ebb away into gradual disuse. On the contrary: It met a violent and shattering end. In 400 C.E., the place was deliberately trashed. Not a single stone was left unbroken. Where for over 300 years countless devotees had lavished love and tribute on the goddesses, now all their heartfelt tributes were reduced to rubble. Christianity was spreading through the Roman Empire following the conversion of Emperor (and later Saint) Constantine, and early Christians, seeing the chance to degrade pagan strongholds, reacted with an orgasmic relish all over Germany. In Mainz, a 30-foot stone column that had been painstakingly carved in honor of a covey of deities, including Diana, Epona, Ceres, and Vesta, was smashed into an amazing 2000 pieces. So at Pesch, the zealots were neither merciful nor charitable.

At the bottom of the sanctuary's well, archaeologists found the broken remains of nearly 150 monuments. Is that any way to treat a mother?

The sanctuary, partially restored, nestles today in a

patch of green forest. The locals call the sanctuary *Heidentempel*, "the heathens' temple." On the shrine's replica stone altars you can sometimes find traces of fresh candlewax: apparently someone is still coming here as a pilgrim and not merely as a tourist.

From each of the altars, the Matronae gaze out calmly, arranged on their benches as always: a young, nubile mother with flowing hair, flanked by two matrons whose huge round hairdos are at once hilarious and mystical. Their sensitive hands cradle the full baskets on their laps. Petticoats peek out from under full, matronly skirts. These goddesses seem too kind, too gentle, to be carved in hard stone. Those great spheres of hair are the pillows you cuddled as a child.

All around, the trees purr and rustle. It is the combined cluckings, the symphony of lullabies, of every mother who ever lived.

Just a few miles away, another partly restored Matronae shrine at Nettersheim illustrates that this whole region was once sacred to these goddesses. Some handsomely carved altars are here as well, bearing Latin inscriptions that show they were donated by pious local policemen during the Roman occupation.

Today, Nettersheim's Mothers overlook a serene undulant landscape, in which cows dream away the days among folds of emerald earth. From their laps, the Mothers offer bread and fruit. Though their eyes are sweet and mild, there is behind those eyes an assumption, an earth-rooted resolve that has no regard for the passage of millennia. They mean to protect you, feed you, keep you safe, forever. You might as well let them have their way.

Getting there: Always open and visible. Admission free. Pesch is 12 miles south of Euskirchen, which is 16 miles west of Bonn. From Euskirchen, go south 8 miles and turn west at Munstereifel; go 2½ miles west through the town of Nothen, and continue 2 miles southwest to Pesch. Signs indicate the parking area for the sanctuary, which you will see about ½ mile before you reach Pesch (actually just a few buildings). A signposted path leads ⅓ mile from the parking area to the sanctuary. To reach Nettersheim from Pesch, go southwest 3

Altars to the Matronae, Nettersheim

miles through Zingsheim, and continue southwest another 2 miles to Nettersheim. Follow the signs leading to the *Tempelbezirk Gorresburg*. It's easy to lose your way, so ask for directions if you're unsure.

Goddesses in Captivity: Museum

Cologne (Köln): Römische-Germanische Museum Despite its name, this museum is not about Romans per se but about Germany during the time it was occupied by Romans. The religous life of the people is fully explored here, including the worship of goddesses—native Germanic, Roman, and imported ones as well.

One section of the museum is devoted to the Matronae, the trio of mother goddesses who were so well loved in this area. The vast array of Matronae altars found nearby and now on display here attests to their popularity.

Other sections include statuettes of goddesses brought in by the Romans, including Minerva, Fortuna, Venus, Cybele, Diana, and, most remarkably, Isis. The cult of Isis spread like wildfire through ancient Cologne, and evidence of her worship was found all over the city, including one site that later became a church. One exhibit explores the connection between Isis and the Virgin Mary, showing how many of Mary's epithets, attributes, and aspects of iconography were directly borrowed from Isis.

As a bonus, the museum's gift shop offers one of the best selections of goddess figurines anywhere in northern Europe.

Getting there: Open Tuesday and Friday though Sunday, 10 A.M. to 5 P.M.; Wednesday and Thursday, 10 A.M. to 8 P.M. Admission: DM3, students DM1. The museum is adjacent to the *Dom* (cathedral) in the center of town. As you face the front of the Dom, the museum is on your right at the back end of the plaza.

Great Britain

GREAT BRITAIN

Britain's history writes itself and keeps on writing.

At first it was written in stone: the sprawling sanctuaries whose sarsens still reach up, like extensions of their prehistoric builders' all-too-human arms, to embrace the swirling universe.

Then, from 650 B.C.E. onward, it was written in bronze and gold, and in the vivid woolen tartans of the Celts, those shining-haired tribes who loved poetry as much as they loved fighting and who revered women's power. This stormy island suited them perfectly; it fired the imaginations of their artists, heroes, priestesses, and priests. Clattering roughshod across the moors, the Celts dreamed of their horse goddess, Epona (worshipped in Wales as Rhiannon). They came bearing gifts to familiar trees, rivers, hills, and wells, knowing each one to be numinous, holy, the seat of some goddess or god. In 55 B.C.E., the Roman army marched in, initiating a series of forays that would result in a 400-year military occupation of England, during which time the Romans ended up building temples to the tantalizing goddesses of the not-quite-vanquished Celts. In 597 C.E., after the Romans had given way to Jutes, Angles, Saxons, and saints, England was officially Christianized. But not without a whimper. This is still a country where garlanded girls are crowned Queen of the May and where popular customs such as rushbearing, church clipping, egg rolling, well dressing, plough blessing, midsummer bonfires, and sea blessing bespeak a firm loyalty, however mute, to the old goddesses and their rites.

Britain's history is written and then lovingly written all over again. It is told and retold; sung; danced; acted out. The old stories are spun out like gossamer banners that spread and billow in the bracing English wind.

Avebury

Prehistoric Sanctuary

Some people build temples. Some people build cathedrals and jam them with candles and bits of colored glass and think they're very fine. But the people who built Avebury 4500 years ago perceived divinity on a much wider scale. No human-sized structure could begin to satisfy their goddess. Whole hills would be altars. Sacred space would roll and ramble over many acres of sweet green land, open to the stars, and encircled, but gently, by a hundred megaliths that stood wide apart like a wagon train. A processional aisle was no mere cramped passageway between pews but a whole country mile of grassy downs and hulking, erect stones.

These builders weren't giants. Their tools were clumsy stone hammers and the sharpened antlers of British red deer. They never knew metal. Yet their idea of a sanctuary required the use of colossal sandstone blocks, some of which weighed 40 tons or more. Given these people's strength and technology, it would have taken two laborers, working in turns, an entire day to cut 4 cubic yards of stone. Once the stones, called sarsens, were cut, they were levered with antler picks onto wooden sledges. A team of pullers hauled the burdens across the downs, sometimes for miles. Setting the stones upright in their proper positions was no easy task, either.

It must have taken over 200 people 10 years or more to complete Avebury. But *what* people, what culture, what religion? They were called the Beaker People because of lipped vessels that they buried alongside their dead. Immigrants from Holland and the Rhineland, they were an energetic society who knew both agriculture and livestock raising. Their homes have vanished. Only by their stones do we know them.

The stones at Avebury, which originally comprised two circles within a larger circle, with gateways at the four directional points—the southern one led to a sextet of concentric stone circles on Overton Hill—certainly served a ritual purpose. The stones reared up and the wind sang through them. The whole whirling cosmos served as roof, walls, windows, and choir. Many other prehistoric monuments lay nearby; this was a sacred district. Perhaps this place knew secrets as great as Eleusis's. But all is lost.

All, that is, except the stones which form a vast, scanty circle, inside of which are the remains of two smaller circles. A hundred pairs of megaliths march southeastward from the circle, over the downs to Overton Hill. Occupying over 20 acres, this is the largest known megalithic monument, big enough, in fact, to enclose part of the modern village of Avebury, cottages, elms, and all. A shallow ditch rings the circle's perimeter: a mere shadow of the yawning moat that originally sank 30 to 50 feet into the earth.

The stones leading away from the circle are of two alternating shapes and were deliberately chosen, it appears, for this reason. Tall pillars and squat diamonds: some say these shapes represent men and women, conjoining in a ritual procession. Others, however, suggest that the stones represent the goddess herself, in her (slim) maiden and (pregnant) mother aspects. The two smaller circles, each with a stone at its center, might have represented the nippled breasts of the Mother, encircled by her huge round belly. These and other theories could, and do, fill volumes.

But rejoicing in Avebury's power, savoring its mystery, lovingly replacing its missing stones, are very recent luxuries indeed. Throughout the Middle Ages until as recently as the eighteenth century, local people's attitudes were very different, and the stones, in a blaze of Christian piety, were systematically burned, toppled, smashed with sledgehammers, and buried. (Perhaps the stones fought back, a little. One of the so-called stone-killers was killed in the process; early twentieth century archaeologists found his shattered skeleton beneath a fallen megalith.)

But stones are patient; big stones have the patience of eons. Avebury's sentinels stand waiting. Victorious in their own way, they are content to outlive both their builders and their breakers, content to kindle the notion that people will cherish them again and summon the goddess from within their long, long shadows.

Getting there: Always open. Admission free. Avebury is in Wiltshire, 7 miles west of Marlborough, 1 mile north of the A4 road on the A361. The circle is around most of the town and is plainly visible in the nearby fields.

Bath

Temple of Sulis Minerva

Sulis Minerva was not a great goddess. She had no legions of worshippers who wept at her festivals. No kings prostrated themselves at her altar. No bard ever sang her myths and legends, for she had none.

Sulis Minerva had but one temple, a single temple in a small settlement on the fringes of the civilized world. Her devotees were regular folk: freed slaves, craftspeople, laborers, retired soldiers. Yet there was *something* about her, some magical, hidden spark that drew the hopeful and curious not only from neighboring towns but from all over ancient Britannia. As reports of her good works spread, seekers came to her from Gaul, Germany, and even farther afield. Now, thousands of years after her shrine was first built, nearly one million curious people come to her temple every year. So even a goddess can be a late bloomer.

She started out as Sul, a Celtic goddess the local Iron Age tribes recognized as the power behind the springs that gushed from the earth at the site we now call Bath. The springs here, the Celts must have realized, were unique, different from all the other springs in Britain, for the water at Bath was steamingly, soul-soothingly hot. To the minds of ancient people, the source of all heat was the sun, and there is some evidence that Sul originally had a solar connection. And it could not have been long before they discovered that Sul was a healer too. Her waters were miraculous: they could wash away disease as effortlessly and smoothly as they flowed out of the ground.

Yet Sul must have been more complicated than that. When the Romans arrived, they not only Latinized Sul to Sulis, but they also paired her with one of their own goddesses to make her more properly Roman. In most cases they merged local spring and healing goddesses with Diana, who seemed to them the most appropriate choice. But here at Bath (or Aquae Sulis, as the Romans called it), Sul was blended with Minerva to produce the Romano-Celtic goddess Sulis Minerva.

This merger is very peculiar and has never been explained. Minerva is a goddess of wisdom, warfare, and handicraft, and she has very little connection with the sun, healing, or springs. The Celts must have taught the Romans more about Sul than we know of her today, for the Romans were always very careful about naming deities and would not have chosen Minerva had they not clearly recognized her attributes in Sul.

Sul, now as Sulis Minerva, took on a new patina, a new all-encompassing glory. She seems to have been at times both healing and warlike; solar, earth-centered, and water-centered; retributive and nurturing; female and male; Celtic and Roman; personal and communal. Yet throughout it all she remained highly localized, all her power focused on this particular spring. She would heal you, but only if you came to her.

And come they did. The pre-Roman Celts undoubtedly had a shrine to her here, but nothing remains of it but a few coins of the Dobunni tribe, thrown in as offerings. The Romans, knowing a good thing when they saw it, razed the primitive shrine and built a beautiful, tall, classical temple and decorated it with the work of the finest sculptors; they contained the sacred spring and channeled its waters into a series of baths used for ritual and healing purposes. The temple was surrounded by a wide precinct, with an altar in front and a special place from which offerings could be thrown into the spring. The usual offering was money, but gems, curses, votive pots, ritual implements, jewelry, and many other items were found. One of the curses, etched in lead and tossed into the waters, bemoans the bisexual adventures of one man's lover: "May he who carried off Vilbia from me become as liquid as water. May she who obscenely devoured her become dumb. . . ."

The last coin given to the goddess as an offering dates from 388 C.E. After that, the Roman Empire collapsed and the temple fell into disuse. Wars, migrations, and the rise of Christianity in the ensuing centuries led to a total restructuring of society. But even in the medieval period people were still coming to the water in hopes of being cured. The name of Sulis Minerva was forgotten. Even so, she continued her favors anonymously, uncomplainingly.

In the seventeenth and eighteenth centuries, the aristocracy discovered Bath, and it became all the rage to "take the cure" in the refurbished healing spring. The meeting place of the elite and the center of upper-class British social life was the Pump Room, built—perhaps not so coincidentally, after all—on the site of the temple and sacrificial altar. People from all over Britain were still, albeit unwittingly, flocking to Sulis Minerva's temple.

Much of the area around the baths and sacred springs has now been excavated. The ruins have been fitted out as a museum, exhibiting the finds at the site.

Walkways now wind past altars dedicated to the goddess, votives found in the spring, sculptures, and masonry from the temple buildings, and scale models of the site as it looked 1800 years ago. From behind a

Bronze head of Minerva from the temple at Bath

railing you can see the temple's front steps. The rest of the temple has never been excavated, lying as it does under the very heart of the city. Near the temple steps, in its own display case, is what once served as the focal point of the whole temple: a gilded bronze head of Minerva, once part of the temple's cult statue. Her once-painted eyes, now smooth, opaque, and blank, still harbor great kindness. They still seem just about able to cure your ills with but a glance.

The most instructive part of the museum is a part that can't be seen at all. The heat from the sacred spring, pulsing with primal power, rolls through the museum's corridors as you approach the source. Only by experiencing the healing, heady warmth of Sul herself can you truly understand the Celts' awe of her.

At the end of the tour, you come upon the baths and the sacred spring, now contained in a lopsided octagonal pool. Wisps of steam rise to an overhanging balcony, where curious tourists peer into the waters and try to fathom their depths. And—when they think no one's looking—they toss a few coins into the holy pool.

Getting there: Open July and August, daily, 9 A.M. to 7 P.M.; March through June and September through October, daily, 9 A.M. to 6 P.M.; November through February, Monday to Saturday, 9 A.M. to 5 P.M., Sunday, 10 A.M. to 5 P.M. Admission: £3.25; children £1.50. Bath is in Avon, 13 miles southwest of Bristol. The temple of Sulis Minerva is in the Roman Baths Museum on Abbey Church Yard, just west of Stall Street in the center of Bath.

Caerleon

Nemesis Shrine

Life is fraught with uncertainty. But the life of a Roman soldier, stationed in the wild wet hinterland of first-century Britain, was more uncertain than most. Here he was, among strangers: the Celts, a dozen rough-riding tribes whose only unifying trait was their penchant for battle. Here he was, charged with holding fast this edge of the empire, to hold it down like a tent spike in a storm.

To a southerner like the Roman soldier, the climate here was ridiculous and cruel. Every wind was an ill one. And even the local diet, *meat* of all things, sickened him. No wonder such a man would think often of Nemesis, his people's goddess of fate. She had put him here. She alone would decide what would happen to him next. Nemesis, unlike sunshine, was one of the few things the Roman could bring along with him from home. In fact, as he must have mused ironically every now and then, Nemesis was the single thing he could never leave behind, even if he tried.

Caerleon, which the Romans called Isca in deference to the river now called Usk, was one of only three permanent military bases in Britain. The others were at York and Chester (Chester is discussed shortly). The Second Augustan Legion established its headquarters here in about 75 C.E. For over 200 years, the legionaries maintained a Roman kind of peace, guarding the Bristol Channel against possible attack while keeping a heavily armed eye on the unquiet Welshmen just beyond the frontier.

A temple of Diana was once here, a logical thing in a city at the very edge of howling wilderness. The temple was once destroyed and once restored, according to Roman records, but its exact location is lost. Fortuna, goddess of luck and fortune, was honored in the soldiers' bathhouse. But the goddess who truly fascinated these men—and their families—was Nemesis, who dangled their dangerous lives on a silver thread. Nemesis's shrine has not been lost. She would never allow that! It occupies a niche in the heart of Caerleon: the Roman amphitheater.

Over 5000 spectators at a time, nearly the entire population of Isca, used to gather here to learn new battle techniques, which were acted out in the amphitheater on a grand scale. They would also come to be entertained by gladiator tournaments. Nemesis's shrine was nestled neatly, like a grotto, into the amphitheater's rounded inner wall, just a heartbeat away from the blood, sand, and clangor. It's a niche, just as a soldier's fears and worries must erupt at his very core while he must, to be a good soldier, compress and confine them in their own small niche in his heart. Two stone benches provided space for worship and meditation, and a seashell-shaped hollow probably once held a statue of the goddess. Soldiers must have visited the shrine before going out to battle, and gladiators must have come here before tournaments to beg for their lives.

Some came to curse. An inscribed lead tablet found here invokes the aid of Nemesis as "Lady Vengeance" in punishing the knave who stole another man's coat and boots.

Nemesis's judgments, while implacably righteous, were seldom sweet. No Mother's Day treats would placate her. It took a soldier's courage to face this goddess.

Caerleon's amphitheater is the most thoroughly excavated one in Britain. Today it slumbers under a plush brilliant blanket of lawn. And yet, still jutting into the amphitheater's heart like a neat, fateful knife wound, is Nemesis's red brick shrine. The theater naps: tired, retired, surrendered. But Nemesis never sleeps.

Getting there: Open March 25 to October 27, daily, 9:30 A.M. to 6:30 P.M.; October 28 to March 24, Monday through Saturday, 9:30 A.M. to 4 P.M.; Sunday, 2 to 4 P.M. Admission: £1; students 60p. Caerleon is in southern Wales, just 2 miles north of Newport, from which there are frequent buses. From High Street, where the Roman Legionary Museum is located, follow the signs south about three blocks to the amphitheater at the southern edge of town. The shrine is the second cubicle to the left of the entrance stairs.

Carrawburgh

Coventina's Well

Jealous goddesses might bristle at the reverence and the lavish gifts that the ancient Britons showered on Coventina. Who was she, anyway? Just a small-time, small-town divinity whose entire domain was limited to a single well in the remote north of England.

"Well," Isis might complain, if she were the whiny type, which she isn't, "*she*'s never even been to Paris or Rome."

"Yes, and," Athena might snarl, if she were small-minded (which by definition she isn't), "she doesn't even stand for anything. Not for wisdom, or for love, or. . . ."

Nonetheless, the Britons doted on her. Wherever they found water welling up sweet and fresh from the body of the earth, these people went wild with gratitude. Who else but a goddess, they reasoned, could pull off such a generous feat, bestowing good water on their rugged island with its limited resources? And so to Coventina's well, they brought jewels and cash . . . and faith in the magical, healthful properties of the water. The Celts were stubbornly local. The little deities inhabiting individual trees, springs, hills, and other familiar landmarks were enough to satisfy their spiritual needs. These were people who, if alive today, would resolutely choose to shop at their neighborhood corner store rather than at the gleaming new supermarket down the road.

As if this were not enough to make other goddesses burn with envy, the Romans, who were here during the third and fourth centuries, took to Coventina, too. The *Romans*, those uptight foreigners, added their own rich tributes to those already heaped at Coventina's feet.

These Romans were soldiers, members of the First Cohort of Batavians, the First Cohort of Cugernians, and the First Cohort of Aquitanians, whose job it was to guard against attack from the north. Their fort, Brocolitia, stood poised directly against Hadrian's Wall, the empire's northern frontier. These Romans were hardly a sentimental lot, yet they found room in their hearts for a simple water goddess. They found time to build her a temple just a few yards to the west of the fort.

Enclosing Coventina's sacred spring and its oblong stone basin, the temple measured 40 feet across and was sturdily angular in the Romano-Celtic style. There was nothing else like it in any of the British military bases. Its west-facing door, now gone, was a handcrafted marvel.

But even good intentions like these can go astray. As the Roman Empire collapsed, the soldiers departed and the natives had a whole new set of worries. Coventina's Well was forgotten. The goddess languished, her waters bubbling for no one, until a British antiquarian rediscovered the site in 1876. Under a layer of stones and gravel that had clogged Coventina's basin for who knows how many centuries, he found a huge mass of artifacts. While the excavation was still underway, vandals sneaked in one night and made off with untold quantities of objects. Even so, what they left behind amounted to 13,487 coins, including some gold and silver ones, as well as brooches, pearls, pottery, clay animals, and other things. These were the amassed tributes to Coventina's gentle goodness; votary objects that long outlived the devotees and their all-too-human prayers, and even the temple itself. The presence of larger objects in the well, such as altars, incense burners, temple bells, and even a rare carving showing the goddess reclining on a leaf, suggests that the sanctuary may have been dismantled in a hurry and its most sacred paraphernalia hastily hidden in the well.

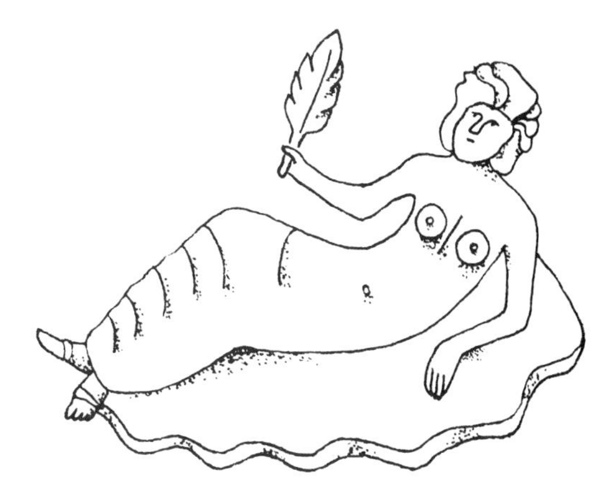

Carving of the goddess Coventina, Carrawburgh

You can still visit the stone basin with its energetic little spring. But poor Coventina! She's not so enviable after all. She came *that* close to disappearing altogether, and her once-pampered shrine just another hole in the ground, in a land where few remember that water is a gift, and divine.

Getting there: Always open. Admission free. Carrawburgh is on Hadrian's Wall, 6 miles northwest of Hexham, which is 22 miles west of Newcastle-upon-Tyne. Coventina's Well is 4 miles west of Chollerford on the B6318 road and next to the northwest corner of the Roman fort.

Charlton-on-Otmoor

"My Lady" Cross

The church cross in Charlton-on-Otmoor wears a dress made of leaves and branches. Perched up high, overlooking the pews, its stubby, green-sleeved arms spread wide as if to embrace the whole congregation. From a trim waist, its long flaring skirt falls gracefully and trembles like taffeta when the church doors open and close.

Every May Day, and again in September when the harvest comes in, loving hands renew the box hedge from which this gown is made, and they weave fresh flowers all down its front, like buttons. They call the cross "My Lady."

Charlton-on-Otmoor is a bramble-hung, thatch-roofed farming village where, for better or for worse, the squawk of the hunting horn still summons riders out to chase foxes across the moor. It is just the kind of isolated place where you'd expect to find ancient customs still surviving, shades of an earlier England still going strong.

The cross has been dressed in foliage for longer than anyone can remember. Its comforting bulky silhouette is etched deeply into every villager's heart, is etched indeed into their very identities. Every woman, man, and child here remembers the first May Day when their parents took them to church to admire My Lady's new flowers. They all remember carrying their own little flower-garlanded crosses through the streets of the village in My Lady's honor, singing. These processions continue to this day, every May 1 and September 19.

The grandparents cherish even richer memories. In the old days, My Lady used to be carried down from her perch on the festival days and paraded through the streets and fields in flowery glory, like a queen. No one knows how or when the custom began. But contemporary scholars, like Celtic expert Dr. Anne Ross, are quick to point out that "in pagan times, (at May Day) images of the mother goddess were carried round . . . and about the boundaries so that the crops might be blessed by her fecundity." Ross goes on to conclude that Ot Moor, "remote, inaccessible . . . witnessed such processions far back into the pagan past."

In her younger days, My Lady, like every good May Queen, had a consort. Another cross, called My Lord, used to stand beside her in the church, in a boxwood robe of his own. He appears in a drawing of the church dated 1823, but by 1840 he had disappeared. Theories are rife. Some say My Lady and My Lord were created to replace statues that had been smashed in the Reformation. Some suggest that the crosses once numbered three, the ancient Celts' most hallowed number. In any case, it's clear that Celtic religion, with its fruitful goddess and its merry rites of spring, lives on in Charlton-on-Otmoor, clad in the most translucent of disguises.

In a somewhat snide England, where quaint customs are often kept alive for no better reason than that tourists expect it, Charlton-on-Otmoor's love for My Lady is sincere and shows no sign of wavering. The thirteenth century church is kept tidy; the sun streams in through mullioned windows to warm every immaculate corner, the pale stone archways with their traces of fresco, the rough beam ceiling, and the plank-and-tile floor. A village woman comes in every day to set out vases of fresh flowers. Even as the seasons wear on and My Lady's green gown goes brown around the edges, the vases of flowers stand stalwartly around like ladies-in-waiting.

Twice a year, in May and September, "the boy down the lane" has the job, along with his mother, of dressing My Lady in a new boxwood outfit. A few years ago, village leaders realized to their horror that Charlton's fields had run out of box hedge. They put out an appeal over Radio Oxford: Now the deacon and his wife go out in their van to collect donations of boxwood from neighboring villages.

And that's how modern technology did its part in saving the life of a British goddess.

Getting there: Always open. Admission free. Charlton-on-Otmoor is a tiny village 11 miles north of Oxford. From Oxford, head north on the A423 road; after about 5 miles, turn right onto the A43 heading toward Bicester. After 2 miles turn right off the A43 to Islip; continue northwest out of Islip, past Oddington, and after 3 miles you'll come to Charlton-on-Otmoor. There is very little public transportation in the area. The church is at High Street and Church Lane, in the center of the village. My Lady is on top of the carved screen and is the focal point of the church.

Chester

Minerva Shrine

If Nemesis, goddess of destiny, made brave soldiers fall to their knees, then Minerva cheered them back onto their feet, into battle, and, they hoped, into victory.

As the goddess of war, she served the Roman army as honorary general, adviser, strategist, captain, soldier, and cheerleader all rolled into one. (Her noble virgin status prevented her from being a camp follower as well.) Along with Jupiter and Juno, Minerva was part of Rome's triad of official state deities, so her worship was also an act of patriotism. As the goddess designated to maintain civilization and protect civilized places, Minerva would have been especially important to men intent on Romanizing the British boondocks. Surely there were times when the Roman soldier, far from home, felt that Minerva was the only woman who truly understood him.

For the largest fortress in Roman Britain—that is, Chester—to go without a shrine of Minerva would have been unthinkable. Her sanctuary was a hulking black boulder that crouched in a field, as bold and startling against the green as a just-awakened elephant. Close by ran the sleek Dee, the river from whose name the Romans derived Deva, their original name for this fortress city.

This natural free-form rock is an unlikely milieu for meticulous Minerva. It's a far cry from the refined and urbane temples built in Rome for Minerva, who as patron goddess of artisans and architects always merited the very best of their efforts. Yet this sanctuary has something of the true war spirit, of sudden violence. The rock is a huge fist slammed onto a boardroom table: "Awright, men, this is what we gotta do. Ready?"

Violence is the operative word here, in more ways than one. A carved statue of the goddess, complete with spear, belt, cap, and attendant owl, originally occupied a niche in the rock. It was there until just a handful of years ago, when vandals destroyed it. The statue had survived for nearly 2000 years, far outliving the Roman legion it was created to inspire. Early Christians called the statue Mary and filled its niche with their own votive offerings, but archaeologists have acknowledged it as Britain's sole example of a pagan statue maintaining its original position—that is, until a few years ago.

A local historian, observing the still-intact statue one hundred years ago, wrote: "I wonder (that) it has escaped ruin so long, placed so near a great city and so low that

Minerva shrine, Chester

it is subject to all manner of injuries." It is ironic to read those words now and to wonder just how anesthetized you'd have to be before you'd mess with Minerva.

After nearly 2000 years, a barbarian army came, with weapons, and Minerva, grown incautious in her old age, let them strike. It just goes to show you that such things could happen any time. Violence is imminent. That is the message of her sacrifice.

Getting there: Always open. Admission free. Chester is on the border of Wales, just south of Liverpool. The shrine is in Edgar's Field (also called Edgar Park), south of the town center across the Dee. Go down Bridge Street, cross Old Dee Bridge: Edgar's Field is just across the bridge, on your right. The shrine is in the rocky outcropping, uphill from the play area.

Chester

Nemesis Shrine

A soldier's life is as tight and regimented as the uniform he wears. The rules he lives by are not of his own making. Strong boundaries surround him: armor, fortress walls, fellow soldiers. Yet he could die violently at any moment, and he could kill just as suddenly. Outside the boundaries, a thousand things are waiting to happen to him. And *that* is the realm of Nemesis, goddess of fate, cool-handed chooser of destinies. At Chester's Roman fortress, as at Caerleon's in south Wales (see the earlier discussion), soldiers built a shrine to Nemesis. They could not get her out of their minds.

Who knew what Nemesis had in store for individuals, countries, armies? Her name means, in a certain sense, "righteous anger." She was the one who condemned selfish Narcissus to fall in love with his own reflection and so to pine away and die. Hers is a specialized kind of discernment, hers a cruel wisdom.

At Chester, men begged her to spare their lives. Her shrine was inside the military amphitheater (as was Caerleon's), an ambitious structure unrivaled in Roman Britain. For well over 200 years, legionaries assembled here for training sessions and to watch the sports they adored: gladiator contests; bull and bearbaiting; bloody cockfights. These life-and-death games couldn't help but remind the spectators of the constant threats hanging over their own heads. So they fell to their knees before Nemesis.

Today her shrine sits quietly at the amphitheater's northern edge. Actually, only half of the once-mighty theater is visible. An Ursuline convent squats, like a victorious gladiator, over the still-buried southern half. The northern part, excavated in 1929, is one of the most orderly ancient monuments in Europe. Where once clashing, gnashing bodies spattered gore across the fine white sand, now a crewcut-trimmed lawn sports potted plants, prim benches, and tourists who calmly munch cheese sandwiches.

But the shrine is a little live spot. Its compact white marble altar, a copy of the original, draws you toward it almost in spite of yourself. You can't resist Nemesis, for in her hands lies all that really matters.

Getting there: Open in summer, daily, 10 A.M. to 6 P.M.; in winter, Tuesday through Sunday, 10 A.M. to 1 P.M., 2 to 4 P.M. Admission free. Chester is on the border of Wales, just south of Liverpool. The shrine is in the Roman Amphitheater, on Little St. John St., near the intersection of Pepper St. and Souters Lane. The shrine room is on the north side of the amphitheater, just on the left side (as you face north) of the ancient entrance passage.

River Goddesses

To live near water is to come to know a strong character, a personality that is ever so much more than human. Rivers are old friends who have the glamor of travelers: always on the move, coming from somewhere, going somewhere else, never quite the same from one moment to the next. Yet they are always right there, close at hand. They're friends for life. They're possessive friends at that: Who could spend any time at all in London without developing a personal relationship with the Thames? Who could bear to turn her back on a river?

To the ancients, rivers, like all bodies of water, were as magical as they were useful and deserved worship as such. Uncomplainingly, rivers carry all manner of things—and people—from place to place. Rivers' relentless, uncheckable flows, their meandering paths, and their ageless constance evoked the very cycle of life itself. Such sinuous nobility could only be divine, and such watery divinity could only be female.

British rivers great and small were ruled by goddesses. The war goddess Aerfen or Aerfon dwelt in the Dee, whose position astraddle the English-Welsh border lent itself to prebattle oracles based on which direction the river's course seemed to be deviating from one day to the next. Verbeia "of the cattle" presided over the Wharfe, whose gentle course through the Yorkshire moors passes by many a ruminant bovine herd, and in whose honor Roman soldiers erected a stone altar that is still on display in Ilkley's Manor House Museum.

The goddess Belisama lived in the Mersey. Devona lived in the Devon; Sabrina in the Severn; Clutoida or Clota, "the divine washer," in the Clyde; and Vaga in the Wye. The rivers Braint and Brent are haunts of Brigantia, the mighty war, water, and livestock goddess after whom Britain itself is named.

These goddesses could be very exacting. Ancient Britons are known to have performed human sacrifice in many waterways; more recent folk rhymes and songs preserve the shadow of those times. "Bloodthirsty Dee, each year takes three," runs one saying, "while bonny Don, she needs none." "River of Dart, river of Dart," goes another, "every year thou claimest a heart." Current superstition still holds that the river Spey demands and takes one human life a year, while the Ribble, which the Romans associated with Minerva, is less voracious and is satisfied with only one life every 7 years.

British rivers continue to fascinate and inspire. Now murky and languid, now sparkling, now mist-hung and hushed, now forbidding, now inviting, they roll and glide through the pages of British literature like the reassuring, strong old friends that they are. The river goddesses roll on too, as ever. Perhaps they don't mind (or don't know) that few people remember their names. And perhaps "Ferry Across the Mersey" is a hymn to Belisama after all.

Getting there: The river Mersey is in the northwest, flowing through Warrington and emptying into the Irish Sea at Liverpool.

The river Braint flows south for a short way across Anglesey in northern Wales, near the town of Llanfair P.G. and parallel to the A4080 road, and empties into the Menai Strait.

The river Brent flows through London and can be seen in areas in the northwest part of the city, including Wembley Park, Perivale, the Brent Valley Golf Course, Osterley, and Brentford, where it empties into the Thames.

The river Clyde flows north through Scotland, through Glasgow, where it empties into the Firth of Clyde.

The river Dee is in northern Wales, flowing from Bala Lake through Chester, where it empties into the Irish Sea.

The river Devon flows for a short way between Nottingham and Lincoln, passing through Newark-on-Trent, where it empties into the river Trent.

The river Severn flows through west England, through Shrewsbury, Worcester and past Gloucester, after which it empties into the Bristol Channel.

The river Wye starts in central Wales, flows south through Hay-on-Wye and Hereford, and eventually empties into the river Severn.

The river Wharfe begins in the Yorkshire Dales, flows through Ilkley and north of Leeds, and empties into the river Ouse.

Sheela-na-gigs

She is ugly. Her head is as round as a turnip, her face contorted into a grimace. Her shriveled breasts hang limply on a skeletal ribcage. And with bold confidence, she reaches down and holds open her vulva.

She is a sheela-na-gig.

This remarkable type of stone carving, found on old churches all over England and Ireland, remains an enigma. Her anomalous presence on Christian buildings seems inexplicable. Scholars still bicker about the origins and significance of sheela-na-gigs, and even the name itself is a bone of contention. The term "sheela-na-gig" was first applied to this type of carving as recently as the 1840s, when an Irish antiquarian, cataloguing old buildings in the Tipperary countryside, asked a peasant the name of the bawdy female image on the local church. "Sheela-na-gig," the man is said to have replied, offering no further explanation. The antiquarian duly reported his findings to his colleagues, several of whom recalled having seen similar carvings in the course of their own research. Sheela-na-gig readily became the generic term for figures like this, although there has never been a consensus on the correct spelling—sheila-na-gig, sheela-na-gigh, Shelah-na-Gig—or on the precise meaning of the name.

Many writers, after careful analysis of the 115 surviving sheelas, are convinced that the carvings represent Celtic goddesses, particularly in their hag or crone aspect. In fact, there is some evidence that sheela-na-gig originally meant "hag." Still others maintain that sheelas are of purely Christian origin: that they were created, like carvings of gargoyles and devils, to remind the faithful of the perils of yielding to temptation. Sheelas, according to this theory, represent the sin of lust.

The truth probably lies somewhere between these two extremes. Some of the very earliest sheelas most probably predate the arrival of Christianity and thus certainly represent pagan goddesses or spirits. The few positively identified surviving images of Celtic deities often show them sitting with their knees apart and legs crossed—a pose similar to that of many sheelas. Furthermore, sheelas are found almost exclusively in Ireland, Great Britain, and Brittany, the lands of the Celts.

Then again, some sheelas were carved as late as the fourteenth and fifteenth centuries and so must have been made by Christian craftsmen in a Christian context. Yet the image, powerful and raw, remained the same.

Taken all together, the sheelas are a unique document showing the centuries-long transformation of a pagan goddess into a fertility symbol or good luck charm and ultimately into nothing more profound than a decorative bit of stonework. Eventually, the practice of placing sheela-na-gigs on churches was discontinued altogether, and prudish church officials began to remove or destroy the sheelas where they found them, shocked by the figures' blatant sexuality.

Despite their exhibitionism, it seems that few sheelas were created with a view toward erotic appeal. Most were deliberately made to be grotesque or ugly. Some seem to represent very aged women, perhaps embodying the concept of the hag. This is enough to convince some scholars that sheelas are not fertility figures after all, despite the obvious prominence and symbolism of the genitals. Instead, runs this theory, the sheelas are protective devices, meant to ward off evil.

That women can banish evil by displaying their genitals is a belief many cultures all over the world share, the ancient Celtic culture included. Sheelas were placed above church doorways probably not for reasons of sexuality or fertility but to ensure the sacred protection of the site, to set it off from the outside world.

Whatever the truth about sheelas, they are among the few precious shreds of evidence for the female side of

Sheela-na-gig adorning the Church of St. Laurence, Church Stretton

Celtic spirituality, whether Christianized or not. Those mentioned here are only a small sampling of the many sheelas still visible throughout the British Isles.

The process of undeifying the sheela-na-gigs took nearly a thousand years. Only now has the redeification begun.

Church Stretton: This sheela was obviously not created for the Church Stretton church. She appears to be much older and was placed, either during or after construction, off-center above a door that some sources say was reserved for the bringing in of corpses. She has a perfectly round head with only the faintest features. Her once-gaping vagina seems to have been deliberately stuffed with a piece of stone or wood. Though she cannot be dated with any certainty, the extremely primitive carving style suggests that she was indeed created by untrained pagan hands.

Getting there: 12 miles south of Shrewsbury, in Shropshire. The sheela is on the Church of St. Laurence, at the west end of town on Churchway, visible on the outside north wall facing the churchyard, above and slightly to the left of a large door.

Holdgate: The Holdgate sheela is sort of a sculpture-in-the-round, attached only by her back to the wall of the church. To get a good view of her, you must stand practically below her, from which point her vagina resembles a huge, gaping maw. She squats and grasps her labia firmly and seems to be on the verge of giving birth. She grimaces as if in pain.

Getting there: 2 miles south of Shipton, which is 7 miles southwest of Much Wenlock, south of Shrewsbury in Shropshire. The sheela is on the Church of Holy Trinity, high up on the outside south wall next to the window of the chancel.

Kilpeck: Universally acknowledged as the last word in sheela-na-gigs, the Kilpeck sheela is actually atypical in its flawless execution and almost comically ultrastylized design. She is only one of hundreds of bizarre and mesmerizing pagan decorations on the Kilpeck church, all of them created by a little-known twelfth century cadre of master carvers now known as the Hereford School of Craftsmen. The Kilpeck sheela is composed mainly of head, hands, and genitals: the shrunken body and legs only serve as a framework for the key elements. Her vagina, which is the focal point of the figure, is almost as big as her face and as long as her legs. Her head is hairless and smooth, with goggling eyes and an oddly flattened nose. She is perfectly symmetrical with one exception: Her mouth curls in a sly, lopsided smile. It is one of the great impenetrable smiles of European art.

Getting there: 8 miles southwest of Hereford, just south of the road leading to Abergavenny. Signs in the village point the way to the church, called the Church of St. Mary and St. David. The sheela is on the outside south wall, on one of the corbels supporting the eaves.

Oaksey: Noted primarily for the absolute enormity of her genitalia, the Oaksey sheela is one of the few to have full breasts and what some consider to be a clitoris. Still, she is far from "attractive" in the modern sense. Her long arms reach to her knees; her hands are like paws, her body like a telephone pole. Her pudenda hang down practically to her heels, and something—a clitoris is as good a guess as any—fills the space between labia that are so swollen as to be thicker than the figure's arms.

Getting there: 6 miles northeast of Malmesbury and 7 miles southwest of Cirencester, east of Crudwell and the A429 road, in northern Wiltshire. The sheela is on the outside north wall of the church.

Oxford: Countless thousands of tourists, students, and scholars pour through Oxford every year without ever knowing that a sheela-na-gig is on display just a few steps away from the most crowded corner of the city. The small, severely weathered Oxford sheela is in a very peculiar pose, her straight legs far apart in what looks like a stiff, lumbering dance. Her genitals are little more than a rudimentary slit, and the hand that once grasped them is now worn away completely.

Getting there: In the Church of St. Michael, on Cornmarket Street next to Ship Street. The sheela is kept in the Saxon Tower (entrance inside the church), open April to October, 10 A.M. to 5 P.M., November to March, 10 A.M. to 4 P.M. (closed during services on Sunday mornings). There is an entrance fee to the tower, but the sheela is actually on display in a small exhibit area behind the cashier, who will let you see it for free if you ask.

Tugford: Tugford's church may be the only one in England to have *two* sheela-na-gigs instead of just one. They sit on either side of the entrance door, and it is generally agreed that they served some kind of magical purpose, perhaps as protective spirits. One of them resembles a hunchbacked gnome, neckless, with very detailed portraitlike features. Like many other sheelas, she reaches under her legs to pull her labia apart. Her partner, a rare, corpulent sheela, is badly damaged and seems to be missing her head. Both are very small but in an easily visible location.

Getting there: 2 miles south of Holdgate, which is 2 miles south of Shipton, which is 7 miles southwest of Much Wenlock, south of Shrewsbury in Shropshire. The two sheelas are in St. Catherine's Church, on the interior wall on either side of the south entrance door.

Well Dressing

The pagan peoples of Europe took nothing for granted. Life, when not a struggle for survival, was an endless series of thanksgivings: thanks for the harvest, thanks for victory in battle, thanks for the healing of sickness, and above all, thanks for water. The Celtic tribes had a special obsession with water. Though the worship of water deities can be found in cultures all over the world, nowhere was it as all-pervasive as in the areas the Celts occupied in historic times: France, Ireland, and Great Britain. Healing wells, springs, and river sources were thought to be divine, and in most cases the divinity in question was female (see the Carrawburgh and Bath discussions in this chapter, and the Aix-les-Bains and St-Seine-l'Abbaye discussions in the France chapter).

The "worship of wells" in England survived far into the so-called Christian era, and the worried clergy repeatedly issued dire proclamations against the practice, but to no avail. Gildas, a sixth-century English monk, described what he believed to be the now-defunct religion of his native land: "fountains, or hills, or rivers . . . to which the blind populace paid divine honor." But the worship of water was never extirpated and for the most part was simply absorbed into the new Christian faith, which actually managed to shoehorn a great number of pagan beliefs and practices into a very narrow theological boot. Most holy wells were rededicated to some apocryphal saint whose attributes conveniently matched those of the well's original deity. And the common people continued to pay tribute to the wells, rededicated or not.

A common way of paying tribute was to garland or decorate a well with flowers and green plants. For hundreds of years, during the Middle Ages, there was no mention or written record of the practice, as it was probably enacted on a casual basis, or in secret. Then, in 1350, according to legend, the Derbyshire village of Tissington was saved from the Black Plague by the pure water that issued from the town's wells. Ever since then, the people of Tissington have left offerings and flowers at the wells in gratitude. The practice reemerged from the dark and spread to other nearby villages, continuing on an irregular basis, becoming especially celebratory when a well was credited with staving off a drought or some other such miracle. Beginning in the early 1800s, these well dressings (as they were now called) graduated from simple flowers and garlands to the elaborate form that they take today.

The townspeople build large wooden frames that are then covered with a thin layer of clay. Then, after collecting thousands of wildflowers and separating their petals into gradations of color, the people spend days crafting intricate mosaics, which they make by pressing the petals, one by one, into the soft clay. These flower mosaics usually depict religious scenes, with messages above, such as "We thank you Almighty God for the gift of pure water." The frames are set up above the wells on a saint's day or a holiday. Different villages participate on different days.

The tradition is now mainly limited to small villages in Derbyshire, in the Peak District National Park. The well dressing season, generally running from May to September, has become a major tourist draw for the area, and the mosaics have become fantastically intricate as the villages unofficially compete with one another.

The most amazing part is the attitude of the villagers themselves. Unlike other modern Christians, who fervently deny the pagan roots of their church-sponsored rituals, the Derbyshire folk freely admit that well dressing is a pagan custom. Even the tourist brochures read (to quote one of many), "Wells were honoured with religious ceremonies and dances in pagan times, and Christianity adopted the ceremony." *So there!*

Sadly, in nearly every case the names of the goddesses to whom these wells were dedicated are now lost forever. The devotion they inspire, however, is not, and probably never shall be.

The following abbreviated list of well dressings concentrates on the most reliable and lavish celebrations. Dozens of other villages also hold well dressings. Inquire ahead of time at tourist offices for the current dates of the well dressings listed here.

Ashford-in-the-Water (June): 2 miles northwest of Bakewell

Bakewell (early July): 12 miles east of Buxton

Barlow (August): 2 miles northwest of Chesterfield

Bradwell (early August): 12 miles northeast of Buxton

Buxton (July): 22 miles southeast of Manchester

Etwall (May): 6 miles west of Derby

Eyam (August or September): 6 miles north of Bakewell

Hartington (September): 13 miles south of Buxton

Pilsley (July): 4 miles northeast of Bakewell, next to Edensor

Stoney Middleton (July): 5 miles north of Bakewell

Tideswell (June or July): 8 miles northeast of Buxton

Tissington (May): 4 miles north of Ashbourne

Wirksworth (late May): 15 miles north of Derby

Youlgreave (late June): 4 miles south of Bakewell

Goddesses in Captivity: Museum

London: The British Museum The British Empire once covered much of the globe. And wherever the soldier and politician feared to tread, the English archaeologist sallied forth anyway. There is scarcely a place on earth that has not at some time been ruled over, fought over, or explored by the British. Throughout it all, they brought home the spoils of empire, the choicest archaeological and cultural specimens of every culture and country under their dominion. And most of these spoils ended up here in the British Museum, the national safe-deposit box. Since almost all cultures throughout history worshipped goddesses, there are goddesses here in incredible profusion, a virtual river of divinity.

Room 40 has goddesses from Roman Britain, including Epona, Luna, and an Anglicized Venus. Rooms 68 and 69 contain thousands of Greek statuettes representing the entire classical pantheon, including Artemis, Hecate, Persephone, Athena, Cybele, and an unusual Greek-Egyptian amalgam goddess, Isis-Tyche. Room 72 focuses on ancient Cyprus, original home of Aphrodite, and she is well represented here. Room 73 has goddesses from the colonies of early Greece, and room 57 focuses on Syrian Astarte. Room 64 is the Isis headquarters: Isis holding a sistrum, Isis with wings, suckling Horus, blessing the world. Also here are other Egyptian goddesses, including Nut, Ma'at, Bast, and many more. And these are only a few rooms out of nearly 100, dedicated to Babylon, Rome, Nineveh, Palestine, Stone Age Europe, Anatolia. . . .

Getting there: Open Monday to Saturday, 10 A.M. to 5 P.M.; Sunday, 2:30 to 6 P.M. Admission free. The British Museum is on Great Russell Street between Bloomsbury and Montague Street. The nearest tube stations are Holborn, Russell Square, and Tottenham Court Road.

Greece

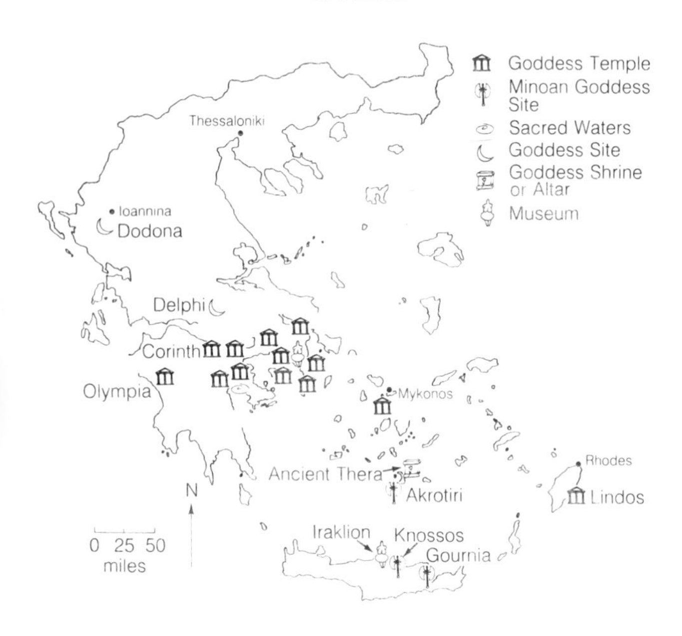

No matter what rhythms pour out of the discos of Athens and Mykonos, there will always be another, more primitive melody to accompany life in Greece: a hymn to a goddess, the strains of a lyre. Like watchful mothers who follow their grown children wherever they go, the myriad goddesses of Greece are always close by, startlingly close. Their names and faces shine in the windows of Greek souvenir shops. Many of their temples, built in love and worship, still stand.

Greece practically wrote the book on goddesses; or, at least, Greece developed the concept into a high art. Neolithic stonecarvers in the seventh millennium B.C.E. rendered austere visions of a broad-shouldered, spoon-faced goddess. On the island of Crete, 2000 years B.C.E., the peaceful, artful Minoans nurtured an enviable society under the beaming eye of their snake goddess. In the warm Greek earth dwelt Gaia, Rhea, Demeter, Hera . . . worshipped by all as supermothers until the barbaric Dorians pressed in from the north with their brutal male-dominated pantheon in tow, touching off a cultural dark age during which the venerable goddesses were left to duke it out with Zeus and his minions. By the fifth century B.C.E., however, classical Greece was in full flower. Athena reigned in her Parthenon, Demeter and Kore shone at Eleusis. This was the Greece of dreams, heroes, and democracy, the golden Greece which, since that time, countless civilizations have longed to emulate.

As you walk the olive-studded fragrant hills of Greece today, the wind-whipped cliffs and radiant island bays, you cross the goddess's noble paths again and again. More than anyplace else, you long to stay here, to don a white robe and, kneeling, relight the sacred fires.

Aegina (Egina)

Temple of Aphaia

She was worshipped here and only here. She was unknown and unloved outside the confines of this airy little scrap of island. And yet Aphaia's temple is renowned as a masterpiece, the finest extant structure of its kind. So Aphaia lives on, after all: famous after all, a local goddess who made good.

The temple is a temple lover's dream, with double avenues of Doric columns still intact, elegantly tall and pale. The temple is practically whole, crowning a high hilltop, enjoying sweeping views in all directions.

Aphaia's domain did not extend beyond the island. But Aegina, though quiet today, was once a remarkably important part of the world. The very first Greek coins were minted here. Also, Aegina was one of the most powerful city-states in preclassical Greece. It was a place renowned for its sailors and traders as well as its skillful potters.

But who was Aphaia? One legend calls her a nymph who resisted the advances of King Minos on Crete. A more interesting legend draws Aphaia as a young huntress, an Artemis-like figure who, while enroute from her native Crete, was captured by pirates. To escape them, she leaped into the sea and swam until she reached Aegina, where she took refuge and eventually became the island's main goddess. She was worshipped from at least the second millenium B.C.E. onward, and her hilltop shrine was established around the seventh century B.C.E. When the power of Athens surpassed that of Aegina in the classical period, Athenians recognized in Aphaia some attributes of their own beloved Athena and did something that was, for them, common: tacked the name of an Olympian goddess onto that of an older, local one. Thus many guidebooks today identify this site as a temple of Aphaia Athena or Aphaian Athena.

The temple suits her, whether nymph or huntress, for a young femaleness pervades the structure and its surroundings. The columns are as lean and straight as young bodies. The stone is pitted now with age, but pure and hard and defiantly attractive. The air is thick with a nymph's complex perfume: herbs, sweet pine, the sea. And the stones bask in an island sunshine that is soft and gentle and eminently flattering. A youthful and feminine place this is, still, despite its age and its scars.

Well-placed signs throughout the site rewardingly identify what used to be where and how it all looked when the temple was at its most vital, in the fifth century B.C.E. They point out that a tall column bearing a statue of a sphinx was once here, but no longer. The gold and ivory statue of Aphaia that once stood at the rear of the temple is gone too. But still here, wide and white, is the outdoor sacrificial altar. A paved avenue leads from the altar to the temple's front door. What must it have been like to burn incense on that broad slab of limestone while the statue waited in the cool depths of the temple, while all around you swirled the night air, laden with its own greater, deeper, eternal incense?

What must it have been like to know Aphaia? The island belonged totally to her, and she to it. To visit Aegina is to search for Aphaia and yet be surrounded by her presence. It is like standing on a crowded railway platform looking for a long-lost sister whom you've never met.

Aegina's temple of Aphaia

Getting there: Open Monday through Friday 8:15 A.M. to 7:00 P.M.; Saturday and Sunday, 8:30 A.M. to 3:00 P.M. Admission: 300 dr.; students and children 150 dr. Take a ferry or hydrofoil from Piraeus to Aegina City on the west coast of the island of Aegina. Then take a bus (the station is to the left as you disembark) heading toward Agia Marina on the other side of the island, and tell the driver you're going to the the Temple of Aphaia. The bus will drop you off at the temple, about 8 miles east of Aegina City. Buses returning to the port all stop at the temple also.

Argos

Temples of Hera

The trek here is hot and dusty. A pair of blue-jacketed caretakers sit on rickety wooden chairs at the foot of the hill, squinting into the Peloponnesian sun and sipping coffee out of dingy glasses. They nod as you walk past. Nothing need be said. Few people make it out here; the ones who do know what it is they're looking for.

A journey to the Argive Heraion is like a journey to your grandmother's hometown, where she first saw life and spent her youth. It's a nostalgic return to a place you've never been. For this is where Hera, presiding mother of the classical world, was first worshipped. This is where her first temple was built, but it's more than that. Hera was honored here before she entered the Greek pantheon, before she was married to Zeus, even before she was given the name Hera.

It's impossible to say when the story begins. Sometime no later than the Mycenaean period the native peoples of this area worshipped the Snake Goddess, the primordial pre-Indo-European goddess who was revered all the way from Crete to Eastern Europe to the Near East. Her holiest shrine in Greece was here on this hill. Her supremacy stood unchallenged. When the Greek kings, according to legend, gathered to swear their loyalty to Agamemnon as the leader of the Greek army in the Trojan War, they met *here*, at the Heraion. Only the holiest of sanctuaries could witness such a pivotal moment in history.

At this stage, we still do not know the name of the Argive snake goddess, who was rapidly maturing into an awesome heavenly queen. In the centuries before the time of Homer, a tribe called the Dorians moved into the area of the Peloponnese. They brought with them their sky god, Zeus. When they learned of the great power of the Argive goddess, they realized that Zeus could not usurp her authority as he was accustomed to doing with lesser deities whom the Dorians encountered. This goddess, they reasoned, was the only one equal to Zeus; she alone was worthy of being his mate. And so they were "married" to symbolize the intermingling of the immigrant Dorians and the native tribes, an intermingling that eventually produced the classical Greeks.

It was the Dorians who named her Hera. There have been many explanations of where the name came from, although the simplest of these is probably the correct one: Hera is just the feminine form of the word *heros* (from which we get "hero") and can be translated succinctly as "lady."

From here the story of Hera and her sanctuary at Argos comes fully into the light. She ascends to her throne presiding over Olympus and becomes the women's goddess. A large temple was built in the seventh century B.C.E. on the site of her sanctuary, one of the earliest temples in all of Greece. In 423 B.C.E., one of Hera's priestesses accidentally let the temple catch fire, and the building was destroyed. A new temple was built shortly thereafter, and it was used by the faithful for at least seven centuries.

Now, however, only foundations and low walls remain to hint at what the temples looked like. The sanctuary's other buildings—an assembly hall, a stoa, baths, and more—tell us a little of how the sanctuary was used in later times, but they too have badly deteriorated.

Address in hand, you climb the hill, looking for the house in which your grandmother was born. You reach the top, but the house is gone. It was demolished long ago. From here the vista extends for miles, across rolling plains and fruit orchards. This was her neighborhood, her domain. Hera, like your grandmother, needs no address now, no house. You hold her firmly in your heart.

Getting there: Open daily, 8:30 A.M. to 3 P.M. Admission free. The Heraion (referred to in books as Argive Heraion, but spelled in modern Greek *Ireon*) is 6 miles northeast of the city of Argos. From there, take the bus heading to the town of Anifi, but get off at the town of Honikas, before the bus reaches Anifi. From Honikas, signs point the way 1½ miles through the countryside to "Ancient Ireon." The walk takes ½ hour. At the site, the oldest temple of Hera is on the highest terrace, and the "newer" temple is on the middle terrace. The columns on the lowest terrace are from a stoa, not a temple.

Athens

The Acropolis

You wouldn't think, stranded on a traffic-embattled Athens streetcorner, that a single cubic inch of this city's poor tortured air could be called rarefied. Ah, but look up. Athena rules this city, she of the clear eyes and clear head. For countless centuries the Acropolis has been her home: It was her first home, her favorite, and she reigns there still.

The hill called the Acropolis soars proud and bright above the tangle of the city. The rock radiates strength, and the three temples that rest upon it express attributes of the goddess.

People were living here as early as 2000 B.C.E.—long before the Athenians built the Parthenon. Primitive goddess figurines, their strong clay bodies striped with paint, their eyes large and watchful, have been found on the hill, proving that this was a sacred site from the very beginning.

A legend tells how Athena and the sea god Poseidon were vying for patronage of the city and the Athenians were forced to choose between the two. To sweeten his candidacy, Poseidon thrust his trident into the hard rock of the Acropolis, at which point a spring welled up out of the earth. Poseidon promised that if he was elected, the Athenians would be given this spring. Athena, on the other hand, offered her emblematic tree, the olive, with its promise of nourishment and silvery beauty. And she was elected. The city was named after her, and the olive tree (so the legend says) grew in the courtyard of what is now the Erechthion.

A third and later structure on the Acropolis is the Temple of Athena Nike, dedicated to Athena as the goddess of victorious battle. Many people regard this delicate temple, clinging bravely to a crag, as the most beautiful of the three.

It is almost too much to imagine the temples whole. How vital this hill must have felt during the Panathenaia, Athens's huge summer festival honoring the goddess, during which a voluminous saffron robe was draped around the 39-foot-high statue of Athena that stood in the Parthenon. It happened on the twenty-eighth day of the month called Hecatombion (falling sometime in what is now July and August). Worshippers proceeded up the Acropolis, leading animals to be sacrificed and carrying the regal robe, the *peplos*, which the women of Athens wove anew for each festival. (Athena is the patroness of weavers.) Dozens of oxen were sacrificed, and a feast of their flesh concluded the ceremonies. As they ate, the participants strove to sense the goddess feasting among them. With this in mind, it is funny to see the list of rules for modern-day visitors, which is carved in stone and placed near the entrance: "It is forbidden to make loud noises (and) to introduce food or animals into the Acropolis."

The path to the entrance gate zigzags upward. The euphoria of climbing, the strange daze, peaks as you reach the ancient gateway, the Propylaia. This gateway was a key spot for participants in the Panathenaia, a place of reckoning where each worshipper in his or her own private way prepared to enter the goddess's ground. Today the visitor crosses the threshhold enthronged, struggling to avoid flying elbows and cameras, and peers over hundreds of heads to see the hill's three temples.

There's no mistaking the hill's centerpiece, the Parthenon, which is, for many, synonymous with the Acropolis itself. Soaring, tapering columns—which draw the eyes upward as if to symbolize wisdom itself—support a carved freize depicting scenes from the Panathenaia. In the Parthenon stood the 39-foot-high statue: over a wooden base were molded thin strips of gold and ivory, giving the statue a pale radiance. Athena was dressed for battle: helmeted. In one hand she clutched a shield. Coiled around her wrist, half-hidden by the shield, was a serpent, which many believe is a clue to Athena's pre-classical origins as a primeval snake goddess. The statue's gold was eventually yanked out by an Athenian tyrant to pay off debts to his soldiers, and the colossal statue itself has long since been destroyed.

In their reverence for the showy Parthenon, most visitors undervalue the Erechthion, the smaller temple to the left as you enter. While the Parthenon is by no means the first shrine to Athena built on the Acropolis, the Erecthion is undeniably ancient. It occupies the site

The Parthenon on Athens's Acropolis

of the original shrine to the goddess, surrounding the olive tree she gave to the city. (The temple is called the Erechthion because one of the legendary kings of Athens, Erechthius, had his tomb inside.)

The petite temple of Athena Nike is off-limits to visitors, roped off as all the temples here have been since officials realized that the stones were rapidly being eaten away by souvenir hunters and smog. From the temple's white walls, in springtime, grow big-headed poppies, red as battle blood.

A museum on the site houses artifacts found amid the ruins. Sculptures and vases depict Athena (and her ancient nameless predecessors) as the countless generations who worshipped on the Acropolis have seen her: from the beak-headed goddess to the goddess enthroned, with long flowing hair; to Athena as she is usually remembered now: with shield and spear in hand.

On this hill, the noble brow of a civilization that worshipped wisdom, you can apprehend a certain stillness among the throng. It is the tense stillness of high places: Athena's stillness, her prerogative: of standing poised, aloof, above it all.

Getting there: Open Monday through Friday, 8:00 A.M. to 7:00 P.M.; Saturday and Sunday, 8:30 A.M. to 3:00 P.M. (The Acropolis Museum doesn't open until 12:30 P.M. on Mondays.) Admission: 800 dr.; students and children 400 dr. Admission also includes entry to the museum. The entrance to the Acropolis is on the west side of the hill.

Corinth

Sanctuary of Demeter

Surely it couldn't be coincidental. There's no earthly reason why a roadside shrine to St. Demetrius should stand *here* of all places, one-third of the way up the mountain of Acrocorinth on an unremarkable section of road that dead-ends after a mile. Why St. Demetrius, who has no local significance and otherwise generates little or no interest among modern Corinthians? Why St. Demetrius, whose name ultimately derives from that of Demeter? Surely the people who erected this shrine must have known that an ancient sanctuary to the goddess Demeter lay just a few dozen yards away. They must have built the shrine out of a sense of piety: maybe not to St. Demetrius exactly, but . . . he's as close as they could get.

This is not the first time Demeter has reblossomed at this site, sprouting up like a new tendril from a long-dormant seed. Her sanctuary here, active for centuries, was destroyed, utterly razed to the ground, along with the rest of Corinth, by the Roman general Mummius in 146 B.C.E. For over a century, the town and the sanctuary were abandoned, unused. In 44 B.C.E., Julius Caesar, feeling perhaps just a bit remorseful, founded a new city on the site of Corinth and repopulated it with colonists. The Demeter sanctuary was rediscovered and quickly rebuilt—all by people who had never seen or heard of the sanctuary before they moved to Corinth. And the mysteries of Demeter became more popular than ever before. You just can't keep a good goddess down.

The common people of Corinth were extremely devoted to Demeter, and to Persephone as well. Archaeologists excavating the site uncovered countless thousands of votive offerings given to the goddesses. The soil was literally riddled with small clay pots, figurines of women and girls, statuettes of piglets, and dolls representing Demeter and Persephone. Almost all the gifts were modest and humble, symbols of the outpouring of love from people who had no money and little to give but tokens of their devotion.

Many of the votives were self-portraits of the supplicants, and the self-portraits were all of women. So the cult of Demeter here was almost exclusively a women's cult. And despite the absence of any written evidence, the excavations have given us a glimpse into what kinds of rites these pious women performed. Over 12 ritual banquet halls have been identified, their outlines still visible among the terraces. During the festivals and initiation ceremonies, the women gathered to dine with the goddess, to laugh and drink and share in her bounty. These women were not satisfied with celebrating Thanksgiving just once a year. Isn't *every* meal a feast of Demeter? And if not, shouldn't it be?

Practically nothing remains of the sanctuary. Still, it is vibrant. No one comes here. No busloads of tourists crawl over the ruins like hungry raccoons. The energy here is untrammeled. Stand in a ruined banquet hall and you can almost hear the chatter, almost smell the fresh-baked bread.

Getting there: Always open. Admission free. The sanctuary of Demeter is on the lower north slope of the Acrocorinth, 5 miles southwest of the modern town of Corinth. Buses run frequently from modern Corinth to the site of Ancient Corinth, which is lower down at the very base of the mountain. From Ancient Corinth, you must walk along the road winding up Acrocorinth. Stay on the right shoulder of the road as you walk uphill. About one-third of the way up the hill, you will see foundations and ruins of the sanctuary on the right side of the road, below you. The entrance through the fence surrounding the site is on the east side, to your right as you face the ruins. The sanctuary and temple area are on either side of the covered mosaic at the top of the site. (If you drive or take a taxi, you will miss the site because it is not visible from cars on the road. Also, there is nowhere to park.)

Corinth

Temple of Aphrodite

An ancient saying went: "A trip to Corinth is not for everyone." Perhaps the homily was created in solemn reverence, but surely every now and then the remark came with a poke in the ribs and an ancient Greek smirk, for it referred to the city's famous Temple of Aphrodite, where one thousand temple prostitutes served the goddess in their own amazing way. In fact, at one time the phrase "Corinthian girl" was synonymous with "harlot," although you wouldn't know it to see Corinth today. The ancient fleshpot is now as staid and concrete a city as any in Greece.

Little is known of what went on at this temple, of what it was that men brought here and what they took with them when they left. Ancient writings make scanty references to the women's "initiating the disciples into the mysteries of love." But the temple was vastly famous in its day. Sacred sex is a far cry from religious practices in the West today, but in many ancient and non-Western faiths, it was (and is) crucial. Sacred sex formed the core of rituals to goddesses in the ancient Near East and Asia Minor, where Aphrodite herself probably had her origins. For us it may be a far cry, but is it really so hard to imagine merging the sublime physical experience with the sublime spiritual one? A culture that worshipped a goddess of love would not even have to puzzle it out. They would know its power instinctively.

The temple, now thoroughly ruined, occupied the highest peak of the Acrocorinth, a stony-topped mountain that looms over the site of Ancient Corinth (whose ruins can still be visited). Numerous peoples built structures on the Acrocorinth over the centuries, most notably the Venetians, whose fortress gives the mountain its present toothy, fearsome, un-Aphrodite-like appearance.

The best way to reach the temple is to walk. It is a major walk, taking well over an hour. A paved road leads halfway up the mountain, winding past fertile orchards and rocky crevasses. Then the ancient path threads its way through the old fortress, past all kinds of ruins, and finally to the Aphrodite temple at the top.

If the temple was so famous, then why does it seem to have been so very small? Today its foundations are all that remain, a square dug into the earth, an incuse queen-sized bed. Where did the thousand prostitutes live; where did they work?

This is a tantalizing site. The goddess was worshipped here as Aphrodite Porne—the titillator—and as Aphrodite Urania—the celestial. At one point, the temple honored Aphrodite-Atargatis, a combination deity whose attributes incorporated those of Aphrodite and the Syrian goddess.

This spot is so loftily remote, so loud with buzzing insects, that you'd expect it to be a shrine to somebody else, Athena, maybe, or Artemis. And who could possibly have the stamina for a liaison, sacred or otherwise, after such a rigorous uphill climb? But consider, again, this hike. It is not a hellish hike, by any means. (For a hellish hike, see the Ancient Thera discussion.) It is just strenuous enough, and the surroundings are just pleasant enough, to invigorate you, to make you keenly aware of your feet, your skin, your lungs, all your parts and senses. It demands all of your body but falls short of hurting you. This is a very physical hike, a sensual one, a hike that in its intense physicality is itself an offering to Aphrodite.

And there is something sexual, something climactic, about finally reaching the top of the mountain. Heart pounding, forehead damp, exhilarated but not exhausted, you sink down among the foundations of the temple to rest. You've made your offering, and far below, on all sides, the land sprawls golden and dimpled like the flanks of a satisfied lover.

Getting there: Always open. Admission free. The temple of Aphrodite is on the top of the Acrocorinth, a mountain 5 miles southwest of the modern town of Corinth. Buses run regularly from modern Corinth to the site of Ancient Corinth, which lies at the foot of the mountain. From there, either walk (45 minutes or so) or take a taxi to the entrance gate of the Venetian fortifications around the summit. From there, climb on foot to the highest (and most northerly) of the three peaks of the Acrocorinth. If you find yourself on a peak that *doesn't* have a view in all directions, then walk the few hundred yards to the peak that's blocking your view. The foundations of the temple are at the very crest of the highest peak.

Delos

Sacred Island

Delos, the dry, rock-bound island that forms the hub of the Cyclades, was for centuries a spiritual hub around which turned the peoples of the ancient world. So many cultures lived and worshipped here: the island's original neolithic inhabitants, then the Mycenaeans, Dorians, Athenians, Naxians, Macedonians, Romans, Egyptians, and others. They all, in their turns, built temples, whose ruins now blanket the island from one side to the other. On this one small bit of land are temples to Artemis (who was born here, the legends say), Hera, Athena, Aphrodite, Demeter, Atargatis, Isis. . . . You could call it a sacred island; just about everyone else has done so. At one time Delos was considered so holy that people were forbidden to die there, and all bodies already buried on the island were exhumed and removed, to dispel all possible taint from this hallowed ground. Or you could call it a supermarket of temples.

Or you could write to the Greek government complaining that the daily ferry from Mykonos, virtually the only means of visiting Delos, allows an absurdly small amount of time for exploring. The island holds so many ruins, so many fragments of worship, that it is as heady as baklava, and it can't be wolfed down in a rush.

Delos starts out flat on one side and rises to a peak—the Mount Kinthos of Artemis's birth—on the other. Except for a few caretakers, the island is uninhabited, as it has been for 2060 years. The absence of residents, cars, and all sounds of modern life makes Delos weird: a hushed, still place surrounded by sea. The island has a haunted feel. From its place beyond the world, with its shadows, lizards, and gaggle of goddesses, Delos extends a welcome that is as eerie as it is sacred.

The oldest shrine on the island was built by the earliest inhabitants in honor of their earth mother goddess. This is the goddess whose carved stone image, usually labeled "Cycladic," is on display in many Greek museums and shops. With her huge spadelike head, minimalist features, and neatly stylized body, she could easily serve as an inspiration for modern sculptors. Her shrine is a small rectangle of stones, hugging the earth at a low-lying spot behind the Oikos of the Naxians. A flat lichen-speckled rock probably served as an altar. The rock faces the shrine at a slant, supported at one end by a fulcrum.

Nearby is a temple of Demeter. Three pitted pinkish columns mark the spot. Abundant seed-bearing, wheatlike plants grow wild among the ruins.

Demeter's temple, like the earth mother shrine, is little-known and unmarked on most maps. Delos's temple to Artemis (called the Artemision) is much more famous. The Ionic temple whose compact remains are visible today was built in 175 B.C.E. on a granite foundation, on the site of at least two earlier shrines. Some scholars believe Artemis "inherited" the island from the Cycladic mother goddess, absorbing some of her rites and attributes. The temples of Artemis and her twin brother, Apollo, were, during the classical period, the religious focal point of the island. During annual festivals called Theoria, crowds of worshippers watched as dancers reenacted the events surrounding Artemis's and Apollo's birth. Choirs sang a *prosodion*, a sacred ballad that narrated the story. And at one point in Delos's history, a would-be invader was so smitten with the island's power that he decided at the last minute to burn 300 talents of frankincense on the altars of Artemis and Apollo rather than attack.

Today the Artemision looks small and unremarkable, but it has a broad view of the water and a wild, rocky islet. When we visited, the dogs belonging to Delos's caretakers, whose cottage is near the temple, were barking manically, screaming their lungs out as if to guard the temple, or at least to prove their allegiance to their true mistress, Artemis.

Worship of Leto, Artemis's and Apollo's mother, was well established on Delos as early as the tenth century B.C.E. It was a faith brought here by Ionian colonists. Leto's temple has finely crafted walls made of tiny stones fitted carefully together and is blissfully serene.

As you start to climb Mount Kinthos, the island begins to look and feel different. The temples and other structures, most of which were built later than the low-lying ones, are more architecturally complex and in better condition. Suddenly the surroundings are green and fresh, in surprising contrast to the desertlike lowlands. The temple of Aphrodite hides coyly, overgrown, near the base of the mountain, enjoying the island's leafiest, shadiest, most refreshing location—just as pleasure-loving Aphrodite herself might do. The walls, now fragmentary, were built of luminous pure white marble, a color and texture suggestive of the pleasures of the flesh: cream, clean sheets, moonlight. A floor made of carefully inlaid stones deepens the sensuality of the temple.

A temple of Isis is farther up the mountain. It has two striking columns and, rarity of rarities, a headless, un-Egyptian-looking statue of the goddess. From this temple, you can see the ruin-studded sprawl of the island and an expanse of calm sea beyond. This, like the nearby Temple of the Syrian Deities (one of whom was the goddess Atargatis), was built to meet the spiritual needs of merchants from the East. The Syrian Deities' temple is equipped with an amphitheater (which attests to its popularity), an altar, and still-intact mosaics.

High on the mountain is Hera's temple, massive and stable as befits the queen of the Olympians. The pale

The temple of Isis on Delos

squarish stones with which the walls are built are unusually large, as if to emphasize Hera's importance and her stubborn stolidity.

There are these temples, and more, and countless jumbles of other ruins in between. For thousands of years this island was populated. Foreign companies had large headquarters here. Delos's great wealth tempted those who were immune to its spiritual charms: the island was ransacked and razed in 88 B.C.E., and all its citizens murdered or enslaved. It was restored, but pirates destroyed it again in 69 B.C.E. That was the last time. The Romans, who controlled Delos, put it up for sale, but no one wanted to buy the island. Much later, the ruins were used as a marble quarry. Finally, in 1873, French archaeologists rediscovered the island and began excavating it. Delos's career had come full circle; its sacredness would once again attract people from all over the world.

And now the boats arrive in the morning and pull impatiently away in the early afternoon, with every would-be pilgrim aboard, staring wistfully back at Mount Kinthos. A sign posted at the harbor reads, "It is forbidden to disembark and remain on Delos before and after the official visiting hours." The boat pulls away and the desert island closes in on itself, and you leave it behind.

Getting there: Open daily, 8:30 A.M. to 3:00 P.M., but visiting hours are actually determined by the ferry schedule. Admission: 500 dr.; students and children 250 dr. Unless you're on an organized tour, the only way to get to Delos is from Mykonos, the nearest island. Ferries leave Mykonos harbor at 10:00 A.M. and 10:15 A.M. (with additional earlier sailings in high season); round-trip tickets are 1200 dr. The last boat back to Mykonos leaves Delos at 1:30 P.M., and you must be on it. Goddess sites on the island include the Artemision, the Earth Mother Sanctuary, and temples to Isis, Hera, Aphrodite, Atargatis, and others. Etched map signs at various places on the island are of some help, but we strongly recommend that you buy a map or guidebook in Mykonos and bring it along to help lead you through the ruins.

Delphi

Shrine of Gaia and Castalian Spring

Delphi was where you went when a problem was burning a hole in your heart. You climbed to the mountain sanctuary, paid your money, made your sacrifice, and a smart woman, a strange woman, heard your question. Slumped down on a tripod she half-sat, half-lay; half-crazy, half-sick. She had breathed the fumes that wafted from a hole in the earth, and she had bathed in the waters that gushed from another. The woman had one ear in another world; she heard voices. She groaned and blurted and mumbled the messages she heard. Her words were unintelligible; they required translation. But it was an answer, a divine one, meant for you alone.

The strange women are gone; they are a breed extinct. Now the pilgrims' questions go unanswered—mostly. But that doesn't stop the pilgrims from flocking to Delphi. For over 1000 years, this place was Greece's greatest oracle, a doorway to the divine in a country where the divine was very, very important. Delphi was a place famous in faraway Egypt, in Asia Minor, and in Italy. Today the buses parked beside the ruins come from those places and even farther.

Legend and history overlap: This is one of those places that has "always" been sacred. Prehistoric inhabitants established a shrine here to Gaia (Ge), the primal earth mother, in the second millennium B.C.E. Two springs on the spot were sacred to her. One of these later became known as the Castalian, in which all pilgrims were required to purify themselves. The other spring emerged from the mountain very near to the Rock of the Sibyl, the great rearing boulder that served as a shrine in the days before temples were built at Delphi. The sibyls (prophetesses) sat here, their low-pitched, often terrifying prophecies based on what they heard the goddess telling them. On this spot the first sibyl, Herophile, is said to have foretold the events of the Trojan War. Plutarch wrote that a goatherd, Kouretas, noticed that his animals behaved oddly in one place near the rock. Investigating further, Kouretas discovered a chasm from which strange vapors were pouring. This chasm, now utterly lost, was to become the main focus of the oracle at Delphi. The resident prophetesses inhaled its fumes and became intoxicated. The Greeks called this a state of enthusiasm, from *en theos*, "with the god."

Mycenaeans settled here around 1500 B.C.E. and maintained the shrine. They brought votives and other images in the shape of the goddess and worshipping women. Already, Delphi and its sibyls were gaining fame. But the goddess who had always reigned here was not, it seems, to be left in peace. After 1000 B.C.E., the shrine became entirely associated with Apollo. The

Doric temple that dominates the site today, and which the visitors come to see, is Apollo's.

Legend has it that Apollo, while still an infant, came to Delphi with the idea of engaging in mortal battle with Gaia's son, the serpentine Python, whose job it had always been to guard the shrine. Baby Apollo killed Python and promptly claimed Delphi as his own, leaving Gaia to mourn and be forgotten. This legend, which is echoed time and time again in Western mythology, clearly represents the violent overthrow of a goddess-based culture by a masculine one. (In a similar vein, countless Christian tales involve saints slaying dragons.)

Apollo's temple was built in honor of his murderous deed. From the seventh century onward, when the shrine at Delphi reigned as Greece's most prominent oracle, the prophetesses still spoke as they always had. But now everyone believed it was Apollo's voice that they heard.

Politicians and generals were among the crowds who jostled outside the sanctuary every morning, waiting for their session with the prophetess. The prophetess—called the Pythia—would begin work only after she had bathed in the Castalian Spring and put on her short white dress. At the temple, she leaned over the chasm and inhaled the fumes and then crossed the temple, where burning pine and laurel thickened the air. Bedazzled, the Pythia climbed into her tripod. The questioner, having made a sacrifice—a honey cake at the very least—was led in to ask his or her question and receive the Pythia's answer. The prophetess sat out of sight behind a curtain. Her words were garbled, and priests stood by her side to "translate" her messages as they emerged.

Delphi was supposed to be the "navel of the world." A stone dome at the shrine, called the Omphalos, represented that navel. While prophesying, the Pythia was in touch with the Omphalos. Some say she held onto one end of a thread that was wrapped around the dome. So, in spite of Apollo, woman imagery was everywhere at Delphi: a navel, female priestesses, even an "umbilical cord" between the two.

The Castalian Spring still emerges from a tall, labial crevice in the mountain. Above the spring, the golden

Delphi's temple of Apollo marks the site of an ancient Gaia sanctuary

mountain face has been smoothed by ancient human hands. Domed niches here once held statues and sacred figurines. Lower down, the waters flow into a pool, where perhaps the Pythia bathed.

The Rock of the Sibyl still crouches, like a brown lion, on a terrace below the Temple of Apollo. The vast wrinkled rock is a kind of throne. To climb it was to take on power and wisdom. And it was an option open to women only. Above the rock, and the old shrine of Gaia, is the Pythia's House. Set deep into the earth, it is shaped like a snake's head. At first the Pythias were local young women whose talent was recognized by the community. Then, after one young Pythia was raped, only women over the age of 50 were allowed to become prophetesses at Delphi.

The Pythias were inspired, in touch, and in demand. The earth spoke to them, the earth's springs cleansed them. Their words were as precious as jewels to the thousands who came here, clamoring. Delphi was after all their place: a place of indisputable, strange women: delirious, ecstatic, enthusiatic, spastic, growling women. They were the most powerful women of their time, reaching dizzily from one world to the other.

Getting there: Open Monday through Friday 7:30 A.M. to 7:00 P.M.; Saturday and Sunday, 8:30 A.M. to 3:00 P.M. Admission: 500 dr.; students and children 250 dr.

The ruins of ancient Delphi are ½ mile east of the modern town of Delphi on the main road. (Signs point the way.) The shrine of Gaia is next to and behind the Rock of the Sibyl, about halfway up the sacred way, next to the terrace wall to the side of the Treasury of the Athenians. You cannot approach it very closely because the area is roped off; the shrine and the spring associated with it are best viewed from the terrace above, which is the terrace just below the Apollo Temple. The best view is from the edge, just next to the Pythia's house. The Castalian Gorge and Spring are a few hundred yards farther east down the road from the main site and are always open and free to enter; steps lead into the gorge to the source. A temple to Athena Pronaia is ½ mile farther east down the road and is, unlike the other two main sites, on the slope *below* the road.

Dodona (Dodoni)

Ancient Oracle

The name that is forever linked with Dodona, Greece's most ancient oracle, is Zeus's. It was to him, the thunder god, that the pilgrims brought their questions, painstakingly scratched onto thin sheets of lead. It was *his* voice they strained to hear in the rustling oak leaves, the cooing of doves, and the clatter of metal vessels hanging in the tree. It was his masculine presence they thought they felt; it was his wisdom that provided answers to their questions.

It wasn't always this way. Perhaps beginning as early as 2000 B.C.E., the pre-Hellenic inhabitants of the area knew Dodona to be sacred to an earth goddess. We do not know her name. But, ironically, we know the name and nature of her son: He was a serpent called Typhon. To lay claim to Dodona, mythology tells us, Zeus appeared on the scene and slew Typhon—just as Apollo killed Gaia's son, Python, and thereby took over Delphi. We only know that the site had become affiliated with Zeus by around 800 B.C.E., and by the fifth century a temple had been built here in his honor. The sanctuary enclosed a huge and ancient oak tree, among whose muscular roots Zeus was said to live. The tree's rustlings were scrutinized by temple priests and priestesses, who interpreted the noises into answers (usually just "yes" or "no") to the pilgrims' questions. (Bird songs and clanking copper vessels added supplementary information, as did the flight patterns of birds overhead.)

But another legend tells of a dove, sometimes a pigeon, who, once upon a time, flew to Dodona from Thebes in Egypt. Landing in a huge and ancient oak tree, the articulate dove, in clearly understandable language, demanded that an oracle be established on this spot. The legend doesn't specify an oracle to whom, but there are clues. Not only are doves, pigeons, and other birds the traditional symbols and emissaries of goddesses, but the ancient Greek word for "dove" also means "old woman." Many see in this legend the arrival of an Egyptian priestess, who brought her goddess, her rites and traditions, to Dodona. (It is also noteworthy that several of the divination methods consistently used at Dodona, even under Zeus's dominion, involved birds.)

Today the ruined temple of Zeus still encircles an oak. But it is a relatively young tree, though large. Early Christians chopped down the original sacred oak (as the Aetolians had destroyed the temple itself in 219 B.C.E.), but modern archaeologists planted a new tree on the site.

Adjacent to Zeus's temple are two ruined temples to Dione: a "new" version and an "old" version. Dione is, in some legends, credited with being Aphrodite's mother. Occasional references to Dione in mythology call her a "sky queen," but no other information is given to support that, beyond the fact that she was linked with Zeus, the sky king. (To quote one writer, Dione was Zeus's "lovely consort.") Local sources suggest that Dodona was Dione's first place of worship. All in all, she remains—sadly—almost a total mystery. But, mystery that she is, Dione's temple and name have managed to find themselves forever connected with one of the world's most significant ancient places.

Zeus was a sky god, but the site, to this day, is decidedly earthy. Mountains shoulder their way in on all sides. Even the sky here is curiously heavy, as if tethered. And no matter how briskly you march through the entrance gates, a leaden slowness soon snakes its way up out of the earth and wraps itself around your legs and ankles. Hardly noticing the change at first, you become rooted, like the oak, immobile, while a tiny, somewhat unfamiliar part of you remains bright and alert. At this ancient sanctuary, whose priests and priestesses used always to go barefoot and never wash their feet, so as to remain hypersensitive to the earth—your body turns to rock, to root, to mulch. It should be frightening, perhaps, but it's not.

The stones here may be Zeus's (*some* of them, at least). But the ground on which these stones lie is potent, a deep blood red in color. Its power reaches up, triumphant, confident, around the broken stones, up through them, beyond them, over them.

Getting there: Open Monday through Friday 8:00 A.M. to 7:00 P.M.; Saturday and Sunday, 8:30 A.M. to 3:00 P.M. Admission: 200 dr.; students and children 100 dr. Dodona is 12 miles southwest of Ioannina, in northwestern Greece. Buses from Ioannina will drop you off at a crossroads 1 mile from Dodona (signs clearly point the way from there). At 4:00 P.M., a bus stops at the site itself heading back to Ioannina (so you don't need to walk back to the crossroads). Within the ancient area, the Oracle Oak and the Sanctuary of Zeus are about 100 yards past the theater and are clearly marked. The "new" temple to Dione is just to the right of the oak; the "old" temple to Dione is the small building just behind the new temple.

Eleusis

Demeter Sanctuary

"*Mystai* to the sea!"

The cry, ringing out among the marbled streets of Athens, echoes down to us through the ages: a rare crystalline moment in the enactment of the Eleusinian Mysteries. Those about to be initiated, the *mystai*, flock joyously to the shore and bathe both themselves and sacrificial piglets in the bracing seawater, a ritual purification essential to the transformative process of the mysteries. Besides this, however, and a few other preliminary public ceremonies, we know little of the actual secret of the Eleusinian Mysteries, for its initiates were sworn to secrecy under penalty of death.

It may seem inconceivable that the central message of the most famous religious experience of the ancient world should remain so impenetrable to modern researchers. Yet of the millions of seekers who were initiated into the mysteries over the centuries during which Eleusis was active, not a single one revealed the secret.

This has only fostered waves of speculation among twentieth century scholars and followers of the Goddess. The same promise of enlightenment that drew pilgrims from all over the ancient Mediterranean world drives modern seekers to a near-impossible search for the unknowable. At least 10 books have been written about the Eleusinian Mysteries, not to mention hundreds of scholarly articles and theses; every book on Greek religion devotes many pages to the topic. (This short entry, in comparison, can only be the briefest overview.) Yet there is very little consensus, and the known facts remain scarce.

The rituals at Eleusis revolve around the well-known myth of Demeter and Persephone, first written down from oral tradition in the Homeric Hymn to Demeter sometime in the seventh century B.C.E. The story runs thus: Persephone, also known as Kore, daughter of Demeter, is playing with friends when she becomes attracted to a certain beautiful flower. As she reaches to pluck it, the earth splits open and Hades, king of the underworld, roars out on his chariot. He snatches Persephone and plunges back to the underworld. Persephone cries out, but only Helios (the sun) and the goddess Hecate hear her wails. Demeter, grieving, searches 9 days and nights for her child, but to no avail. Finally she speaks to Helios and Hecate and learns that Hades has taken Persephone to rule as his queen in the underworld and that Zeus aided Hades in the abduction. Demeter dresses herself as a crone and wanders the earth in misery. She rests beside a spring, where she meets the daughters of the king of Eleusis. She is invited to come and work as a nursemaid in the royal household, where she performs her duties admirably. Late at night, she holds the infant prince in a flame in order to make him immortal. One night the boy's mother catches her in the act and screams in horror. Demeter then flings the child down and reveals herself as a goddess. She demands that the people of Eleusis build a temple for her. They comply immediately, and Demeter sits in the temple, mourning. As she mourns, the earth is laid to waste, for she, the creator of nourishment for all humankind, lets no grains grow. The human race almost perishes from starvation.

Zeus finally relents and orders Hades to return Persephone to her mother. Hades obeys but gives Persephone a pomegranate seed to eat just as she is leaving. Because of this snack, she must spend one-third of every year thereafter in the underworld and the other two-thirds on Olympus with her mother. Mother and daughter are reunited, and the world springs into blossom. Before she departs for Olympus, Demeter teaches the people of Eleusis her secret rites, which give the initiates a special blessing and which may never be openly discussed.

And there the story ends. At the basic level, it explains why vegetative growth is cyclical and seasonal. When Persephone is in the underworld for one-third of every year, Demeter mourns and nothing grows. The earth lies fallow. When Persephone returns, the sprouts shoot up and the earth is fruitful for 8 months. Scholars used to assume that the fallow months were the winter months and that Persephone returned in the spring. This, however, has been shown to be incorrect. Demeter's name comes from *de*, meaning "grain" (though some say it means "earth"), and *meter*, meaning "mother." So she is the Grain Mother (not the "Corn Mother," which is an unfortunately confusing Britishism that has crept into American academia and left many students wondering how she could be the Corn Mother when corn is native to the Americas, not Europe: The British call corn "maize," and their term "corn" means grains in general). Demeter is specifically the goddess of grain, not of all plant life. In Greece, grains are planted in the fall, grown in winter and spring, and harvested in June. The fallow months, then, are the *summer* months, when it's too hot to grow anything. Persephone returns in the fall.

This is a clue to the mysteries, as they were celebrated in the Athenian month of Boedromion, in late September according to the modern calendar, at the time of the Greek grain sowing. The mysteries were a festival celebrating the return of Persephone and the start of the fruitful season. This fact has led many to suggest that at a climactic moment in the mysteries, a priestess impersonating Persephone emerged from an underground chamber before the dazzled eyes of the initiates.

The myth also explains why the mysteries are celebrated at Eleusis and why the initiation takes 9 days: in commemoration of Demeter's 9 days of wandering. But for a clearer picture of the goings-on at Eleusis, we must turn to later writings that tell, up to a point, what happened at the mysteries.

On Boedromion 14 (September 22), the priestesses and priests of Eleusis carried the secret "cult objects" (whatever they might have been) in a procession from Eleusis to the Eleusinion in Athens. On the following day, sacrifices were made, and the mysteries were inaugurated with a blessing of the initiates. Boedromion 16 was marked by the cleansing in the sea, mentioned above. Afterward, each initiate sacrificed his or her piglet and threw it into a pit, a supposed symbolic killing of the old self. The next 2 days saw more sacrifices and the arrival of *mystai* from areas outside Attica. Boedromion 19 was the beginning of the sacred procession back to Eleusis, held in public, though the rule of secrecy was in theory already in effect. The priestesses placed the cult objects in baskets on their heads and led thousands of *mystai* from the Eleusinion in Athens 13 miles along the Sacred Way to Eleusis. A priest in front carried a statue of the young god Iakchos, whose symbolic birth may have been enacted later in the initiation. At one point the singing, chanting procession crossed a bridge at which the worshippers were mocked and humiliated by specially trained insulters.

That night, the exhausted *mystai* arrived at Eleusis by torchlight. They gathered in a huge ritual hall called

During the ancient Eleusinian Mysteries, thousands of initiates gathered on the steps around the Telesterion

the Telesterion for a secret ritual involving drama, movement, and dance and in which few words were said. The *mystai* were asked simply to perceive what was enacted and through that perception be transformed.

We have some hints that the initiated *mystai*—called *epoptai* after they completed the initiation—were privy to a great secret about death and the afterlife. In this way the Eleusinian Mysteries were *similar* to Christianity and other eastern cults, for *epoptai* apparently believed that they would have an afterlife experience that was in some way better than that of noninitiates.

Other myths, stories, and writings about the mysteries present a great deal of conflicting evidence. Some say Kore and Persephone were simply two names for one and the same goddess. Others imply that the two are indeed distinct. In some versions, Persephone is a virgin; in others, she has a son. Hades is often equated with Pluton, god of wealth; elsewhere, Pluton is Demeter's son. One ancient writer claims that the climax of the ritual is the showing of a single ear of grain, reaped in silence. Elsewhere we are led to believe that there was a sexual aspect to the ritual, or that Persephone miraculously reappears in the finale. Each version may have an element of truth, or they may all be wrong. We'll probably never know.

Because the site of the mysteries is today surrounded by intensely ugly industrial slums, Eleusis is not on the mass tourism circuit. But the ruins do attract a steady stream of amateur archaeologists, religous historians, television documentary crews, writers, mystics, scholars, and, more and more, people interested in the Goddess on a personal level. The site is a virtual tangle of ruins, ranging from the earlier Mycenaean-era initiation hall to flamboyant late Roman embellishments.

Clamber up the few remaining yards of the Sacred Way and stand in the plaza-like remains of the Telesterion, now missing its wall, roof, and columns. What was revealed on this spot? What did the goddess give to her people? It seems unfair that we are denied the privilege of her company. It has been 1600 years since the last initiation. Still, you want to raise your fists and shout toward Olympus, "We're back! Tell us your secrets once more. This time we won't forsake you!"

Getting there: Open Tuesday to Sunday, 8:30 A.M. to 5 P.M.; closed Monday. Admission: 200 dr.; students and children 100 dr. Eleusis is on the coast, 11 miles northwest of Athens. Take bus 853 or 862 from Eleftherias Square in Athens to the main street of Elefsina, the modern name of Eleusis; a sign points the way to the archaeological site (3 blocks toward the water). If you miss the sign, ask anybody and they'll point the way. The Telesterion and the Sacred Way leading up to it are on your left as you enter through the modern entrance; the modern building housing the museum is on the hill above the back of the Telesterion and becomes visible only after you've walked uphill about 100 yards on the Sacred Way.

Gournia (on Crete)

Minoan Town with Goddess Shrine

Gournia (or whatever its true ancient name was—we'll never know) was a happy town. Its inhabitants lived a life as busy, contented, and peaceful as that of the bees these Minoan people so deeply respected. The people of Gournia lived securely nestled into a hillside, on a beautiful island with a soft climate, in a society that valued pleasure and art and in which war was unknown. Bustling about their marketplace, creating tools and artworks in their studios, paying their respects at the hilltop palace, and worshipping their goddess at the public shrine, the people of Gournia lived a charmed life—only to have it all end in one great cataclysmic spasm. The volcanic eruption and earthquakes and tidal waves that destroyed many other Minoan settlements around 1450 B.C.E. (see the Thera, Akrotiri discussion later in this chapter) also obliterated Gournia. It is almost as if their goddess vouchsafed these people their golden moment, their supreme place and time, their ease, their clear awareness of her, while all the time she foresaw their city's destruction.

While Crete's most famous Minoan site, Knossos, is a palace complex, Gournia was an ordinary town. In fact, it is the best preserved and most extensively excavated (by women archaeologists, interestingly) Minoan town on Crete. Strolling its crooked streets, and the little agora that bustled 3600 years ago, the visitor has a sense of immediacy, of lives lived fully.

Unlike other ancient peoples, the Minoans did not fortify their cities. Elsewhere in Europe, the threat of invasion was a brutal and constant fact of life, a fact that influenced everything. But in the Minoan world, town planning was merely a matter of how to fit streets and structures most pleasingly and usefully into the landscape. Attack and defense were not even issues, so people were free to pursue all the other unwarlike realms of life.

Gournia's sacred area was—and is—at the top of the hill. It is not a temple, but a one-room shrine. Today it is virtually indistinguishable from the homes and studios that surround it: All are ruined, roofless. All are built of the same gray stone. The archaeologists who excavated Gournia established that this unassuming space was a shrine—in fact, the earliest known civic shrine surviving today—on the basis of the things they found inside, which included Horns of Consecration (see the following Knossos discussion), pedestals, a tripod altar, and best of all, a clay statue of a snake goddess.

Beloved by the Minoans, the snake goddess is believed by many to be the primordial forerunner of the Olympian Athena. The Archaeological Museum in Iraklion (discussed at the end of this chapter) has on display several snake goddess statues found on Crete. They stand wide-eyed, as if astonished, with snakes wrapped around their outstretched or upraised arms. No depictions have ever been found in Minoan art of male deities: only goddesses. Scholars are convinced that this was a strictly goddess-oriented culture.

From Gournia's little shrine, you look toward the sea over a gently curving lip of land, which gives the view a natural frame. All the artifacts originally found here are gone, but an interesting large rock can still be seen in the irregularly shaped courtyard in front of the shrine. Flat-topped like an altar, it has a round, bowl-like depression in its center, obviously hollowed out by human means. It is also a different kind of stone than the gray limestone of which all of Gournia is built. This one, this altar, is smoky dark, with white quartz veins and starbursts erupting across its surface. And another curious feature of the shrine is a niche in its corner, specially reinforced with smaller stones, that leads through the wall into an adjoining room.

The sense of contentment that still saturates this site—the shrine as well as the whole ruined city—is almost paralytic. Our own minds can barely grasp the kind of security that the Minoans enjoyed. They had nothing to fear and a faith in a kind goddess, a faith that was as fully meshed and integrated into daily life as eating and sleeping.

Getting there: Open Tuesday through Saturday, 8:30 A.M. to 3:00 P.M.; Sunday, 8:30 A.M. to 2:00 P.M.; closed Monday. Admission free. Gournia is 10 miles southeast of Agios Nikolaos, along the main north coastal road in eastern Crete. There are frequent bus connections between Agios Nikolaos and Gournia. The site is set back about 200 yards from the main road; signs clearly point the way. To find the shrine, climb through the ruins to the very crest of the hill, where trees are growing. Turn, face the bay, and go a few feet toward it (north) until you come to an irregularly shaped courtyard. This is the courtyard in front of the shrine room that, as you face the bay, is now on your left and behind you. You can distinguish the shrine from the surrounding rooms because it has a small passageway through its rear wall connecting to a niche on the other side of the wall. The larger rectangular courtyard farther south from the bay is the courtyard of the palace.

Knossos (on Crete)

Minoan Palace and Religious Center

For well over 3000 years, the palace of Knossos was a mere figment. Most scholars were thoroughly convinced that the legendary palace of King Minos, like Troy (which was eventually discovered) and Atlantis (which wasn't), had simply never existed.

By the end of the last century, the island of Crete was a funky backwater and showed no traces of having ever been anything but that. Sir Arthur Evans, a dashing British archaeologist with something to prove, went to Crete and bought a hill for a song. The hill was the mound called Kephala, which local lore had always associated with the legendary palace. Evans's colleagues scoffed, but in March 1900 he found, buried in the earth, the remains of a palace and temple complex richer and more beautiful than he had ever imagined. The mazelike array of frescoed rooms, stairways, and colonnades had been once destroyed by a natural disaster, then painstakingly rebuilt, destroyed again by an even more serious natural disaster, and finally abandoned around 1190 B.C.E.

Greek mythology tells the story of Knossos's Queen Pasiphae, who ruled Crete alongside King Minos, who was a son of Zeus. The queen became irresistibly attracted to a huge white bull that Poseidon had given to the royal couple as a gift. Disguised as a cow, Pasiphae managed to mate with the bull. The result, to King Minos's horror, was the Minotaur, half-man and half-bull, with violent tendencies. This murderous beast was eventually killed, to everyone's relief, by the Athenian hero Theseus—who could not possibly have pulled off the task without the help of the princess Ariadne, whom Theseus later had the gall to abandon on faraway Naxos.

History, and the articulate ruins of Knossos itself, tells a much better story. Through artifacts and clues uncovered during Evans's 25-year stint at Knossos (although the ancient written materials have never been deciphered), we learn of a palace complex that served as the royal and religious headquarters of a peace-loving, sensuous society whose like would never be seen in the world again. These people were the Minoans. Their realm encompassed Crete and Thera, and while they vanished along with Knossos and Gournia, their influence seeped into many later civilizations. Over 3500 years ago at Knossos, Minoan men and women mingled freely, exchanging ideas as easily as they exchanged glances. The men, with their wasp-waists and cascades of curling hair, enjoyed a matter-of-fact equality with their female counterparts, whose bodies, with full breasts bare above flowing skirts, were as free as their spirits. At Knossos, women gathered and milled the grain, and men baked the bread. Both sexes braved the sacred sport of bull-jumping, unique to their culture, in which athletes somersaulted over the backs of charging bulls. And at Knossos, as in all Minoan places, everyone—men and women alike—worshipped the same goddess.

The queen who reigned at this palace did double duty as a high priestess, communing with the goddess in private rituals and representing her to the populace during public ones. Worshippers came to Knossos, in the hundreds, to make offerings.

The Minoans' origins, though still somewhat mysterious, probably lay in the Near East. Their civilization reached its glory point in the second millennium B.C.E., enjoying a level of art and sophistication that has led historians to pinpoint the Minoans as the virtual inventors of what is now thought of as European culture. While most of their contemporary peoples lived in a stressful world of wars and bad weather, the Minoans were blessed with unbroken peace, which led to a whimsical, lively style of art and architecture. The classical

Greeks' dogged, careful realism could never match the pulsing rhythm of those earlier Minoan designs.

Minoan religion too reflected a serene and creative lifestyle and was to influence the beliefs of later cultures. Statues were found at Knossos and all over Crete depicting the Minoan snake goddess, full-skirted and bare-breasted like the women who worshipped her, and holding aloft a pair of snakes. In some depictions, she gazes with huge hypnotic eyes at snakes as they twine around her arms. She is an ancient, ancient goddess and was worshipped both outdoors and indoors. Minoan families often kept and fed live "household snakes," honoring them as protectors of the home and emissaries of the goddess. Aspects of the Minoan snake goddess, whose name, if any, is lost to us, were absorbed by the classical Athena and Hera. In her original form, on Crete, this goddess reigned alone, independent and universal. Sir Arthur Evans, after decades of collecting artifacts depicting her and her priestesses, declared that in Knossos's salad days, religion was matriarchal, and that "Clearly, the goddess was supreme."

In love with the palace he had rescued from oblivion, Evans carefully reconstructed many of its shattered or vanished elements. This was a controversial action in its time, but the visitor to Knossos today cannot help but be grateful. Thanks to Evans, colors abound at Knossos: across columns and walls flow the favored Minoan colors: sun-gold, earth-black, and a warm red-brown that lingers in the memory and the senses. It is the color of nourishment and pleasure.

One vivid fresco (a reproduction) shows a procession of worshippers, each carrying a uniquely shaped vessel filled with offerings to the goddess. Each wears a differently patterned garment. Originally, 350 women and men were depicted in the fresco.

Around the palace's central courtyard spreads a honeycomb of rooms: shrines, crypts, and storerooms, laced with stairwells and passageways. Signs label some of the rooms, but even so, the site is bewildering. It's easy to see how classical Greeks, exploring the ruined site some centuries after its abandonment, believed that it had acutally been a huge maze. Through their misun-

Reconstructed Horns of Consecration, columns, and frescoes at the Minoan palace of Knossos

derstanding, the word "labyrinth" came to be associated with Knossos and with all mazes.

But "labyrinth" did not originally mean "maze." The word referred to the *labrys*, or double axe, a potent religious symbol for the Minoans. The symmetrical, butterfly-shaped symbol adorned many Minoan buildings. The Shrine of the Double Axe at Knossos is, today, tiny and barren, although the wooden gate protecting it is marked with graffiti from lesbian visitors, who have claimed the symbol as their own.

Although very little is known of Minoan religious practices, it is generally believed that double axes were used to sacrifice sacred bulls—perhaps the same bulls that performed in bull-jumping tournaments. Bulls were important here; their horns are the inspiration for that other Minoan mainstay, the Horns of Consecration, whose twin peaks decorated every Minoan household and which were found at Knossos in great profusion. Sir Arthur Evans constructed a huge set of Horns of Consecration at a key point along the palace's western wall. There is an unmistakable rightness about gazing out between the horns at the distant, sharply conical mountain that they so perfectly frame.

Deep within the complex, the priestess-queen sat in cool quietude. Her Throne Room still holds her gypsum seat, the oldest throne ever found in Europe. Its narrow, scalloped, high back suggests a regally graceful woman. A duplicate of the throne, in wood, is provided for visitors to sit in. Its seat, like that of the original, is delicately hollowed out to fit human buttocks, a typical gesture of Minoan hospitality, of their attention to comfort and sensuality.

More than anything, the palace at Knossos is a *big* place, where people gathered in great numbers to do things together. Out in the central courtyard, athletes took bulls by the horns while the throng watched and held its collective breath. And in the red-and-green-paved procession hall at the palace's west entrance, they lined up, hundreds of them, with their offerings. This was a lucky crowd, an enviable one. This was a community that had the world in the palm of its slim brown hand. You can't help but feel the twinge that comes with having been born 3000 years too late.

Getting there: Open Monday through Friday 8:00 A.M. to 7:00 P.M.; Saturday, Sunday, and holidays, 8:30 A.M. to 3:00 P.M. Admission: 500 dr.; students and children 250 dr. Knossos is 4 miles southeast of Iraklion, on the northern coast of Crete. Buses run frequently from Iraklion to Knossos every day. To find the sites discussed in the text, buy a detailed map or guide beforehand. At Knossos, trying to follow written directions only makes things more confusing.

Lindos (on Rhodes)

Temple of Lindian Athena

If the Acropolis in Athens is Athena's business address, then Lindos is her vacation home. Never was a sea so cobalt blue. Never was a breeze so bracing, as sharp as a slap from the goddess's own hand. It ruffles your wits as it does your hair. Twin sapphire bays nestle at the foot of Lindos's sheer cliff, a precipice so sheer as to be worthy of none but brave Athena. No question about it: This spot begs to be used as sacred ground. This place was a temple waiting to happen.

Long before a temple was built on the hilltop, a huge natural cave in the cliff's southern face was used as a shrine. This cave, called the Voukopion, is more easily seen from the sea than from the hilltop itself and is not accessible to the visitor today. In the ninth or tenth century B.C.E., a tiny shrine was constructed inside. Little cow-shaped statuettes were recently discovered among the cave/shrine's foundations.

A mother goddess was worshipped here, long before Athena was known in these parts. The goddess's name may or may not have been Lindia; she may or may not have been Mycenaean. She may or may not have presided over vegetation. A long-standing tradition held that only fireless, that is, bloodless, or fruit and vegetable, sacrifices were performed at her shrine. But recent discoveries of charcoal- and bone-strewn altars have made a hash of this theory.

All we really know is that she was here, worshipped on this site as early as 1500 B.C.E. As later populations moved into the area, the Olympian Athena was grafted onto the older goddess. An ambitious temple was built here, dedicated to Lindian Athena (also known as Athena Lindia). It became one of the religious meccas of the ancient Mediterranean world, and to this day it is held to be one of the most beautiful religious structures ever built.

The first temple on the hilltop, built in the early sixth century B.C.E., burned to the ground in 348 B.C.E. It was soon rebuilt in the Doric style, with eight columns and an altar. Later additions, erected in the fourth and third centuries B.C.E., included a *propylaia*, or gateway, modeled after the one on the Acropolis in Athens. Under the gateway, worshippers prepared themselves to enter sacred ground. Also here was a complex featuring 42 majestic columns, arranged to frame the approach to the temple.

Now, as in ancient times, the visitor reaches the site by means of a steep ascent. It begins in the town of Lindos, from which a narrow stairway girdles the hill. Then the Sacred Way (as it was called) continues through stone tunnels, opening onto a grand staircase over 60 feet wide. Now, as then, the excitement mounts with every step. The Sacred Way was deliberately designed to surprise the pilgrim with new sensations every few steps as the pilgrim approached the temple. It still works.

Remains of the temple of Athena's propylaia *at Lindos on Rhodes*

Today, seven of the eight original columns tower at the brink of the cliff, braced against the wind. The stone is pitted, yellow as honeycomb, and warm to the touch. (The site also includes the ruins of a later Roman temple, and even an Orthodox chapel thrown in for good measure.) Piles of broken stones include many with still-legible ancient Greek inscriptions.

Among these stones once rested a massive statue of Athena. The statue is now lost. To this day, scholars argue whether the goddess was depicted standing or seated, bejeweled or plainly dressed. Also here among the columns stood legions of smaller statues of Athena, as numerous and as plaintive as votive candles burning in a modern church. The ancient custom at Lindos was for every pilgrim to donate an image of the goddess to the temple as a token of her or his visit. Now the temple is bare. These little statues too are gone, and the custom that brought them is gone: perhaps forever . . . and perhaps—trusting the magnetism of this site—perhaps not.

Getting there: Open Tuesday through Sunday, 8:30 A.M. to 3:00 P.M.; closed Monday. Admission: 500 dr.; students and children 250 dr. Lindos is 30 miles south of Rhodes City, along the southern coast of the island. Buses run between Rhodes City and Lindos several times daily. There is a short but steep climb from the modern town of Lindos to the top of the ancient acropolis. The temple of Lindian Athena is the small building at the far tip of the acropolis, right on the cliff edge. The sacred cave is below the temple, set into the cliffside, and is inaccessible and not visible, except from the sea.

Mycenae (Mikines)

Temple of Athena

Despite Mycenae's near-mythical status as the legendary home of Agamemnon and Clytemnestra, as the leading Greek city in the fight against Troy, and as, according to Homer, the most powerful city in Europe during the time of the *Iliad*, it was by the sixth century B.C.E. a ruined ghost town, a half-buried mountain of stones, as ancient-seeming to the classical Greeks as their own cities seem to us today. Centuries after Mycenae was destroyed and abandoned, it was reoccupied and revived for a short time in the 500s B.C.E. And it was during this last chapter in the city's history that the Greeks built on the summit of Mycenae's acropolis a seemingly incongruous temple to Athena.

Why Athena? Masculine Mycenae, with its history of random violence and battle-scarred kings, hardly seems a fitting place of worship for a goddess so rational, wise, and sophisticated. Yet Athena did not spring so neatly from Zeus's head, fully equipped with armor, helmet, and a prepackaged mythology. This is a temple to the true Athena, the ancient Athena, the Athena much older than the Mycenae of Agamemnon.

Homer, writing of the Trojan War, tells of the Olympian gods—Poseidon, Athena, Aphrodite—helping and interacting with the heroes. But he was writing at least 500 years after the fact, and the Greeks of the Mycenaean era, in the thirteenth century B.C.E. and earlier, did not have the same Olympian pantheon that Homer knew of and that we envision today. Archaeologists have discovered precious little about the religion of the pre-Doric, Mycenaean Greeks, but one salient fact does seem clear, and that is that they were probably not polytheistic at all but worshipped a single deity: a goddess.

A comparison of finds from the Mycenaean era with those of a few centuries earlier on Crete reveals a close connection between the religion of the Minoans and that of the Mycenaeans. Many suggest that the Mycenaeans are in part descended from the Minoans, who may have migrated to the mainland after the destruction of Crete. In any case, it is fairly sure that the Mycenaeans worshipped a version of what we now call the bird goddess or snake goddess.

In an unmarked area below the palace on the south side of Mycenae's acropolis, several snake and goddess figurines were discovered in rooms that were apparently used for religious purposes. The extant foundations of the Temple of Athena on the summit are actually just the most recent structures in an area referred to in some guides as "the temple area." The sixth century B.C.E. temple was built on top of even earlier ones, going back to a time before the Dorians, perhaps even before the Mycenaeans, to the era of the so-called "Pelasgians," the original earth-centered tribes that inhabited this peninsula.

This is not a temple to the Olympian Athena, the civilized Athena of textbooks, but to the aspect of Athena most closely connected to her actual roots: the Athena, snake curled at her feet, owl perched on her shoulder, who is the direct descendant of the snake or bird goddess of old. It is not incongruous at all; no other deity would do.

A young tree now grows in the center of the temple, springing bravely from the raw rock. The summit is windswept, with a powerful, crystalline view over the surrounding lands. The temple, being more recent than the cyclopean structures below, is ignored by tour groups and bypassed by most visitors. You are here alone, but you know that this is, in fact, the most ancient place of all.

Getting there: Open Monday through Friday 8:00 A.M. to 7:00 P.M.; Saturday and Sunday, 8:30 A.M. to 2:45 P.M. Admission: 500 dr.; students and children 250 dr. Mycenae is 8 miles north of the city of Argos and 1½ miles northeast of the modern village of Mycenae (spelled Mikines). Buses run directly from Argos to modern Mikines several times daily. From there you must walk uphill to the site. The first entrance you come to is for the tomb area; continue past it to the entrance of the acropolis, the towering ruin-covered hill to your right. The Temple of Athena is at the very crest of the acropolis; only rectangular foundation walls remain. A sign identifies it. The ancient cult area where the figurines were found is on the south slope, below the palace, but it is difficult to reach, and individual structures are impossible to identify amid the jumbled stones.

Nafplion (Nauplio)

Spring of Kanathos

A Greek myth describes how Hera retired every year to the Spring of Kanathos, near her native Argos. Here she bathed, and so—miraculously—regained her virginity.

One wonders why the goddess of women and marriage, the divine wife and mother among the Olympians, would want to do such a thing. Virginity seems the antithesis of all that the experienced, mature Hera represents. Obsessively regenerated virginity seems especially so. But mightn't "restoring her virginity" mean something not entirely sexual, like "renewing her spirit"? Mightn't she have been escaping to the countryside in order to rest? Divine bones grow weary, like anyone else's. (It is worth noting that at various temples, Hera's priestesses ritually bathed statues of the goddess, to prepare her—and thus the world—for the yearly

Pool fed by the Spring of Kanathos, Nafplion

cycle.) If that makes sense, then the Spring of Kanathos, still visitable today, is not enigmatic at all.

What better place for Our Lady's bathtub? High on a hill, where citrus orchards scent the air, where pink roses bob on every fencepost, the Spring of Kanathos still bubbles softly. An Orthodox convent, begun here in the twelfth century C.E., has grown up around the site, and today the goddess's bathtub sits just outside the convent's wall. The divine bathwater is eagerly drunk by the aged black-clad nuns, who collect it in huge plastic buckets. (Local farm families also cherish the restorative properties of the spring and gather it in huge quantities to use at home.) Up the hill from the spring, close to the convent's front entrance, is a tiny white chapel that houses an unusual icon depicting the Virgin Mary standing before a well.

Serious bathers and nuns alike can tell right away that this is a meditative spot. Because the Spring of Kanathos is a mythological site rather than a historical one, nothing is known of how it supposedly looked in ancient times. There is no indication that it was ever used as a shrine. Today the spring trickles into a stone cistern, above which are carved ornaments. These designs are undoubtedly a product of the convent and can be given a Christian interpretation, but still they whisper insistently of the goddess. The images include cats and cypress trees, fish, cornucopias, a sheep, and a cow (Hera was often called "cow-eyed" or "cow-faced").

Nearby, on the verge of the hill and also fed by the spring, is a large rectangular pool. Fat goldfish loll in the dark green murk, drunk with warmth and safety. If the water were just a teensy bit clearer, if such things were permitted, if a convent were not so close by, then the temptation would be irresistible: to sink down into its placid, sun-streaked depths, feel the smooth walls against bare back and shoulders, and relax as Hera did, to restore, to forget, and forgive. . . .

Getting there: Always open. Admission free. The Spring of Kanathos is at the convent of Aghia Moni, which is near the suburb of Aria, just east of Nafplion. From Nafplion, go east, past the old train station, and continue out of town on Asklipiou Street. After ½ mile you'll come to a sign on the right side of the road that reads, "To the Monastery of Aghia Moni," pointing to the right (south). Go right and continue on the paved road. When you come to a T-shaped intersection, turn right toward the hills. Follow the winding road up the hill to the convent. The road will end in a small parking area; the spring is just to the right of the parking area, through a small whitewashed archway and down a few steps.

Olympia

Temple of Hera

Imagine a time in which all nations gather every 4 years to celebrate a festival in honor of the great Earth Goddess. Imagine that this festival is the world's largest and most prestigious. Now imagine, if you can, that not a single one of the festival's participants even knows who the Earth Goddess is, and that she is never mentioned in any of the celebrations.

Too difficult? Too absurd? It shouldn't be. That time is now, and that festival is the Olympics.

When the Olympics were revived in 1896 (largely because of interest in the excavations at Olympia), the religious aspect of the ancient festival was entirely abandoned.

In the ancient world, the Olympics were primarily a pious celebration; the physical competitions were a secondary theme. When they were finally outlawed in 393 C.E. by a declaration of Emperor Theodosius I banning pagan festivals, the Olympics had already degenerated to a point where the prayers and sacrifices were no longer being made. Prior to this degenerate period, and throughout most of their recorded history, the Olympics were dedicated to Zeus.

Zeus hardly qualifies as an Earth Goddess, we daresay. But the celebration here goes back much further than 776 B.C.E., the first year in which the Olympics were recorded. Prehistoric tribes settled here at the foot of Mt. Kronion, the hill at the north side of the ruins. The area was dedicated as a sanctuary to the great Earth Goddess, identified by various writers as Ge, Gaia, Rhea, or Meter. The hill was sacred to her consort, Kronos. Festivals were held here in the goddess's honor. Sometime before 1000 B.C.E., aggressive tribes from the north moved into the surrounding area. Due to their influence, linguistic and otherwise, the deities were given the names Hera and Zeus.

The original natives still controlled the area, and the celebrations, centered around a primitive Gaia temple (now known as the Metroön), began to grow in importance. In 776 B.C.E., physical contests were introduced as a part of the ever-expanding festivities. Shortly thereafter, the people built a new temple to Hera next to the smaller, older Metroön. But the immigrant peoples, known in historical times as the Eleans, seized the area militarily in the sixth century B.C.E. They took control of the festival, which they had named the Olympiad after Mt. Olympus, home of their god Zeus, and gave Zeus equal billing as the guest of honor. In the following decades, the Olympiad became the most important event in the Greek calendar, serving as a time of gathering and political reconciliation for the whole Greek-speaking world. And each year Zeus pushed Hera a little more to the side, so that by the fifth century B.C.E., the games were dedicated almost entirely to him. A huge temple was built in his honor between 468 and 457 B.C.E. Only hints of Hera worship remained. Special footraces, called the Heraia, were reserved solely for young women of the native people, and off-year festivals were held in honor of Hera and Gaia.

Today the site still holds the magnetic power that it always has. Two small rivers converge in the distance. The trees, planted by archaeologists, echo with chattering birds. The sun streams through the leaves. The air is fresh. This is what you always imagined Greece would be like. This is the Greece that nurtured the goddess.

The early goddess-oriented history of Olympia can still be seen at the excavations. Faint traces of the primitive dwellings are discernible near the base of the hill. On one side of them are the foundations of the Metroön, on the site of what probably was the original Earth Goddess shrine. On the other side is the temple of Hera, much older than the ruined temple of Zeus, though, ironically, in much better condition. In fact, this Hera temple is one of the first Doric temples ever built, yet it remains the most intact temple in Olympia.

The Olympics were held here every 4 years for nearly 1200 years, but the games have left Olympia behind. Now they roam the globe, visiting a different city every time. One constant, though, is the Olympic flame, brought to each new site at the opening ceremonies. But brought from where? The Olympic torch, the symbol of international cooperation, is carried all the way from Olympia. Every 4 years, months before the games begin, a special ritual is held here in Olympia, in which the flame is lit by women in the role of the priestesses of Hera. They gather here, in the temple of *Hera*, not Zeus, to initiate the celebration.

Imagine that.

Getting there: Open in summer, Monday through Saturday, 7:30 A.M. to 7 P.M.; Sunday, 8 A.M. to 6 P.M.; in winter, daily, 8 A.M. to 5 P.M. Admission 400 dr.; students and children 200 dr. Olympia is on the western side of the Peloponnese, 12 miles southeast of Pyrgos. Trains run to Olympia from Patras and the mainland. Within the sanctuary, the Temple of Hera is on your left as you enter the site, just behind the circular foundations of the Philippeion, near the foot of the hill called Mt. Kronion. The Metroön is about 50 yards east of the Temple of Hera and is much smaller, directly in front of the row of little treasuries at the foot of Mt. Kronion.

Rhamnous (Ramnous)

Temples of Nemesis and Themis

The natural human impulse, when you sit upon a desolate coastline and look out to sea, is to think enormous thoughts. (Life, death, destiny, etc.) So it is chillingly appropriate to find, in exactly such a place, a temple to Nemesis, the Greek goddess of destiny and retribution.

Temples to Nemesis are rare indeed, in a Greece that is crowded with shrines to Artemis, Athena, and Aphrodite. They are rare, perhaps, because Nemesis is such a dread goddess, so portentious and unsettling. She is, potentially, the bringer of both consummate joy and unbearable misery. She waits, unsmiling, around every one of life's corners and behind every action that humans perform. Her decisions are final. She is a spoilsport.

The ruined but still impressive temple overlooks the Aegean on a bluff near an ancient fortified outpost of Athens. As if Nemesis's worrisome ministrations were not enough, the site also has a temple to Themis, the goddess of justice and law. Themis's smaller, older temple stands cheek by jowl with Nemesis's larger one, and together they reign over this gloomy, sea-bound place.

Temples to Themis too are rare, even though she was one of the oldest and most deeply revered Greek goddesses of all. Themis was a daughter of Gaia, the primal earth mother, and all the Olympians held her in awe. Themis was the Greek goddess most savvy about human nature and its consequences and is thus often depicted holding a pair of scales. (Aspects of Themis and Nemesis were eventually absorbed by the abstract quasi-goddess Justitia, who became the modern blindfolded, scale-bearing symbol of justice.) Interestingly, the concept of moral responsibility, so central to the Judeo-

Christian tradition, is nearly absent from Greek religion, with the exception of the worship of Themis and Nemesis, who ensure retribution for human wrongdoing.

Themis's temple, built in the late sixth century B.C.E., predates Nemesis's by about a hundred years. Both temples were constructed of local gray limestone. While the Nemesis temple (the one closer to the sea) was much larger and more architecturally ambitious than the Themis temple (12 columns as opposed to Themis's 2, for example), Nemesis's was never completed, probably because of the Peloponnesian War. Statues of the goddesses were found in the ruins. The Nemesis statue, famous in its own time, had been reduced to fragments by the time of the excavations. Originally, it wore a deer-studded crown, and the goddess held an apple bough in one hand and a carved bowl in the other. Themis's boldly resolute statue now resides in the National Archaeological Museum in Athens (discussed at the end of this chapter), where it is one of the most striking pieces in the collection.

Portions of finely made walls and floors remain. The floor of Nemesis's temple is riddled with graffiti chiseled painstakingly into the rock. The walls of Themis's temple are built of primitive-looking polygonal stones rather than standard rectangular blocks, suggesting that this temple was built in imitation of an even earlier one that occupied the same site. Piles of gray stone lie about. The most striking feature of the temples today is a pair of white marble thrones, one of whose still-barely-readable inscriptions claims it for Nemesis; the other was inscribed to Themis. Side by side the thrones sit overlooking the silent landscape. Dare you place yourselves on these thrones, even for a moment? Dare you take on that responsibility?

A solemn air hangs over this site, a site whose lonesomeness is quite deliberate, and which has been this way always. The constant wind soughing through the hunched pines is like the voice of ghosts; it casts a spell of silence, a baleful finger held to the visitor's lips. The sea here is part mirror, part window, part dark slate tablet on which all is written and imagined. It is a tablet as profoundly blank and full of possibilities as the face of Nemesis herself.

Marble thrones of Nemesis and Themis, Rhamnous

Getting there: Open daily, 9:00 A.M. to 3:30 P.M.; holidays, 10:00 A.M. to 4:30 P.M. Admission free. Rhamnous is on the eastern coast of Attica, 30 miles east-northeast of Athens, 3 miles north of Agia Marina. From Athens, take the bus heading to Agia Marina from the bus station at 39 Mavromateon Street, and tell the driver you want to go to Rhamnous; he'll drop you off at an intersection 1½ miles south of the site. A ½ hour walk north will bring you to Rhamnous: look for a gate and a small caretaker's booth on the right side of the road (the ruins are not visible from the road).

Sounion (Sounio)

Temple of Athena

Athena, in sober silence, guards this cape, the peninsula that Homer called "the holy promontory of Athens." The Greeks asked her to take on this job when they built this temple in the sixth century B.C.E., and she has no doubt done it well, for Cape Sounion is to this day resolutely Greek, a proud part of Attica: Athena's chosen domain.

The temple rests on a hill overlooking a cove. It was built in the Ionic style, made of limestone and sun-dried brick, with four massive columns inside a rectangular

Rectangular foundation of temple of Athena, Sounion

hall. A colonnade ran along the outside. The statue of the goddess—called Athena Sounias here—stood at the back of the shrine facing the eastern doorway, through which it had a clear view of the sea.

Invading Persians smashed the temple, as well as the smaller shrine that stood just to the northeast, in 480 B.C.E. By 450 B.C.E. it had been rebuilt, this time in marble. It was considered an offbeat temple because the ornate details—that is, the colonnades—decorated its sides and not its front. But who needs an ornate front, mere masonry, when the sea serves as your glittering doormat?

Not one of the temple's columns remains today. Only a flat rectangular foundation and scattered stones greet the visitor. But the foundation is neat and powerfully defined, and the outdoor altar that once served the smaller northeastern temple still basks in the sun, radiating reverence. And nothing will ever smash the perfection of the location itself, for it was obviously chosen with care.

Sit in the middle of the ruined temple, gaze out to sea as the statue of Athena Sounias once did. The Aegean from this point is as broad and docile as a whale's back. Soon you'll notice that the bluff directly in front of you drops roundly down to the sea, forming a symmetrically bulging near-horizon. The bluffs rising up on either side of this cove splay sideways, so the effect is exactly like that of crouching on a huge rounded belly and peering out at the sea from between a pair of enormous thighs.

It is a sensation that grows and deepens once you become aware of it, a sensation of being held, protected, guarded.

To the southwest of the temple of Athena Sounias is another, higher hill, and on it a well-preserved fifth century temple of Poseidon. The big white temple, with its rows of slender Doric columns, is a major tourist draw. Buses roar up that hill from sunrise to sunset, disgorging hordes who swarm delightedly over the monument and then roar away, never noticing, much less visiting, the modest, flattened temple of Athena, a ruin that even the Athenians—the goddess's children—today dismiss as "only rocks."

So you sit alone with Athena Sounias; you sit watching the sea from between two amazing thighs, while around you grow amethyst-colored thistles, so like the battle-clad goddess herself. You sit, in quiet vigilance, in the most enviable position of all, and watch the clamoring crowds *over there* and have a soft chuckle with Athena about who is and who isn't wise, after all.

Getting there: Always open. Admission free. Cape Sounion is 35 miles south of Athens at the southern tip of Attica. Buses leave often for Sounion from the bus station at 14 Mavromateon Street in Athens; the buses will drop you off at the parking lot below the famous temple of Poseidon.The temple of Athena is *not* on the tip of the peninsula; it is about 500 yards inland from the temple of Poseidon. From the parking lot, walk away from the cafe building (and the crowds) back (north) down the road to the bottom of the slope, and look for a fence with an open gate in it to your right. Go through the gate and climb 100 feet up the small hill; the ruins of the temple are on the top.

Thera, Akrotiri

Minoan Colony

Imagine living in a city that is totally devoted to the goddess: a town whose many shrines are dedicated wholly to her, where every man, woman, and child loves her, where her name and her rituals are as well known in every kitchen as they are in the darksome caves on the outskirts of town.

Akrotiri, once home to some 10,000 people, was such a city. It was a well-rounded community; its inhabitants were sailors, traders, craftspeople, homemakers, architects—and priestesses. Its most celebrated residents, most likely, were its artists, a skilled and worldly clique whose travels in Egypt and other distant lands influenced the scenes they painted on walls all over Akrotiri.

A massive volcanic eruption decimated Akrotiri, as it did most of the Minoan world, around 1450 B.C.E. Volcanic rocks rained down like bombs on the town, smashing walls and crushing houses, some of which were two and three stories tall. The inhabitants, forewarned by earthquakes about the coming disaster, escaped in a hurry, probably by sea. Erudite, wealthy, beautiful Akrotiri was no more.

Like other Minoan towns that flourished in the second millennium B.C.E., this was a place in which male gods were unknown but in which the goddess was supreme: she, and only she. Some of Akrotiri's now-famous wall paintings depict the goddess and her devotees, and even the most worldly of the paintings are alive with special plants and animals that are traditonal emblems of the goddess and of human faith in her.

It is weird to visit Akrotiri today. Not because the town is ruined—you come expecting that—but because the entire site is now under a huge corrugated plastic roof, and probably will be forever. The Greek government ran out of money for the project before the Akrotiri excavations could be completed; thus the site squats in permanent limbo. The roof is there to protect the delicate walls and the wealth of artifacts known to be just under the surface. Here and there, crates lie stacked on pallets, ready to be shipped to museums. But otherwise no work goes on here. Visitors walk along a single avenue, constrained on either side by ropes and railings, unable to see most of the site. What you can see beyond the railings is tantalizing, although the roof and artificial lighting make you feel that you are wandering around a shopping mall.

Mural of Minoan priestess, found at Akrotiri

Keep trying to imagine this place in sunlight, and in the milky light of the moon. Keep trying to imagine this as a real, living town, whose ships carried traders (never warriors) to distant lands. This was a town with paved streets—and with shrines.

At least seven shrines have been discovered among the ruins of Akrotiri. They were identified by the presence of low, tablelike altars (for bloodless sacrifices) and ritual cookware, notably animal-shaped vessels, and nippled pots that the archaeologists call "breasted ewers." Sacred meals seem to have been an important part of worship here, but very little else is known about this goddess or the ways people worshipped her. The few written records the Minoans left have not been deciphered, so the scholars base their theories principally on wall paintings.

One of these paintings was found in a shrine room (visible, thankfully, as you walk through Akrotiri today), which is now rather condescendingly called The House of the Ladies. It depicts several women who appear to be dressing themselves for a ritual—a meeting with a priestess or even with the goddess herself. One of the women has unusually elongated breasts and is thought by some to be lactating.

Another painting, found in what is now identified as Room 4 on the "Triangle Square," a former public meeting area, depicts a young priestess. Dressed somberly, fully covered from neck to ankles, she holds a censer in her reverently upraised arms.

Alas, the paintings are gone. So are the animal-shaped pots, the breasted ewers, and of course the people of Akrotiri themselves. But still here, standing about like perplexed citizens, are enormous clay storage vessels. Big enough to take a bath in, the vast pots are roundly feminine and decorated with large fanciful spirals, a favorite motif of the Minoans and many other goddess-worshipping peoples. Also here, lying where it was found in front of a house, is a stone rendition of the Horns of Consecration (see the previous Knossos discussion), the stylized bull horns through which Minoans framed their view of the world. A hole drilled in the hollow between the "horns" shows where the *labrys*, a double ax, once was affixed. This religious symbol was placed on Minoan houses the way we might fly a flag on our homes: to proclaim the household's allegiance, to mark it as the domain of the goddess—she, and only she.

Getting there: Open Tuesday through Sunday, 8:30 A.M. to 3:00 P.M.; closed Monday. Admission: 500 dr.; students and children 250 dr. The site of Akrotiri is 6 miles southwest of the capital city, Thera (also spelled Fira), and just ½ mile south of the modern town of Akrotiri. Buses run from Thera directly to the site several times daily. There is a single roped-off path leading through the ruins.

Thera, Ancient Thera

Sanctuary of Isis and the Egyptian Deities

In many of life's best adventures, the approach is everything. Think of climbing Mt. Everest, for example. Think of eating an artichoke.

The same is true for Ancient Thera. The speckled gray ruins of the city sprawl glittering in the sun and wind: ancient houses, graveyards, streets, even a theater beckons to you. But by the time you get close enough to see them, who cares? Struggling up the 1800-foot

The rock-cut niches in Thera's Sanctuary of the Egyptian Deities

cliff, virtually swimming uphill through slippery oceans of gravel, has given you a whole new perspective on life. Whimpering, choking, thrashing past the castaway bloodstained handkerchiefs of previous climbers, you have honed and sharpened your new philosophy: namely, that apart from basic survival, little really matters.

You reach the high plateau, steadying grieving legs; you cross the gate into the ancient city, and then the wind begins. Bracing isn't the word. Tearing, screaming across the summit and into your very bones, the collected gusts of all of Europe buffet Ancient Thera. No doubt they buffeted it when "Ancient" was not yet part of its name, when men and women actually *lived* up here. (Archaeological evidence has shown that one of the deities these people worshipped was Boreas, god of the north wind. For good reason.)

And then, like the first sweet glimpse of heaven after a painful death, the southern view assails you. From the bottom of the dastardly cliff spreads an elegant, endless black blade of beach, edged in silver. And far beyond, the wide Aegean, whose deep generous blue is like a balm for the eyes.

Maybe that is the lesson of this place: the relative insignificance of humans, their structures and their history. What more, beyond sea and sweat, does any person really need to know?

A wide variety of divinities, both male and female, enjoyed worship from the city's 2000-plus years' worth of inhabitants. The martial Dorians, relishing this site for its natural defenses, settled here from about 1000 B.C.E. onward, eventually giving way to archaic, classical, Hellenistic, and Roman developments, each of which entailed its own deities. Demeter, Kore, Athena, Aphrodite, and the goddess Tyche had temples here; Aphrodite and Tyche, as well as the sanitary goddess Hygeia, were also worshipped at small household shrines inside people's homes.

During the Hellenistic period, in the third century B.C.E., Ptolemaic Egyptians, of all people, took over Thera and commandeered it as a military base from which they controlled the central Aegean. Wherever Egyptians went, their goddess Isis was sure to follow. With her consort Serapis and the jackal god Anubis, Isis enjoyed worship at a shrine at the southern tip of Ancient Thera.

At the verge of the cliff, you crouch—too acrophobic to stand upright—and admire the rock-cut sanctuary. Four house-shaped niches jut into the soft rock, deep enough to have held statues and sacrificial offerings. Two cisterns once held water for use in the ceremonies. On the flat ground, interspersed with the gravel, you can see infinitesimal chips of ancient pottery, seashell, and bone: the remnants of sacrifices? For priestesses and worshippers, the view from here must have been positively trance-inducing.

Isis, the Alexandrian, traveled well. Poised up here with the whole Aegean for her altarcloth, she is Isis of the sea. Perched up here on this impossible, wind-stabbed cliff, she is Isis the Healer. It is she who gives you the strength, the nerve, to climb back down again.

Getting there: Open Tuesday through Sunday, 8:30 A.M. to 3 P.M.; no one admitted after 2:30. Closed Monday. Admission free. Ancient Thera is 7 miles south of the capital city, Thera (also spelled Fira), on the east coast of the island, next to the town of Perissa Beach. Frequent buses run from Thera to Perissa Beach, but from there you must climb the mountain to the ancient site. From the town, walk toward the base of the mountain, and follow the paved road until it peters out in the cleft between the two peaks. Continue on the trail until it too peters out, and then just keep climbing. No matter which route you take, you'll eventually come to the path that will lead you up to the car park near the entrance to the site. (If you've rented a car or scooter in Thera, you can drive to the car park by heading south from Thera, through the town of Messa Gonia, toward Kamari Beach on the north side of the mountain. About a mile before you reach Kamari Beach, a road branches off to your right and leads, after miles of steep hairpin turns, to the car park at the site. There are no buses.) A path leads up from the car park to the entrance of the site. To find the sanctuary of Isis, walk all the way through the extensive ruins to the south side of the mountain, overlooking Perissa Beach. Keep going until you reach the lowest, most southerly point of the site. A sign in front of the rock-cut niches reads, in German, *Heiligtum Der Agyptischen Gotter*. (Be forewarned that the climb from Perissa Beach takes an hour and is difficult; however, the only equipment required is a pair of good shoes and a strong heart.)

Vravrona (Vravron, or Brauron)

Sanctuary of Artemis

On the day we visited, shreds of bloody tissue and bone were strewn across the entrance to the site, the remnants, no doubt, of some wild kingdom drama. *Not bad,* we mused, stepping gingerly over the bits, *for a goddess of the hunt.*

The lush, humid marshland of Vravrona has long been sacred to Artemis, mistress of wild things. There was a settlement here in the Neolithic period; it flourished in the second millennium B.C.E. Although the town vanished around 1300 B.C.E., a shrine persevered here, which was at first focused on an ancient local mother goddess. Later it culminated in the cult of Artemis Brauronia: Artemis of the Bears.

This was more than just a temple. In classical times, Athenian families sent their young daughters here to be trained in the service of the goddess: to learn her secrets, her rites, and her ways.

By all means, tour the adjacent small museum before visiting the ruined sanctuary. The museum houses the artifacts found in the vicinity, which tell a story so tantalizing, so irretrievable, as to make you wish you had been one of those pious little girls who grew up at the shrine. Bronze mirrors, once polished to a high gloss, stand in the museum's cases, as do weaving implements, vases in the shape of women's heads, clay jewel boxes decorated with scenes from mythology, and brilliant and detailed jewelry, some of which was found at the bottom of the temple's sacred spring. One necklace is made with beads in the shape of tiny bears.

Statuettes found in the lower strata depict the earlier mother goddess—a strong stick of a body, molded quickly and feelingly in clay, with short, outstretched arms and a small pinched head. And dozens of classical-era statues and reliefs show Artemis as we know her: hunting, riding on a bull, enthroned but casual, her loose hair crowned with a full-moon-like diadem. In the biggest and best of the statues, Artemis stands as if poised to run. Lithe, her robe breeze-tossed, one knee bent, the goddess looks disarmingly natural, with laughing eyes and the half-smile of a young woman who poses—but ever so impatiently—for a photograph.

As you wander around the museum, note the way wild birds have chosen to nest in nearly every windowsill: They have made big exuberant leafy homes, and the museum echoes with their chirping. It is as if they cannot bear to leave her, longing to be near her now as always.

The sanctuary itself crouches in the shadow of a rippling, striated outcropping whose jagged sides are pitted with caves (just the right size for bears). Marshland encroaches on all sides, and in fact flooding was the reason the sanctuary was finally abandoned after centuries of use. Incessant cries and rustlings of birds, insects, and lizards make the air as wild and alive as it ever was, though the temple's columns and walls are broken. A model in the museum shows how the complex used to look, in its fifth-century heyday: sprawling and

Sanctuary of Artemis, Vravrona

low, with a Mediterranean toast-colored roof, a wide green courtyard, and a long breezy porch, supported by columns. The sanctuary faced onto wilderness and it dwelt amid wilderness. Its shape and colors were in perfect harmony with nature, allowing people to mingle easily with the outdoors, with the fresh air so beloved of Artemis—to be forever half in- and half outdoors, as if to seal oneself off completely would amount to sacrilege.

The sacred spring is just west of the temple complex. Behind the complex, to the south, is the crumbled structure known as the tomb of Iphigenia. As early as the eighth century B.C.E. this spot was considered holy, in memory of the heroine who, legend has it, took refuge here, carrying a primitive wooden statue of Artemis. She dedicated Vravrona to the goddess (who, one legend says, had miraculously saved Iphigenia from being sacrificed, having deftly replaced her with a stag), and she served here as priestess.

Another legend tells how Artemis, horrified when a mortal happened to kill one of her sacred bears, demanded that, as compensation, Athenians send their little girls to her shrine. The girls, aged 5 to 10, were called *arktoi* (bears), and in fact they imitated the sacred beasts during a ceremony they learned and practiced at the site every 4 or 5 years. The "bear dance" was a key part of this ceremony.

Vravrona was known as a place where young girls matured. Marble statues of the *arktoi*, now in the museum, were found on the site and reveal the little faces as sensitive and wide-eyed, lips parted in expressions beautifully tender and open. One girl fondles the ear of a rabbit, which she cradles in the folds of her long robe. Another child holds curious fingers over the delicate heart of a bird.

On the western flank of the sanctuary are the rooms where the *arktoi* lived. Originally lined with cots and couches, the rooms resembled the crowded dormitories of a modern summer camp or convent school. And in fact that is the feeling that pervades this whole sanctuary complex, still. You can feel it, the sweet companionship: This is a place of women-in-the-making, of young girls; a devout and happy encampment where secrets were shared and where soft voices melded with the sounds of wild things.

Getting there: Museum is open Tuesday through Sunday, 8:30 A.M. to 3 P.M.; closed Monday. Admission: 200 dr.; students and children 100 dr. The ruins are fenced off and seemingly closed indefinitely, despite hours posted on the gate. However, though you can't get in among the ruins, you can see them at close range from behind the fence. Vravrona is on the eastern coast of Attica, 20 miles east of Athens. From Athens, take a bus from the station at 14 Mavromateon St. to the town of Markopoulo; there you can transfer to a bus that will drop you off at the Vravrona museum. The site is about 500 yards back along the road from the museum, on the other side of the hill. It is also possible to take a blue #304 bus from Athens to the modern town of Vravrona. From the end of the line, walk along the main road, then go down to the shore and along the short path through the marshy area to the museum; or stay on the main road for 1½ miles and turn left at the first paved road, which will lead you to the ruins. (Better yet, drive.)

Goddesses in Captivity: Museums

Athens: National Archaeological Museum The greatest artifacts of thousands of years of Greek creativity are here, sealed behind glass in a hideous modern building. Yet they never lose their spiritual and cultural relevance. This museum houses the choicest discoveries taken from ancient sites and smaller museums all over Greece, and so—not surprisingly—it contains more representations of goddesses than any other museum in the world.

To list all the goddess images in this collection would take a whole book unto itself. Even the museum guides sold at the front counter are woefully incomplete. Moreover, some of the most intriguing displays are labeled only in Greek, or not at all, and the various rooms are not clearly numbered, so that trying to find specific things becomes a needlessly difficult adventure. Our recommendation is that you simply wander at random from room to room. Still, here are a few marvels for which you should keep an eye peeled:

Room 4, the large central room, contains (among innumerable Mycenaean treasures), primitive pinched-head goddess figurines found at various sites, and thirteenth century B.C.E. frescoes from Tiryns, which clearly show how Mycenaean religion and culture can be traced directly to goddess-centered Minoan Crete.

Room 6 houses the stunning Cycladic collection, with hundreds of goddess figurines from as early as 3200 B.C.E.

Room 19 has reliefs and statues of Demeter and Persephone as well as a small but notable Aphrodite.

Room 29 contains the striking statue of Themis that was discovered at her temple at Rhamnous (discussed earlier). When found, the statue was in near-perfect condition.

Getting there: Open Monday, 12:30 P.M. to 7:00 P.M.; Tuesday through Friday, 8:00 A.M. to 7:00 P.M.; Saturday and Sunday, 8:30 A.M. to 3:00 P.M. Admission: 600 dr.; students and children 300 dr. The museum is located at 44 Patission St., north of Omonia Square.

Minoan Snake Goddess, Iraklion's Archaeological Museum

Iraklion (on Crete): Iraklion Archaeological Museum Visitors to the Minoan ruins on Crete are often disappointed to learn that the most attractive frescoes, statuettes, votive offerings, pottery, and double axes have been removed from the sites. Fortunately, just about every important (not to mention unimportant, but still amusing) Minoan artifact ever found was dutifully housed in a single, convenient museum. The sites on Crete, denuded of their treasures, tell only half the story of a great civilization; the rest of the story can be found here. A sampling:

Room 4 houses both of the world-famous faience snake goddess statues. Rooms 7 and 8 contain hundreds of double axes in bronze and precious metals, some of which are several yards tall and others which are so tiny that you need a magnifying glass to see them clearly. Rooms 9 and 10 display many large terracotta statues of goddesses, including the intriguing "opium goddess." Upstairs are the frescoes found at Knossos and a detailed scale model of the palace.

Getting there: Open Tuesday through Sunday, 8:00 A.M. to 7:00 P.M.; Monday, 12:30 P.M. to 7:00 P.M. Admission: 500 dr.; students and children 250 dr. On Eleftherias Square, a few blocks east of the center of town.

Hungary

HUNGARY

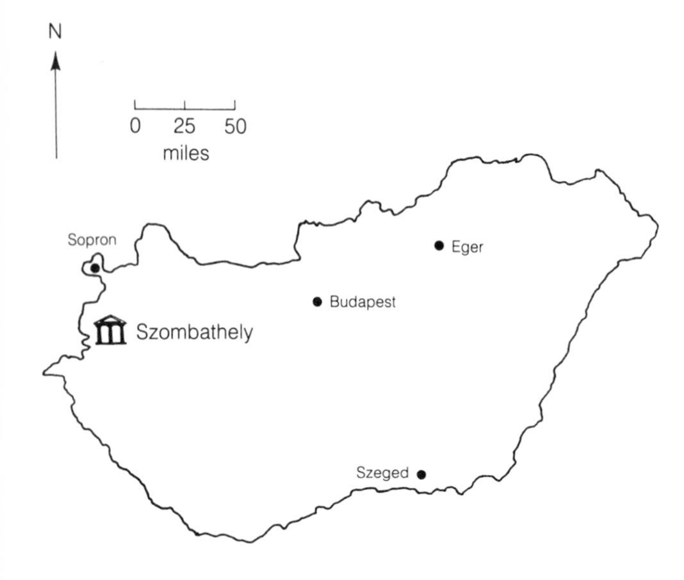

Hungary is an odd duck, one of Europe's oddest. Its people and their language are unique, absolutely unrelated to any others, east or west, with the singular—and startling—exception of Finland. The Finno-Ugrics, ancestors of the Finns and the Hungarians, rode as one people out of what is now northern Russia. One segment rode north; today they're sweating in saunas. The others rode south and became geographically isolated from the Finns; today they're bottling Tokay wine.

But those migrations took place in the eighth and ninth centuries C.E. Previously, Hungary had been, like much of Europe, a Celtic land. With their reverence for the goddesses and gods of nature, the Celts thrived here, only to be conquered by the Romans in 10 C.E. At that point, the areas south and west of the Danube became part of the Roman province of Pannonia. The Roman goddesses found a new home here, having been welcomed, no doubt, by the Celtic goddesses, who in turn had filled the shoes of still earlier goddesses, like the one who inspired the sensitive, wide-eyed, mother-suckling-child clay sculpture unearthed at Zengovarkony and crafted some 6000 years ago. The Roman deities settled in for a four-century stint, after which time Hungary became a raiding ground for Attila's Huns and the aforementioned Finno-Ugric Magyars, who brought with them the strange tang of the north.

Szombathely

Temple of Isis

Hungary is the land of gypsy fiddlers, of paprika on restaurant tables alongside the salt and pepper. It's all very Eastern European, down to the horse-drawn haycarts, the statues of Russian soldiers . . . and a temple of Isis.

"Hold on," you cry, "it's not *that* exotic."

No, it's not. But the ancient Romans, those wild rovers, thought little of congruity as they plastered their empire all over the globe, from the green fields of Cumberland all the way to the Danube. Wherever the Romans colonized, they carried Roman culture, which was duly installed alongside that of the local population.

And Isis, once they discovered her in the saddlebags of Egyptian merchants, became one of the Romans' favorite ministers of culture. They loved her, and they established temples to her from one side of their empire to the other: just as the Americans, having gone off to war and "discovered" pizza in the taverns of Naples, immediately made it their own and then hawked it to a waiting world.

And, just as the Americans remodeled pizza to fit their own tastes—sticking pineapple on it and forever fiddling with its crust—the Isis whom the Romans introduced to the peoples of Europe often scarcely resembled the original Alexandrian Isis. (The Roman version dressed differently, for one thing. Would *you* wear a skintight, sheer sheath in Cumberland?) But her meaning was always the same: hope, healing, and kindness.

And so to the Danube. Present-day Szombathely is an indecisive-looking place, slipping back and forth between old-world gentility and concrete-block, rather humorless modernism. Starched, bow-tied waiters glide among dark wood tables, the steam from bowls of goulash obscuring their smiles. And yet the streets outside are grim, deserted on a Saturday.

Two thousand years ago—before the new world *and* the old world—a Roman town, Savaria, was on this spot. Even here, on the windswept plain at the northeastern edge of the Roman Empire, Isis found a home.

A temple of Isis was uncovered recently in Szombathely. Local archaeologists had long known of the existence of Savaria. Various statues, inscriptions, and altars were continually being discovered (including some dedicated to Nemesis and Luna, which are now in Szombathely's Savaria Museum). But the discovery of the ruined temple was really exciting, for few temples have ever been found in this distant part of the empire. Reconstruction of the so-called Savaria Iseum began in earnest, and you can visit the results today.

Don't laugh.

The white marble frieze with depictions of women and grapes, the fancy Roman capitals, and other original fragments are supported and held together with slabs and tubes of poured cement, whose flat gray surfaces contrast hugely with those of the original materials. Granted, a few of the structures have been done in a nice natural green stone. (Isis likes green.) But reconstructed altars, staircases, and floors of the large temple (it occupies half of a city block) are all made of cement, giving the ancient Iseum a striking resemblance to the cubist Hotel Isis across the street.

Efficient Socialist archaeologists did this job in the spirit of their own time and place. The Iseum is now the showpiece of Szombathely. And through your smirking, know that Isis is really there, having the last laugh. She always knew she would live forever; she knew she would always turn up in the most surprising places. And here

Reconstructed temple of Isis, Szombathely

in a place where religion is almost illegal, *Isis* surfaces. Dressed in concrete, dressed in gray, she folds her arms in Hungary and laughs a satisfied, smug laugh.

(There's pizza in Szombathely too.)

Getting there: Open daily, 10:00 A.M. to 5:00 P.M.. Admission free. Szombathely is 130 miles west of Budapest, 8 miles from the Austrian border. The easiest way to reach it is by train from Sopron, which is accessible from both Budapest and Vienna. The Isis temple is on the street called Rakoczi Ferenc u., in a park near the intersection of Thokoly Imre u., a few blocks south of the center of town. The reconstructed temple is unmistakable, right in the center of the park; the foundation ruins are behind the cement facade.

Ireland

Ireland owes much to its goddesses. Everywhere you look in this brimming island, you see their handiwork. In the bookstores full of poetry, in the peaty soil; in the mother love, the pewter brooches, the eloquent laughter rippling out of a pub late at night, you spy Brigid, goddess of poetry and metalcraft; Maeve, the "drunken woman" and battle queen; Badb; Macha; Morrigan, the spiteful crow-headed goddess; Danu, mother of all.

It is the bold blood of the Celts that flows, barely diluted, through the people of Ireland today. It is the Celts' lusty, restless goddesses whom we remember. Artistic, warlike, the Celts passed on their proud stubbornness to modern Ireland, a country that always goes its own way in the world. Pigheaded? Yes, but pigs are among the goddesses' favorite animals. Those Irish who came before and after the Celts were just as interesting. Prehistoric people built great stone monuments for burial and worship. And then, later, an individualistic brand of monks and nuns kept literacy alive while the rest of Europe slipped grimly into the Dark Ages.

Modern Ireland is unclassifiable, elusive, as if the constant rain that sweeps this island makes it slippery, changing color as often as the sky and sea. Ireland is saturated—with tears, blood, memories, urges—and seems forever on the verge of welling up and overflowing. The goddesses stand by, waiting for the deluge.

Kildare

Fire Sanctuary of Brigid

Among the Celts, the fire goddess Brigid was "the bright one, the bright arrow." Strong, brilliant, and popular, she was every woman's idol. Three-faced and magical, she was every man's mystery. The mistress of poetry, smithcraft, and healing, Brigid was an awesome, tireless dynamo, a triple-stranded braid like the ones that twine and meander through Celtic art to this day.

Other Irish goddesses drift lonely and forlorn, mere wisps of mist, over the land they once ruled. And yet Brigid still blazes across every green field, every pebbled shore.

The early church, recognizing this goddess's hold over the Irish, went into their drawing rooms and came up with St. Brigid, a fifth-century superwoman who (they said) could turn stone into salt and hang up her cloak on a sunbeam. Thus was bright Brigid kept alive. Today she is Ireland's favorite saint, along with St. Patrick, and she rivals even the Virgin Mary in the warm hearts of the Irish.

In a dark land, Brigid had been a goddess of light. Her annual festival at the beginning of February later became known as St. Brigid's feast day, a pagan holy day since ancient times. Called by the Celts *Imbolc* or

Imbolg, that day marks the yearly loosening of winter's death grip; this is the tremulous moment when the first shy stirrings of new light, life, and hope can be felt in the earth and in people's spirits. The festival is still celebrated, as it always has been, with the jubilant lighting of candles.

Appropriately, the goddess's primary shrine was a fire shrine. At Cill Dara, "the place of the oak"—later Anglicized to Kildare—it is said that a sisterhood of priestesses tended an eternal flame in the goddess's honor. For how many generations this tradition was maintained we do not know; at some point, a transition occurred, and St. Brigid, with her nuns, took out a 1500-year lease on the property (with option).

It is from the saint's biographers and other Christian writers that we learn about the continuing usage of Brigid's shrine. Its rites and conditions under the tutelage of the nuns are so reminiscent of the goddess as to strongly support the popular (but subversive) theory that a certain fifth-century high priestess, named Brigid as were all the goddess's high priestesses, was converted to Christianity and became the saint. Few hard facts are actually known about St. Brigid, anyway: She was born in County Cavan, where a hill still bears the name Knockbride; her father was a "pagan chieftain"; the convent she founded at Kildare served as the model for every Christian sisterhood that was to spring up in Ireland thereafter. Brigid's seventh-century biographer, Cogitosus, admitted that it was difficult for him to separate the saint's legends from the goddess's; he complained that it was difficult to "translate" his material "into a Christian context."

The eleventh-century chronicler Geraldus Cambrensis wrote of the shrine at Kildare, with its "miraculous fire of St. Brigid. This they call inextinguishable." During the saint's lifetime, he wrote, "twenty (women) served their Lord there, she (Brigid) making the twentieth." After Brigid's death, "nineteen always remained and the number was not increased, and when each had kept the fire in order in her own night, on the twentieth night the last nun put faggots on the fire, saying, 'Brigid, keep your own fire, for the night has fallen on you,' and the fire being left so is found still burning in the morn-

Kildare's Fire Sanctuary of Brigid

ing." The fire was encircled by a fence made of twigs, and this sacred enclosure was strictly off-limits to men. Male trespassers "escaped not, without enduring punishement." The women stoked the fire with bellows and fans, but never with their own breath.

Cambrensis was writing some 500 years after St. Brigid's demise, and yet these traditions were still going strong. Several bishops ordered the fire extinguished, lambasting the shrine's "pagan overtones." But they met with resistance, and the fire stayed. Brigid's fire was not extinguished until the time of the Reformation, when convents and monasteries were systematically disbanded. So in the end, the fire went out because of its "Catholic overtones," not its pagan ones.

Today a low stone wall, rectangular and not circular as in ancient times, marks the site of Brigid's sanctuary. As neat, tidy, and understated as the transition from goddess to saint, the reconstructed shrine speaks little of its life as a spiritual magnet for Irish women, both in the goddess's time and for centuries afterward. The ground here is cold, cold, cold, crouching in the shadow of the Cathedral Church of Brigid. The cult of Brigid, like all tired creatures, has retired indoors. But all is not lost. In the stained glass window, St. Brigid is depicted with a crimson flame crowning her head. The red sparks flash as the sun catches them, and she is a beacon.

Getting there: Open daily, generally daylight hours. Admission free. Kildare is 32 miles southwest of Dublin, from which run frequent buses and trains. The Cathedral Church of St. Brigid is just off the main square in the center of town. Brigid's Fire House, as it is called, is in the churchyard, surrounded by graves, on the north side of the church (the back side, which is not visible from the church's entrance gate).

Kildare

Tobar Bride (Brigid's Well)

Tobar Bride bubbles up out of the rich earth—a gift. The waters offer themselves, every drop, to your wounds, your pain. The well is a virtual salve factory.

Just a mile away from here, down the dreamy country lane, is Brigid's most famous monument: her ancient fire sanctuary. Generations of priestesses tended her eternal flame. A fire sanctuary . . . and this water sanctuary, practically elbow-to-elbow, both in the name of the same goddess. What kind of spiritual schizophrenia *is* this, anyway?

But Brigid is the most versatile of goddesses. The ancients perceived her as threefold, a one-woman holy trinity who enjoyed dominion over three crucial aspects of Celtic life: poetry, smithcraft, and healing. So fire and water are both hers, after all: the fire that melts the metal and the water that cools fevers and washes wounds.

The early Christians squinted shortsightedly at the threefold goddess and made her into a kind saint who helped and converted people. She was remarkably capable, but she was still human. One of the many legends about St. Brigid tells how she prayed to God to make her ugly so that her father wouldn't be able to find her a husband and thus she might maintain her chastity and enter a convent as she desired. God obliged, and the now-hideous Brigid went cheerfully to a nunnery. As soon as she had taken her vows, however, her good looks returned.

Painted "Brigid's cross" marks stone arch at Tobar Bride, Kildare

Tobar Bride is dedicated to Brigid the saint, not quite the goddess. As such it is immaculately kept, primly decorated, with a clear Christian conscience. And yet the deep serenity of the well, the soothing murmur of the little stream as it ripples past the lifelike statue that wears a nun's habit, reaches deep down just as Brigid the healer reaches with knowing hands into a deep place and does her good works.

Is it an accident that every Irish woman, brought up to emulate St. Brigid just as her foremothers emulated the goddess Brigid, seems to be, herself, a little like a well? A source, a lifelong outpouring of kindness and care?

Getting there: Always open. Admission free. Kildare is 32 miles southwest of Dublin, from which run frequent buses and trains. Tobar Bride is 1 mile south of Kildare. From the center of town, follow the signs leading to the Japanese Gardens. About 300 yards before you get to the gardens, a small white sign indicates that Tobar Bride is off to the right, down a small road. Follow the road 100 yards, after which another sign points left down a lane. Follow the sign. The well is on the right side of the lane. Another unmarked Brigid's Well is farther along the main road past the first sign, about 50 yards before the Japanese Gardens entrance, on the right side of the road.

Killinaboy

Sheela-na-gig

Hidden in a quiet corner of western Ireland, amid soft green hills and lakes wreathed in fog, lies the village of Killinaboy. A country road separates Killinaboy from an overgrown field in which the crumbling skeleton of a church, roofless for centuries, stands in silent memory of an Ireland long vanished. In the life of these gray stones, a year is nothing, nor is a decade. Five hundred years ago these walls were already old.

Even today, the main entrance to the church, a gaping portal in the south wall, commands attention. For some reason it feels like the only "right" way to enter the church, though there is access to the interior in many places where the walls have collapsed. Just as you step up to the door, you notice, above the lintel, a weather-worn carving. It is of a woman: a fierce, powerful woman, naked, her legs wide apart. Though nearly a thousand years old, the figure is compelling, mesmerizing, a jolt to the senses. Carvings of women with openly displayed genitals were once common features on churches all over Ireland and England, though scarcely more than 100 of them survive today. Their ancient name, if any, is lost, and they have acquired the name "sheela-na-gig" almost by accident, although no one is quite sure what the term means. The debate rages among modern scholars about the religious and/or magical significance of sheelas and whether or not they originally represented Celtic deities. (For more details, see the Sheela-na-gigs discussion near the end of the Great Britain chapter.)

Sheelas are probably the remnants of a woman-centered pre-Christian religion, a religion so passionate, so deeply rooted in this soil that it survived even the onslaught of Christianity. Early Christians in Ireland and England thought it a natural thing to place sheela-na-gigs in commanding places on their churches and castles. At Killinaboy, as elsewhere, people entered the church through her door; she blessed and protected people who passed under her vulva. The common folk probably felt more strongly connected to the spiritual power of the sheela-na-gig than they did to any other symbol in the church.

The church at Killinaboy was part of an early religious community in an area with many prehistoric ruins and was most probably built on top of an earlier sacred site. Killinaboy is named for a female saint, St. Inghean Bhaoith; the church was named Cill Inghean Bhaoith, which, pronounced rapidly by a native tongue, becomes Kill-in-a-boy. Tellingly, the sheela-na-gig here is *itself* sometimes referred to as Inghean Bhaoith, which suggests that the church was named after the figure, and the town named after the church, rather than the other way around. St. Inghean Bhaoith, who supposedly founded the religious community here, may very well have been a mythical figure. She may in fact be the personification of the feminine spirit of the place, now represented by the sheela-na-gig.

Sheela-na-gigs still hold spiritual power for many people in modern-day Ireland. Stone dust collected from the figures' genital areas is reputed to have magical properties. In some regions it is customary to touch or rub sheela-na-gigs for good luck or for other, more profound reasons. Comparison of photos of certain sheela-na-gigs taken 50 years ago with recent photos of the same ones reveal that in 50 years they have become unmistakably smoother and more worn away. The evidence of recent rubbing is clearly visible.

Historians say that Ireland was thoroughly Christianized many centuries ago. The sheela-na-gigs, if they could talk, might have a different story to tell.

Getting there: Always open. Admission free. Killinaboy is 2 miles north of Corofin, which is 8 miles north of Ennis, in County Clare, northwest of Limerick City. The Killinaboy Church is in the ruins of the monastic site on the north side of the road; the ruins are visible from the road and from Killinaboy. The sheela-na-gig can be seen above a round-topped doorway in the outer south wall of the large abandoned church.

Knocknarea

Queen Maeve's Grave

This is one of those Irish places that floods you with a choking, unreasonable sadness. The country is full of such places; many, like this one, are next to the sea. Like the fog smothering the shore, the sorrow socks you, and you want to sob and roar and shake your fists like a mourner at an Irish funeral.

And well you should, for they say Knocknarea is the grave of a goddess. The occupant in question is Maeve, also known as Medbh, Medb, and Mab. In most current books of Irish mythology, she appears only as *Queen* Maeve, a rowdy, insatiable woman whose selfish desire to possess a powerful brown bull results in oceans of bloodshed between the clashing armies of Ulster and Connaught.

Here we see in action a favorite tactic of the myth collectors of the British Isles. In an attempt to banish wild and powerful goddesses from the land where they had been so much adored, writers systematically demoted goddesses to the status of mere mortal queens. (Poor Brigid, on the other hand, became a saint, but biographers are quick to point out her royal connections: her father, they say, was a "pagan chieftain.")

As a goddess, Maeve had ruled over war—like Athena, but without Athena's cool head. Maeve's wars were skull-battering cataclysms, brother against brother, part of the legacy that makes this such a sorrowful, ghost-ridden country. Also as a goddess, Maeve ruled rulers. She was the patroness of sovereignty itself, and every Celtic king maintained a special relationship with her.

As a queen, Maeve was willful. Of course, she still loved war, commanding an army of her own. She rode out to battle in the forefront of legions of men, and she sat up nights planning treacherous strategies. Just as every king consorted with the goddess Maeve through ritual and worship, so too did Queen Maeve require the intimate companionship of countless kings and heroes. Usually she settled for about 30 lovers per day. If human queens were this interesting, we wouldn't need democracy.

From a distance, the flat-topped mountain of Knocknarea, rising gently beside the sea, looks like an altar draped in moss-green flannel. Like an overturned bowl on its summit is the 35-foot mound called Misgaun Maeve, "Maeve's Cairn" or "Maeve's Grave." Its gray stones stand out starkly against the green. As you clamber upward, gaining with every step an ever-widening view of rain-soaked pastures and sad, silvery bay, it overtakes you: the melancholy, the sorrow.

Science tells us the mound is most likely a passage grave, built by Stone Age people around 3000 B.C.E. But legend, as the mound's name shows, marks it as the tomb of Maeve. In the Celtic belief system, goddesses, like mortals, did not necessarily live forever. The athlete goddess Macha, for example, died in childbirth following a footrace. And so on Knocknarea, especially at twilight when the world goes soft and slack, you mourn for fiery Maeve, who battles no more. In the fields below, cows ruminate: mild dull descendants of Maeve's prized Brown Bull of Cooley.

The mound has never been excavated, partly because the local residents are leery about opening it up. Science is no match for legend, and no archaeologist can stand up against Maeve.

Getting there: Always open. Admission free. Knocknarea mountain is 5 miles west of Sligo. Buses from Sligo will get you only within 2 miles of the site. The

Queen Maeve's Grave, Knocknarea

mountain is an imposing landmark, so it's hard to get lost. Whatever route you're taking, simply follow the road leading in the direction of the mountaintop. You will eventually come to a narrow path leading up the mountain between fields of grazing sheep and cows. Follow the path all the way to the end; the cairn is at the peak of the mountain. The climb is a bit steep in places and takes about 45 minutes altogether.

Mulhuddart

Holy Well

The Irish are as nonchalant about their 3000 holy wells as they are about their haunted castles, banshees, fairy mounds, and other uncannyisms that irreparably divide Ireland from the realm of the ordinary. To a foreigner like yourself, it is charming, downright thrilling, that so many water wells are decorated and treated as shrines to which pilgrims come bearing flowers and prayers. Yet the news agent, when you ask directions, looks up mildly from her high-octane cup of tea and beams, "First left after the schoolyard, love; then it's in that big cluster of trees," as if you'd asked for nothing more supernatural than a mailbox or a gas station.

Mulhuddart's is a rank-and-file, workaday holy well if ever there was one. Hugging the side of a busy road, it uncomplainingly stews in the exhaust of cars and trucks. Like many other Irish wells, it sports a whitewashed concrete shelter with blue trim. Blue and white are traditionally the Virgin Mary's colors. But it doesn't take a scholar to appreciate the fact that they are also the colors of water; water, springing fresh from the earth as if by magic, is what is *really* being celebrated at a holy well, and what has, from ancient times up to the present, fascinated people all over the world. Ireland's holy wells, like those throughout the British Isles, hark back to a time when people acknowledged springs to be the homes of gentle, healing goddesses, who were consulted and celebrated with great respect.

A statue of Our Lady of Lourdes leans crookedly in an alcove, like a child's toy put hastily away after playtime. An inscription on the side of the shelter, incised in an idiosyncratic script, reads "O Blessed Mother and Ever Virgin Gl/orious Queen of the World Make Inte/rcession . . . O Sacred Virgin Obt/Ain for me Force Aga/Inst Thy Enemies." No one seems to mind that the well's water, through years of neglect and clogging, seems mighty scarce indeed.

Glimpsed from the corner of your eye, the domelike shelter resembles a cairn, one of those stone burial mounds which the ancient Irish built so solidly and hugely that their rounded bulks still loom, undisturbed, all over the landscape. Then again, adorned as it is with plastic flowers peeking aridly out of a drinking tumbler, this well could pass for a big, stolid dollhouse.

Dollhouse, cairn, shrine—and all by the side of the road. It is very, very Irish to mix things up so casually, to juggle the elemental and artificial, maudlin and miraculous, as naturally as a cook juggles the ingredients for Irish stew . . . and then to eat it up for supper, with plenty of salt and beer.

Getting there: Always open. Admission free. Mulhuddart is a suburb of Dublin, 8 miles northwest of the city center. Take bus 38A from Middle Abbey Street in Dublin all the way to the end of the line in Mulhuddart, where you'll get off on Lady's Well Road. Walk back one

Inscription to the Virgin Mary on Mulhuddart's holy well

block, and turn left on the main road heading north. Go north about one block, and you will see the well on the left side of the road, at a corner of Lady's Well Park, which is now in the process of being developed into a housing tract.

Rathcroghan

Queen Maeve's Palace

One of Ireland's goriest—and thus best-loved—sagas begins as the "beautiful and proud Maeve, queen of Connacht" and her husband, King Ailill, are lying cozily in bed one night in their palace at Rathcroghan. What begins as pillow talk soon escalates into a heated boasting match. What else would you expect from Maeve, the war goddess *cum* queen whose appetites made men's legs turn to jelly?

That night, king and queen began comparing their hordes of prized possessions. Ailill bragged of his cauldrons and his jewelry. Maeve laughed and had her own brought out to show him. They were every bit as fine. Ailill counted his servants and gloated over the number. But Maeve had just as many. Starting with the least valuable items and working up through the entire inventory, they compared flocks of sheep, stables of horses, pigs . . . until finally their respective herds of cattle were brought out. Maeve saw at once that she had lost, for Ailill owned a huge white-horned bull whose equal she did not begin to possess.

In fact, so great was this bull that no one owned its equal, save one man, Daire Mac Fiachniu of Ulster, whose Brown Bull of Cooley was a legend in its own time. In a competitive fury, Maeve set out to steal the bull. Her efforts resulted in an all-out war between Daire's Ulstermen and her own army of Connacht. In the end, after much bloodshed; after Maeve tricks the hero Cu Chulainn into slaughtering his own boyhood companion; after Maeve's daughter, Finnabar, dies of shame when she learns that Maeve has been offering her, like candy, to a different soldier every day . . . after all this and more, Maeve acquires the precious Brown Bull, only to have it tear Ailill's white-horned beast limb from limb, then go stomping back home to Ulster, where it finally commits bovine suicide.

The world is an exciting place for a woman who knows what she wants.

Maeve was a wild and primal Irish goddess before the straitjacket of mythology tamed and demoted her to the status of mere human queen. Nonetheless, she remained outlandish, swashbuckling, and fearsome.

Her palace at Rathcroghan is associated with the entire royal line of Connacht, rulers both real and legendary. Here, Ireland's pagan kings were inaugurated. Some, including Dathi, the last pre-Christian monarch, were entombed nearby.

A mound, 25 feet high and 70 feet across, is still known as a residence or seat of "Queen" Maeve. Flat-topped, like a wardrum, it commands a haughty view in all directions. Once surrounded by structures befitting a palace, the mound now stands in the middle of a pasture. The saga tells that it was here that Maeve and Ailill began their fateful snit, here that Maeve assembled her army before setting out for Ulster. As Irish writer Eileen O'Faolain describes it, "Daily they began to arrive . . . around her palace at Rathcruachan, companies of men in flowing kilts and long beards from the far south and west, giant-sized warriors from the fat lands of Leinster . . . the flat land around the royal palace of Maeve was one great warrior camp waiting for the word of the Queen to move off to war."

Her army went off to scream and die in Ulster. In place of those brave soldiers, what do you see at Rathcroghan today? Cows and bulls, their brown, black, and white silhouettes dotting the landscape for miles around. They stamp and chew and softly moan as if to mourn for the long-lost heroes, the Brown Bull of Cooley and the White-Horned Bull of Ailill. Perhaps they moan for the goddess whose throne they now dare to nibble. Perhaps she would have found one among them worth warring over.

Getting there: Always open. Admission free. Rathcroghan is 2½ miles northwest of Tulsk, which is about 15 miles north of Roscommon. The mound is about 200 yards off the south side of the road, on your left as you are going northwest from Tulsk. A gate through a fence allows access across a field to the mound. Many other smaller mounds are in the area, so you may become confused as to which one is Maeve's. If you are unsure, ask any of the neighbors and they'll gladly point you in the right direction.

Italy

ITALY

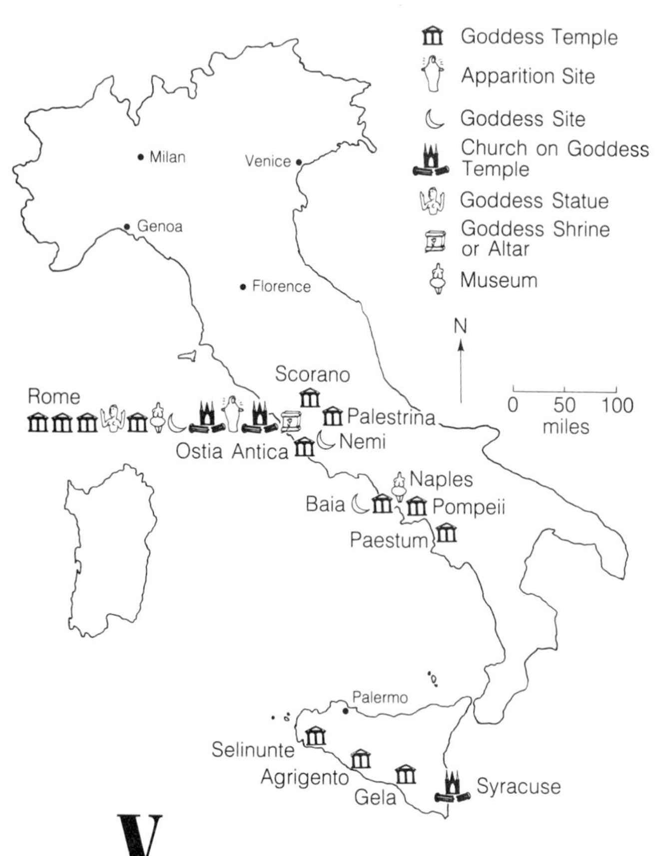

You could leapfrog across Italy's temples from one end of the country to the other; there are so many of them. You could play a vast game of croquet using their columns as wickets, knocking boulders from Rome to Pompeii.

This sun-blessed country has inspired no fewer than three great civilizations to flourish here, to dream, build temples, and worship, all the while fortifying their place in world history. A great civilization requires mighty goddesses; Italy's goddesses are the familiar archetypal Olympians of the Greeks, the mysterious underworld queens of the Etruscans, and the divine hybrids-in-togas of the Romans. The Etruscans fostered an artistic, highly technological world in central Italy—Etruria—roughly between the eighth and sixth centuries B.C.E. The Greeks established colonies all over southern Italy between the seventh and fourth centuries B.C.E. and built the Doric temples that are still hailed as the country's finest. The Romans, feeling their oats around the fifth century, admired both those civilizations. They leaned so heavily on the Etruscans as to swallow them up completely, and they seduced the Greek deities right out from under their straight noses, blithely switching their names. As the Roman Empire expanded to encompass virtually all of Europe, here at home the goddesses enjoyed constant attention. On them were showered the sumptuous gifts, the elaborate temples and festivals that only a people on top of the world can afford. For that moment of glory we, leapfrogging golden temples to our hearts' content, are ever grateful.

Agrigento, Sicily

Demeter Sanctuaries

The cities of the ancient Greek world were sadly lacking in the basic amenities that now seem so essential for urban life. They had no running water, no windowpanes, no leash laws, no police force, no toilets. Their streets were unpaved. They had no hospitals, banks, or pricey cafes. Ah, but nearly every Greek town had one essential feature not to be found in a single modern American city: a temple of Demeter. The Greeks may not have had windowpanes, but they had their priorities.

Agrigento, called Akragas by its founders, was a colony established in 582 B.C.E. by the people from nearby Gela, which itself was founded by Cretans and Rhodians. After the colonists had settled into Akragas, they went on an inspired temple-building spree, erecting a phalanx of grandiose temples for which Agrigento is still justly famous. They built a sanctuary to Demeter too. But they didn't stop there. For some reason now lost, they built a second Demeter sanctuary. Then, incredibly, they built a third.

Akragas may have had more Demeter sanctuaries than any city in the ancient world. Why Demeter was so popular here, we will never know. An odd feature of her worship at Akragas, though, was that it emphasized her Chthonic, or earth-centered, aspect over her grain mother aspect.

One of her sanctuaries stood on the eastern end of the hill overlooking the area now known as "the Valley of the Temples." The Greeks cut a terrace into the solid rock of the mountainside, and on this they built a marble temple. Demeter's temple still stands on this spot, but it is hardly recognizable as such, for it was later converted into a chapel and is now known as the Church of San Biagio. Greek temples generally faced east, but early churches faced west, so a door was cut in the temple's rear wall to create the front entrance of the church. Adjacent to the temple are two round altars used in Demeter's rites. One of these was of a type called a *bothros*, with a central opening into which liquid offerings, such as wine, were poured so that they would soak directly into the soil.

Downhill from this temple, on the back side of the hill, is the so-called Rock Sanctuary of Demeter. Two caves (both now fenced off) were dug into the cliff face. When first discovered, they were filled with votive statues of Demeter and Persephone. In front of the caves was a building of unknown function, now a tumbled pile of masonry. Some of its blocks, still in place, were cut to serve as water channels, though we can only guess what the function of this water was in the ritual.

Over a mile away, on the far end of Agrigento's famous row of temples, is the third Demeter sanctuary, appropriately dubbed the Sanctuary of the Chthonic Deities. Demeter, Persephone, and possibly pre-Greek, native Sicilian underworld deities were honored here with sacrifices and libations. The whole area is dotted with altars and *bothroi*. Most were in the open air, though some were enclosed in rooms for the enactment of secret rites.

Yet another temple of Demeter stood near the altars and ritual buildings. This one, however, was not converted into a chapel, and so it was thoroughly destroyed. A small corner of the temple was reconstructed in the 1800s and mistakenly identified as a temple of Castor and Pollux, which is the name by which most guidebooks still refer to it. This reconstruction, though very picturesque and reproduced on posters, postage stamps,

Stone-cut water channels at the Rock Sanctuary of Demeter, Agrigento

and postcards all over Italy, is actually totally erroneous, a Frankenstein's-monsterlike concoction using blocks from many different and unrelated fallen temples.

If a native of Akragas were alive today, the first question we'd ask her would be, "Why did your city have *three* Demeter sanctuaries?" And she might very well retort, "Why does *your* city have more than one church, more than one school, more than one theater. . . ?"

Getting there: The Temple of Demeter and Church of San Biagio is open irregular hours, generally Monday through Saturday, 9 A.M. to 1 hour before sunset; closed Sunday, though there are no official opening and closing times. Admission free. The Rock Sanctuary of Demeter (Santuario Rupestre) has the same hours, admission, and directions as the Temple of Demeter. The Sanctuary of the Chthonic Deities, also known as the Temple of Castor and Pollux, is open daily, 9 A.M. to 1 hour before sunset. Admission free. To reach the Church of San Biagio, from Piazza Marconi in front of the train station, follow the signs pointing to the Valley of the Temples down via F. Crispi. Turn left after about ¼ mile onto via Demetra, heading east. Just where it turns uphill is a gate on the right side of the street and a sign pointing to the Sanctuary of Demeter. Go straight through the gate and up the dirt road, then take the ancient rock pathway going up the hill to the church, clearly visible above you. The outdoor shrines are right between the church and the cut-away hillside. To reach the rock sanctuary from San Biagio, take a path leading downhill, keeping to the left when in doubt. All paths eventually lead to a stone stairway winding down the steep side of the hill. The stairs lead directly to the rock sanctuary. To reach the Sanctuary of the Chthonic Deities from the main part of town, follow the signs to the Valley of the Temples, all the way down via dei Templi to Piazzale dei Templi, just opposite the Temple of Hercules and west of the Temple of Concordia. A signposted gate on the west side of Piazzale dei Templi leads to the Temples of Zeus (Giove) and the Chthonic Deities. Go through the gate, past the Temple of Zeus and related ruins, all the way to the far end of the site, where four columns hold up part of a temple roof. This, and the shrines around it, is the sanctuary of the Chthonic Deities, erroneously named the Temple of Castor and Pollux.

Baia

Temple of Diana, Cave of the Sibyl, and the Sacred Grove of Hecate

A jade-green sea, melting to glassy translucence against a white crescent of beach . . . silken sky . . . the sea teeming with good things, an endless banquet: These delights were no less irresistible to the ancient Romans than they are to people today. The sunny beach resort, stocked with well-oiled hedonists, was not a concept born yesterday.

The ancient Romans enjoyed resorts, and Baia was their favorite. From the first century C.E. to the fourth, emperors, senators, and other fun-loving Romans flocked to this coastal town, whose abundant natural hot springs had been engineered, in typical Roman fashion, into a complex system of baths. The Romans built here a huge temple of Diana. (Archaeologists are almost positive the building was sacred to Diana, though no inscription has been found that identifies it as such.) The divinely healthy and physically fit goddess, who so treasured her own bath that she destroyed the man who dared to spy on her as she bathed with her nymphs, was often associated with Roman thermal resorts—as in France's Aix-les-Bains.

Since Baia was so important a resort (the poet Horace wrote, to translate loosely, "There's nothin' like it!"), this Diana temple was appropriately palatial, the equivalent of a Monte Carlo Casino or an Avalon Ballroom in a time and place in which travelers did not leave their spirituality at home. An enormous dome crowned the temple: its repetition of soft rolling curves was perfect for a water sanctuary.

Today it seems almost as if some jealous god has deliberately dashed and trampled once-lovely Baia. Most of the ancient city now molders under the sea, and the temple of Diana is half gone, its once-perfect dome now resembling a ragged, oversized bandshell.

Arched doorways and niches, set into the remaining semicircle of temple walls, help show the grand scale on which this temple was built. So does the massive half-dome, as golden brown as the skins of the ancient bathers. The dome's curve might well be that of an incredulously raised eyebrow, for while it once sheltered the rich, famous, and pious, it now shelters a garbage dump and a few humble backyard gardens. Has Diana come to this? A royal palm tree, ramrod-straight, stands just outside the broken wall, heightening the sense of despoiled splendor.

Some of Baia's popularity stemmed from its proximity to the important ancient city of Cuma (Cumae), the

Remains of domed Diana temple, Baia

oldest Greek colony in Italy and the seat of the Cumaean Sibyl. From the sixth century B.C.E. onward, seekers visited the sibyl in her cave. They braved the long and spooky subterranean hallway so that the seeress, in her chamber, might provide divinely inspired answers to their questions. The sibyl's cave and entranceway are every bit as awe-inspiring today, damp and chill and eerie. Hewn out of soft sallow stone, they were deliberately constructed to make the visitor ill at ease. This effect has survived through the ages.

Homer wrote of the Cumaean sibyl in the *Odyssey*. Virgil, in the *Aeneid*, tells how his hero, Aeneas, visited the sibyl with questions about his dead loved ones. She led him to nearby Lake Averno, on whose shore was located one of the legendary portals to Hades. Aeneas descended; but without a sibyl to guide you, you'll never find your way. The lake, actually an extinct volcano's crater, 100 feet deep in the center, is ringed by a deep forest. Very deep, and dark enough to be known as Hecate's sacred grove, Hades's back garden, and to shelter the comings and goings of Hecate, Persephone, and others who know the way.

Getting there: The Temple of Diana at Baia and the grove of Hecate around Lake Averno are always open and free to visit. The Cave of the Sibyl is at the archaeological site of Cuma, open daily, 9:00 A.M. to 6:00 P.M. Admission L2000. Baia is 12 miles west of Naples. From the Montesanto metro station in Naples, take the Ferrovia Cumana train line to Baia. The Temple of Diana is just across the tracks from the station platform. However, to reach the temple, you must exit the station and take the overpass that crosses the tracks right next to the platform; then go down into the garden area, heading toward the large half-dome. (Be careful not to trample people's gardens.) To reach Cuma from Baia, take a bus from across the street from the Baia station. (Make sure to tell the driver you're going to the Cuma archaeological site, which on road signs is called "Antro della Sibilla.") To reach Lake Averno from Baia, take the Ferrovia Cumana back one stop to the Lucrino station. From there, follow the signs ½ mile north to the lake.

Gela, Sicily

Temples of Athena and Sanctuary of Demeter

The Greeks were not the first to fall in love with Gela's fruit-bearing valleys and sparkling swath of shore. Nor were they to be the last. The Sicans (aka Sikels), the original native inhabitants of Sicily, lived here in the second millennium B.C.E. Greeks from faraway Crete and Rhodes founded a colony here in 690 B.C.E., which flourished for 200 years. Gela was sacked by Carthaginians in 490 B.C.E., then resettled, then destroyed again by neighboring armies in 280 B.C.E. It remained a wasteland until the Middle Ages. Now it is one of the cornucopias of modern Italy.

But it was the Greeks who made Gela famous. Naturally, they brought their goddesses with them to Sicily. On Gela's acropolis, a wild bluff overlooking the sea, they built a temple to the Greek Goddess Most Likely to be Found on Bluffs Overlooking the Sea: Athena, of course. Gela's acropolis no doubt reminded them of their beloved Lindian Athena, who guarded a splendid bluff back home at Lindos, Rhodes (see the discussion in the Greece chapter). Later, to commemorate a victory over Carthage in the fifth century B.C.E., a second Doric temple was built here in Athena's name.

Athena was a good choice for the Gelans, considering the many invasions their town was to suffer over the years. But the museum adjoining the acropolis reveals that other goddesses were also honored here, most notably, Demeter. Traditional offerings to the vegetation goddess were figurines depicting women carrying piglets. Dozens of these figurines were found at Gela, as were statues of Demeter and her daughter, Kore. (Traveling around the region today, or tucking into a meal here, you can see that it is still very much Demeter's country.)

As principal deity, Athena's image dominates the museum. Some of her statues have a distinctively Asiatic appearance and have been compared with those left as offerings at the goddess's temple in Lindos. The museum's cases also hold row upon row of woman-shaped votive statuettes. The little terracotta women stand solemnly at attention, all eyes staring foreward, like an auditorium of schoolgirls preparing to salute their principal.

On the acropolis, little remains of the sanctuaries. Of one temple, virtually nothing is visible. On the site of the other Athenaion, a single orange-gray column stands in abject solitude. Cruelly echoed by refinery smokestacks on the horizon, this lonely column is like a last soldier in Athena's army: bereft, abandoned by all companions, but still holding out, standing firm, in the goddess's name.

Lone column marks Gela's temple of Athena

This is an eloquent loneliness. It reminds us of our own loneliness here at Gela and at places like Gela. So alien in time, in fashion, in culture from the people who built the temple and the many generations who worshipped in it, we stand on the denuded bluff like that last soldier, holding out, waiting for the others to return.

Getting there: Open Monday through Saturday, 9:00 A.M. to 1:30 P.M. and 3:30 P.M. to 6:30 P.M.; Sunday, 9:00 A.M. to 1:00 P.M. Admission free. Gela is on the southern coast of Sicily, 45 miles east of Agrigento. The temples are on the acropolis and in the park adjoining it, at the far eastern end of town, at the end of Corso Vittorio Emanuele. The Doric temple of Athena is among the trees of the park, beyond the main acropolis ruins.

Nemi

Grove of Diana

Under the violet sky of an ancient Italian dusk, torches crackle and flicker in the darkening forest. A sinuous procession winds through the sacred groves of oak, back and forth down the steep slope; ecstatic women raise flaming firebrands to the newly risen moon. Around a lustrous marble shrine, the worshippers throng, their torches a circle of blazing light reflected in the silver stillness of Diana's lake just below. The night rings with invocations and paeans of profound antiquity.

This shrine, this grove, are the precinct of Diana, goddess of woodlands, of wild animals, of the moon, fertility, and childbirth. Here, in the woods around Lake Nemi, Diana herself is said to have dwelt. The lakeside shrine was the center of her cult, a cult whose popularity eventually spread throughout the Mediterranean world. Her origin was here, her birthplace, her home.

Diana's divinity is of primordial importance. Evidence of her worship found at Nemi dates to the beginning of the Roman era and even earlier, to the time of the aboriginal Italian tribes who looked to her for guidance when this peninsula was but a primitive wilderness. The many devotional artifacts found at Diana's shrine tell us a great deal about her, but not everything: to complete the picture, we need to know the legends and mythology surrounding the goddess. The temple at Nemi inspires us, drives our need to know. Who is Diana?

Like many of the Italian goddesses and gods, Diana has kept her secrets. By the time the Romans began to write of their deities, another pantheon was making its presence felt. The Romans were smitten with Greek culture, and very early on they paired Hellenic divinities with their own. Thus Jupiter became indistinguishable from Zeus, Juno from Hera. Venus became Aphrodite, Vulcan became Hephaestus. And so Diana too was melded with Greek Artemis. Their attributes became identical, as did their images, their rites. Even Diana's mythology was reshaped to be the same as Artemis's. Diana's original legends were never written down, and so they will always remain a secret.

One legend does survive, however, and that legend has been the subject of unparalleled scrutiny. The story is of the priests of Diana and the strange ritual by which they succeeded one another. Sir James Frazer's 12-volume study, *The Golden Bough*, a work that revolutionized the field of anthropology, concerns itself entirely with this legend and its significance.

Diana's priest must be, according to custom, a runaway slave. He lived here in the grove of Nemi. As her priest and King of the Wood (*Rex Nemorensis*), he was, symbolically at least, married to the goddess. He spent his reign guarding one particular oak tree that was especially sacred to Diana. He would drive away anyone who tried to break off a bough, either from the tree itself or, more likely, from the mistletoe that grew on the tree. If another escaped slave succeeded in removing a bough—Frazer's "golden bough"—he earned the right to slay the reigning priest and take his place. This succession of priests, each one slaughtering his predecessor, extended from the early Iron Age well into the Christian era.

Frazer spent the better part of his life exploring the meaning of this baffling ritual. He proved, with an argument so fluid, so thorough, so beautifully precise as to be irrefutable, that the Rex Nemorensis was the embodiment of the sky god, that his death renewed the yearly cycle of life, and that Diana was the true Goddess herself, mother of the earth. Her rites and worship at Nemi are a crystalline window to the time when the Goddess, in her purest form, was revered the world over.

Diana's festival day in Rome was on the Ides of August, the thirteenth of the month. Throughout the Roman world, women paid tribute to their goddess on this day. To begin the festival's solemnities, each woman ritually washed her hair. Then each proceeded to a Dianic temple, where she gave thanks and offered the goddess votives, which were often in the shape of a lamp or, most strikingly, a uterus. Diana watched over fertility and childbirth, and the terracotta uteruses were given in gratitude for a painless delivery or as a request for fruitful conception. The worshippers were, in essence, consecrating their wombs to Diana. In the evening, torchlight processions wound their way through cities, towns, and forests to holy places, where celebrations lasted well into the night.

Slaves also loved Diana, for on her day they were permitted to live and travel as freely as any citizen. Lenient slave owners often chose August 13 as the day to emancipate their servants.

The Roman emperors became fascinated with the cult of Diana and turned her holy day into an outrageous extravaganza. Caligula built two vast, luxurious barges and set them afloat in tiny Lake Nemi, where they became part of the overblown state-run celebrations. The barges eventually sank, and in 1928, Benito Mussolini ordered the lake drained and lowered so that they could be recovered. The barges were installed in a museum on the shores of the lake, but they were spitefully burned by retreating Nazis in 1944. They were replaced by scale-model reproductions, but the museum has been closed for many years. The lake's water level was never restored to normal.

Evidence of votive offerings at Nemi dwindled during the imperial period, as the area became a resort for the wealthy. The natives were driven from the region, and few rural locals remained to attend Diana's rites.

Later, the month of August was lengthened, and the Ides (the middle of the month) moved from the thirteenth day to the fifteenth. After the empire was Christianized, August 15 became known as the Assumption Day of the Virgin Mary. On Assumption Day in Rome, women thanked the Virgin and offered votives, usually small oil lamps or, later, candles, just as hundreds of years earlier women had offered votive lamps to the virgin Diana.

Nowadays, Nemi is more famous for its strawberries than for its goddesses. The temple and sanctuary the Romans built are mostly covered by garden plots where berries and vegetables grow, and there is little left of it to be seen. The most impressive parts of the ruins are the retaining walls of the sanctuary's terraces: long rows of graceful domed niches hold back the mountainside. A small corner of the sanctuary remains excavated, exposing a jumble of marble and masonry.

But it is not in these ruins that Diana lived, and still lives. It is in the oak groves that encircle Lake Nemi—

the lake once known as Diana's Mirror. The moon's reflection still floats on the lake, as achingly perfect as when it moved women to chant and pray. The woods, remembering the women, are dark and alive, wild and fertile.

Getting there: Always open. Admission free. Nemi is 17 miles southwest of Rome, on a promontory overlooking Lago di Nemi. The temple is below the town near the shore of the lake. To reach the temple, either drive on the via Appia Nuova (SS7) from Rome, or take a bus from near the train station at Albano to Genzano di Roma, which is on the southwest side of the lake. From Piazza Dante Alighieri in Genzano, you can drive or walk 1½ miles along via Diana, which curves along the western side of the lake and continues past the Museum of Roman Ships. *Or* you can take a local bus from Genzano to the town of Nemi. From the place where the bus drops you off, walk 3 blocks down Corso V. Emanuele, out the city gates overlooking the lake, where you turn right on Belvedere Dante Alighieri, which becomes via Tempio di Diana, which also winds down the hill for 1½ miles. (There is also a footpath leading through the woods down from Belvedere Dante Alighieri, but it is overgrown and you may end up wandering onto private property.) Either way, you'll eventually reach via Navi di Tiberio, which ends in a path called Vicolo Sonnemi, which leads to the temple. However, there are no street signs in this area, so the best thing to do is ask, "*Dov'e tempio di Diana?*" of any of the local strawberry gardeners and they'll point the way. You'll know you've reached it when you see two rows of semicircular niches meeting at right angles in the hillside.

Ostia Antica

Temples of Ceres, Bona Dea, Magna Mater, and Bellona

Ostia was Rome's outpost at the mouth of the River Tiber. A thriving, pivotal kind of place, its bustling streets held shops, marketplaces, baths, sporting fields, theaters, studios, restaurants, mills, guildhalls, and mansions. Ostia enjoyed the sophistication and genius of the capital city that it supported as well as something extra: As a shipping port and food-and-supplies warehouse for all of Rome, Ostia constantly felt the touch of foreign cultures. All kinds of people from all over the world met and mingled here, some just passing through, others settling down and forming tightly knit communities.

Of course, they worshipped here too. In those years when every land and culture had a religion of its own, it was taken for granted that an immigrant would bring along the familiar goddesses, gods, and traditions of home and set them up alongside whatever new and strange ones were encountered along the way. Thus in international Ostia, where characteristic Roman tolerance ensured that people could worship whomever and however they wished, an interesting variety of temples thrived.

Excavations in Ostia revealed no less than seven temples dedicated to the Persian sun god, Mithras. There were also Syrian temples, Egyptian temples, Phrygian temples, a Jewish synagogue, and even a Christian basilica. The standard Roman pantheon was faithfully represented as well. Ostia's temple of Ceres, the goddess of grain, stands behind the amphitheater. This goddess was important to everyone who liked to eat, but especially so to the city's many residents whose livelihood was the importing and exporting of foodstuffs. Today, the temple's twin columns and headless statues make it the classic ruin, eminently photographable.

Presenting quite a different picture, a temple of Bona Dea can be found on the far outskirts of town. Unlike most of the others worshipped in Ostia, Bona Dea was a strictly local goddess. Her name, delightfully blunt, was Latin for "Good Goddess": no more and no less. She was a women's goddess. Men were forbidden to explore her mysteries. A famous scandal of ancient Rome concerns a young nobleman who, disguised as a woman, sneaked into a building where a Bona Dea ritual was being performed. His ruse was soon discovered, and the furious women punished him soundly. Nevertheless, the event sparked off a powder keg of

Temple of Ceres, Ostia Antica

gossip that actually moved Caesar to divorce his wife, who was a bigwig in the Bona Dea cult and had been present at the ritual. (Caesar claimed that any wife of his must be absolutely above all possible scandal. Historians tell us that he had long been searching for an excuse to divorce her.) While most of Ostia's remains are in an excellent state of preservation, Bona Dea's shrine is not. Crumbling away in its forgotten corner, this shrine makes the visitor feel like an intruder, a discoverer, or a liberator. Brick-walled chambers, a courtyard, and the remains of a pool all huddle under a thick tangle of weeds. It is as if the sanctuary, in the absence of its priestesses, is trying hard to clothe itself, to hold intact its mysteries.

The Phrygian earth and fertility goddess, Cybele, who was irrepressibly popular in the capital and all over the Roman Empire, had a faithful retinue of followers in Ostia. So substantial was her following here that a special corporation, the Hastiferi, existed for the sole purpose of maintaining the large precinct which was dedicated to her. This sanctuary, on the edge of town, comprises a raised shrine to the goddess and a smaller one devoted to her lover, Attis. Between the two stretches a wide field known as the Campo della Magna Mater. Magna Mater—"the Great Mother"—was what the Romans called this Near Eastern goddess. In her fierce love for Attis, a love that drove him crazy, killed him, and eventually brought him back to life, people found a force that was both passionate and maternal. As you climb the nine marble steps up to Cybele's temple today, turn swiftly to glimpse, across the field, the shrine of Attis—beautiful, difficult Attis—that is half-obscured behind tall waving grasses but that is, thankfully, for Cybele's sake, never out of sight.

Annual celebrations held in the Campo della Magna Mater around the time of the spring equinox dramatized Attis's resurrection. The festival began on a sad, stark, stricken note, as befits a time of mourning. Then, with the symbolic rebirth of Attis, the party exploded into feverish, often bloody abandon: the "sacred frenzy" that made worship of Cybele so famous and, to many, so attractive. In later years, the ceremony culminated with the sacrifice of bulls in the goddess's honor.

Another part of Cybele's precinct is a compact temple dedicated to Bellona, an ancient local goddess of war who managed, somehow, to escape the usual Greco-Roman fate of being absorbed into the large personalities of Athena and Minerva. Bellona's traditions came to be linked with Magna Mater's, so that today, Bellona's ruined shrine, with its weed-choked mosaic floor, squats protectively just behind the temple of Attis. Bellona also guards the back gate of Ostia, the Porta Laurentina, to which her shrine is closer than any other.

Fortuna, the goddess of fortune, was known and loved in this avidly commercial city. Her temple, known as the Domus Fortuna Annonaria, was one of the largest structures in Ostia and was decorated with statues of Fortuna and other goddesses. The mosaic floor in one of its chambers depicts a she-wolf, that most potent and motherly of Roman symbols. On the day we visited, this temple was closed for restoration. We were crestfallen. But it is not for us to determine our own fortunes, after all, is it?

Getting there: Open daily, 9:00 A.M. to 6:00 P.M. Admission: L4000. Ostia is 15 miles southwest of Rome, near the coast. From Rome, take the Metro to the Magliana station; once there, transfer to the commuter train, which takes you directly to Ostia. The entrance to the archaeological site is a few hundred yards from the station, on the other side of the footbridge crossing the highway. To find the temples in the ancient city, you will need a map or a guidebook; the best is the free brochure the tourist office in Rome distributes.

Paestum

Temples of Hera and Athena

Today, Paestum is one of Italy's archaeological showcases, a once-magnificent city whose well-preserved temples now pose on a perfect lawn like a trio of large, obedient pets. But Paestum, bless its old soul, has had a difficult time of it these past 2700 years.

For one thing, none of the succession of peoples who marched in and out of the city were content to leave its goddesses alone. The huge central shrine, originally built in honor of Hera, was later "rededicated" (the *nerve*!) to Poseidon. The temple just to the left of it, also built for Hera, was at one point actually held captive inside a medieval Christian basilica, whose walls were built directly around the temple's. And archaeologists excavating a sixth-century temple at the far end of town at first declared it a sanctuary of Ceres, then amended their diagnosis to a temple of Athena, and to this day are not exactly sure for whom the temple was meant. (It might have been for any of several deities.)

Founded by the Sybarites, the city was a Greek outpost for centuries, only to have been invaded and taken over by the Lucanians—a local tribe—and then raided and occupied by the Romans. The greatest and strangest indignity was yet to come. The sea rose and surged through the town, and, as if it were gloating, kept Paestum submerged for many years. Eventually the shallow waters were drained away to expose the drowned ruin with all its houses, shops, avenues—and temples.

Any one of Paestum's temples would do an ancient city proud. The larger of the Hera temples is one of the

Two temples dedicated to Hera, Paestum

best preserved in the world, a situation for which we have the sea to thank: by submerging the city and its structures, it effectively prevented vandalism. The temple, with its regiments of massive golden-yellow columns lining all four sides, stops you dead in your tracks, commanding almost as much awe as Hera herself. The temple's heaviness offers a kind of comfort that is distinctly this goddess's, and the sense of well-being grows as you cross the smooth floor, double rows of columns rising in reassuring symmetry all around you. The British novelist Bryher (a pseudonym) was so touched by her visit here that she wrote a novel, *Gate to the Sea*, in which an aging Greek priestess of Hera struggles to maintain this shrine, and the goddess's dignity, in the face of an oppressive, repressive Lucanian occupation.

At Paestum, the goddess was worshipped as Hera Eileithya: she who safeguards childbirth. Figurines found in the shrines, now on display in the museum across the street, depict Hera calm, Hera with hands on hips, Hera with lips curving in a don't-you-worry smile. There is an amazing number of Hera statues on display here, so many that it becomes suddenly intolerable and stifling to live in a modern world in which people no longer feel the need to surround themselves with such things. The museum also displays an array of votive statuettes in the shapes of human body parts, which people offered to Hera either in thanks or in prayer for healing. Among these statuettes are terracotta eyes, arms, penises, and some uteruses that bear a strong resemblance to oven mitts.

Paestum's other temple of Hera crouches close to the ground, columns running, fully intact, all along its length and breadth. You'd never know, to look at this Greek masterpiece, that it was once totally covered with a Christian basilica. Christian shrines indeed swallowed a great many pagan ones, but most never disgorged their prey. In this case, however, the basilica's walls and trappings were peeled away to expose the Hera temple, and the Hera temple is all you can see on that spot today. Oddly, on the day we visited, we heard the repeated and nearby screams of a peacock, though we never saw the bird. (Surely its keepers knew that the peacock was one of Hera's sacred animals.) To us, it sounded like a cry of victory.

The graceful structure known as the Temple of Athena stands on a slight rise and is long and narrow. A great many figurines were found here, attesting to the temple's long continuous usage. A fence, however, prevents visitors from entering the temple. (The Hera temples are not fenced.)

The invaders robbed Paestum, crawled all over it, changed it. The Church tried to swallow it, the sea to drown it. But Paestum was once alive, so alive. The wind sweeps in from the sea today as if to blow you right away; as if you are the ghost after all; as if to clear the town's streets once and for all, so that its citizens, having waited out yet another invasion, can once again return.

Getting there: Open Tuesday through Sunday, 9:00 A.M. to one hour before sunset; closed Mondays. Admission: L3000. Paestum is 60 miles south of Naples, on the coast. Trains stop at the Paestum station very infrequently. It is easier to take a train to Agropoli, 5 miles south of Paestum, and take a bus to the site from there. The two Hera temples are directly in front of you as you enter; the one next to the entrance was the one later dedicated to Poseidon. The one farther to the left is the one later converted into a basilica. The Athena temple is about ¼ mile to your right as you enter, at the other end of the ruins.

Palestrina

Temple of Fortuna Primigenia

The Romans were, perhaps more than any other civilized people, obsessed with religion. They were acutely aware that every aspect of human existence was watched over and guided by the gods. Smooth relations with the powers-that-be were the key to success. Thus the Romans built shrines, temples, and sanctuaries for every imaginable divinity, local and foreign, female and male, powerful and insignificant. Generally, the size of each shrine depended on the importance of the divinity to whom it was dedicated. Every Roman household had a little shrine—usually just a niche—to the gods that watched over the food in the cupboards. Modest-sized temples were built to the various gods in the Roman pantheon. Occasionally, rulers or communities particularly enamored of a certain god or goddess built large temples.

Only once, though, did the Romans go completely overboard. Only one deity ever excited such awestruck devotion in the Roman psyche that they totally lost their sense of proportion and built a temple as big as a city.

That deity was Fortuna, one of the few Roman goddesses to transcend the Roman tendency toward divine specialization. Fortuna determined the outcome of every venture, guided the fate of every individual. Mighty Jupiter looked like a one-trick pony in comparison. Both he and Juno supposedly sat on Fortuna's lap, suckling like babies at her generous breasts. It is a testament to Fortuna's role in western religious thought that even Jehovah absorbed some of her characteristics in his transition from the vengeful, tribal Yahweh to the all-knowing, all-seeing, capital-G God of today.

So it comes as no surprise that Fortuna earned herself a big temple. To say that her sanctuary here at Praeneste was the biggest in Italy hardly does it justice. It was so impossibly vast that even the grandiose temples of Rome or Athens looked like dollhouses in comparison. Today the ruins of Fortuna's temple serve as the foundations for the modern city of Palestrina. The *entire city*—churches, streets, shops, mansions, hundreds of houses—manages to fit quite easily inside the former temple.

The sanctuary was eventually built over, covered up for centuries, until the city was bombed during World War II. When the rubble was cleared, a section of the long-lost temple was at last revealed. The sanctuary covered one side of a large hill, at a site called Praeneste. The Romans cut four immense terraces into the hill, turning it into a stairway fit for a goddess. These terraces were smothered with ramps, porticoes, arches, oracle halls, plazas, statues, and shrines. The whole sanctuary was symmetrically organized around a central axis that led eventually to the focal temple building at the top of the hill, containing the cult statue of Fortuna.

Even today, the layout of the sanctuary is clearly visible. The city is only a thin veneer over the grand structure of the sanctuary. The paved streets run parallel along the 2000-year-old terraces. Buildings and walkways are ranged along the ramps. The deep half-domes built to support the lower terraces of the temple are still perfectly intact, now used as garages, storage sheds, cafes, bus stops, and car repair shops. Next to the church in the center of town on the second terrace are sacred chambers where supplicants went for oracular advice.

The holiest temple building at the top of the hill was incorporated into a palace built by the aristocratic Barbarini family beginning in the fifteenth century C.E. The palace has been converted into a museum showing finds from the area, including many small statues of Fortuna. The prize of the collection is a 20-foot-wide, 16-foot-high mosaic of sumptuous craftsmanship, which shows the Nile Valley during a flood. It once decorated part of the sanctuary and is now regarded as one of the finest mosaics of the ancient world.

The palace itself is part of the exhibit, as you can still see and enter the remnants of the small circular temple building that once held the statue of Fortuna.

Statue of Fortuna at her sanctuary in Palestrina

The palace's semicircular front steps were once the seats of a theater that faced the temple's altar.

Fortuna, like most Roman divinities, gradually evolved over the centuries, acquiring new names and aspects as her power burgeoned. She may have started as an Etruscan goddess primarily concerned with fecundity. Traces of this early aspect survived in one of her Roman festival days, April 1, on which women stormed the men's public baths where they held special lustration ceremonies. On this day she was known as Fortuna Virilis.

At Palestrina her title was Fortuna Primigenia, "the first born." But she was also Fors Fortuna, Fortuna Mammosa, Fortuna Muliebris, and many others. Whatever her aspect, she was a favorite of poor folk, of slaves (whom she graciously admitted to her festivals), of emperors, and especially of women. On April 11, people traveled to her oracle at Praeneste, where she revealed individuals' futures by means of wooden lots drawn at random. Her biggest festival was on June 24, when the entire populace would head outdoors for a drunken party.

Fortuna's many attributes included the cornucopia, the ship's rudder, and the wheel. The cornucopia represented the bounty that the goddess could bring; the rudder marked her as a divine captain who guided the lives of people and nations. The wheel lives on today in the Wheel of Fortune; and Fortuna herself lingers on in the popular mind as Lady Luck, the ersatz goddess of modern gamblers.

The Romans knew, however, that all life was a gamble and that every day was yet another spin of Fortuna's wheel.

Getting there: The lower parts of the sanctuary are visible anytime and free to the public. The upper section, including the museum and the parts of the temple enclosed inside it, are open daily, 9 A.M. to approximately 6 P.M. (earlier in winter, later in summer). Admission: L3000. Palestrina is 22 miles east of Rome. Acotral buses leave for Palestrina from in front of Rome's Termini station and will drop you off in the lower part of the town. Walk up through the town to the Barbarini Palace at the top of the hill, which contains both the museum and the main temple remains.

Pompeii

Temples of Isis and Venus

One can't help but wonder, when strolling the paralyzed streets of Pompeii, whether a citizen of that city, magically revived and brought back there today, would bear a grudge against the deities he or she had so faithfully worshipped, so conscientiously placated.

"How could you have let this happen to me—to *us*?" the outraged Pompeiian might demand, shaking an angry fist.

"Well, my child," the divinity might respond in cool, considered tones, if this was a joke told onstage by a comedian, "you *asked* me to get rid of your mother-in-law."

In every place where, as in Pompeii, a whole community has been wiped out—the Warsaw ghetto, for example—the human mind strains to figure out why it happened. But the gods, who are after all in a position to know, remain ever silent on the matter. The goddesses who had been worshipped at Pompeii—Venus and Isis—were among the sweetest and most sympathetic of deities. Nevertheless, their lips are sealed.

Pompeii was an ordinary Roman town, existing in undistinguished normalcy when, in 79 C.E., Mount Vesuvius erupted and buried it in waves of hot ash, which scorched and suffocated all that it touched. It was curtains for the inhabitants, but a fiesta for the archaeologists who came along centuries later. Most ancient cities, by the time archaeologists appear on the scene, have either been long abandoned, sacked, built over, dismembered by vandals, or otherwise tampered with. But Pompeii afforded a glimpse of a town at its most vital and virtually gift-wrapped, so that scholars and other visitors might thoroughly inspect not only its streets and buildings—which any ancient town might have—but also things like fresh graffiti and half-eaten meals.

Pompeii's startled citizens, plaster casts of whom lie in attitudes of horror and resignation all over the city today, cannot escape our prying eyes any more than they could escape Vesuvius. And so we tiptoe along their streets feeling guilty, like the voyeurs that we love to be.

Venus was an important goddess in Pompeii (speaking of voyeurism). But the temple dedicated to her, which now crumbles away behind a fence, is in far worse shape and is far less popular with tourists than the town's more famous venereal site, the bordello, whose walls—with their convenient built-in beds—bear the traces of erotic frescoes.

One of Pompeii's most poignant monuments is its Temple of Isis. It must have been breathtaking. Now enclosed on all sides by protective walls and only visible through a metal gate, the temple is still amazingly intact. Its dozens of narrow columns suggest reeds along the Nile, while a peaked, red-tiled roof is resolutely Mediterranean. Bits of delicate carving barely evident behind the tall weeds are clues to the former splendor and importance of this sanctuary, which was one of the first centers of Isis worship to be established outside of Egypt. Frescoes once brightened these walls. Jars of sacred Nile water occupied a place of honor. The temple was damaged in an earthquake in 62 C.E., after which it was carefully restored.

Little did the restorers know how short-lived their work would prove to be. And little could they have guessed how very appropriate was Isis as their city's primary goddess. For she, who knew well the meaning of suffering, was a goddess of compassion. When her brother-husband, Osiris, was murdered and parts of his dismembered body strewn far and wide, Isis's grief was as deep and as wide as the Nile. Then, with a resourcefulness born of sorrow, she collected the scattered organs and limbs, invented the art of embalming, and so revived Osiris. Isis's, then, was a religion of resurrection and of hope.

Did the people of Pompeii learn enough from her, in the time allotted them, to bear the agony of those last stifling moments? Did she hold their hands, wipe their brows with a cool cloth; did she soothe their pain?

Getting there: Open daily, 9 A.M. to 1 hour before sunset. Admission: L5000. Pompeii is 13 miles southeast of Naples, at the foot of wily Mount Vesuvius. From the Naples Central train station, ride on the private Circumvesuviana train line to the station called Pompeii Villa dei Misteri, which is just outside the entrance to the site. Trains run very frequently. The Temple of Venus is a few yards inside the Porta Marina entrance, on your right through a gate in the wall. The Temple of Isis is behind the large theater on via Iside.

Rome

Church of Santa Maria in Ara Coeli

If St. Peter's Basilica is Rome's masculine masterpiece, then the Church of Santa Maria in Ara Coeli, built on the site of an ancient temple of Cybele, is its feminine counterpart. Because it is so large, and because this hilltop sanctuary has been visited faithfully for over two thousand years by countless generations of women, Santa Maria in Ara Coeli feels more like a village than like a church. On the afternoon we visited, elaborate floral arrangements, left over from a morning wedding, still twined about the pews. Clusters of local women and their children were busy with clippers and shears, gathering bouquets to take home. Meanwhile, groups of nuns, many of whom had traveled halfway around the world to come to this spot, glided about in companionable silence.

But if this is a village, it is the most elegant village in the world. It is surrealistically rich. Fifteen sparkling chandeliers frame the main altar, and cadres of chandeliers run the entire length of the nave, drawing the eyes upward to a ceiling ablaze with gold leaf.

So confidently has this cathedral established itself as a bulwark of Christian Rome that little is known, appearancewise, of the ancient temple whose position it usurped. Cybele (whom the Romans also called Magna Mater, or "Great Mother") was a powerful Near Eastern goddess. In one legend, her young lover, Attis (who technically was her grandson) was unfaithful to her. In a fit of shame, Attis castrated himself and bled to death under a pine tree. Cybele's followers—including many self-castrated priests—celebrated Attis's resurrection every year around the time of the spring equinox. Cybele symbolically arrived in Rome in 204 B.C.E., personified by a special black stone that was brought here after a sibyl had prophesied that only Cybele's presence in the city could save Rome from an attack by the Carthaginians. Rome was saved, and as the Romans grew to adore Cybele and her passionate rituals, they built temples to her all over the empire. The site now occupied by this church is one of them.

Stairway leading up to Santa Maria in Ara Coeli, Rome

On this site, decades before the birth of Jesus, Octavian, later known as Augustus, saw a vision of what he described as "a beautiful lady." Dressed all in white, the lady told him that if he would build her an altar on this spot, she would put his heart at ease and see him through the tangle of political dilemmas that were currently troubling him. She was as good as her word, for Augustus eventually became the first Roman emperor and enjoyed unparalleled power and success. He was even, eventually, deified by his people. Augustus's vision took place not only before Jesus' birth but probably before Mary's as well. Yet the Roman Catholic church takes credit for the vision, flying bravely in the face of history, insisting that the lady whom Augustus saw was the Virgin Mary.

Most of the Catholics who visit Santa Maria in Ara Coeli today come to see a jewel-encrusted statue of the baby Jesus, which resides in a room of its own to the left of the main altar, near the gift shop. The statue, affectionately known as Il Bambino, sports a large head and tight swaddling clothes, which give it a limbless, pluglike appearance. People all over the world have great faith in the statue's ability to grant favors and aid causes. On display are cards and letters that children have sent to Il Bambino; one of these expresses a dire and immediate need for a set of Lego. It is worth remembering that worshippers of Cybele, while loving the goddess best of all, kept a tender spot in their hearts for young Attis—poor mutilated Attis—in whose weakness they saw their own falterings and whose resurrection gave them hope.

Ara Coeli means "Altar of Heaven." And certainly the monumental stone stairway leading up to the cathedral is an approach worthy of such an altar. But an altar to whom? The cathedral's air of confidence is that of a younger sister who, after a long and impatient wait, slips into the comfortable, well-proven shoes of her elder sibling. Without a doubt, the church's ambience would be quite different were it not for the invisible presence of its ancient predecessor.

One of the images in the church's marble floor depicts a high-stepping bull crowned with a star. It is intriguing to find this here, for along with lions, bulls were Cybele's sacred animals. They were regularly sacrificed to her in Rome. Also, prominently placed above the main door is a stained glass window that depicts not a biblical scene, not a saint, but three enormous, plump honeybees. That's all. Three bees: The number three has long been sacred to goddess-worshipping peoples and to Christians alike. Bees: They look so startlingly natural in contrast with all the other decor in the church. Efficient and mysterious bringers of sweetness, worshippers of their own queens, bees figure among the traditional helpers and companions of goddesses. Delphi itself was said to have been built by bees. Demeter's priestesses were called *melissae*—"bees." And bees, like those forever enshrined in the stained glass window, were associated with Persephone, Artemis—and Cybele.

Getting there: Open daily, 7:00 A.M. to noon and 4:00 P.M. to sunset. Admission free. On Campidoglio hill, immediately behind the Vittorio Emanuele II Monument; the stairs leading up to the church start on Piazza Aracoeli, at the northern end of via del Teatro di Marcello.

Rome

Church of Santa Maria in Cosmedin

Most churches in Rome are holy jewel boxes. The air inside is cool and still, but so heavy with gold and with piety that it's rather hard to breathe. Such places, in their grandeur, are deliberately set apart from the outside world, like little islands or castles, or like somebody's idea of heaven.

Santa Maria in Cosmedin is different. Stepping through its modest doors, you don't feel as if you have abandoned the world of the living. A clear, shifting light plays across the festive mosaic floor, and the sounds of laughter—real human laughter—come bubbling in from outside.

The source of the laughter is La Bocca della Verità ("The Mouth of Truth"), a gigantic stone face chiseled countless years ago and brought here from the ruins in which it was discovered. Strictly an ornament, it has no functional connection with the church or with the ancient temple that preceded the church. But The Mouth is a local landmark nevertheless. Visitors line up for a chance to slip their hands into the gaping stone mouth. A long-standing Roman legend has it that the Bocca can spot a dishonest person and will bite off the hand of any liar who dares approach, but will spare all virtuous persons. (On the day we visited, one man sidestepped fate by thrusting his hand into the Bocca della Verità's eye.)

As one of Rome's oldest churches, unmodified and unremodeled, Santa Maria in Cosmedin retains a folksy, battered warmth, which is most notable in the bright, simple paintings that march across its walls. Many of these, painted directly on the plaster, depict floral and geometric motifs rather than Christian ones. The stone columns that line the nave and the rear are so aged and worn that they seem to bridge the gap between this site's two incarnations: its present one as a Catholic church dedicated to the Virgin Mary, and its ancient one as a temple dedicated to the Roman grain goddess, Ceres.

The temple stood to the right of what is now the church's main altar. But the temple was not incorporated into the nave, and its precise site, now part of church property, remains closed to the public. All we have left is the temple's successor, the church itself, but the church provides several clues to its former identity.

Ceres was one of the Romans' oldest and most fundamental goddesses, presiding, like Demeter, over the growth of edible grains. While Ceres's companion goddess, Tellus (sometimes called Tellus Mater), personified the fertile earth, Ceres was the spark that made things grow and flourish in the soil. And just as surely as she ensured the birth and health of the grain, so she ensured its death, so that people might obtain and eat it. Ceres was a nature goddess, but only insofar as nature aided humans. She has not been forgotten: in even the most unspiritual of supermarkets, the goddess's name is echoed in the word "cereal."

All Italians were grateful to Ceres; she was the one who put the bread on the table. Here in Rome, far from farm and field, she was well appreciated. Her temple was built in 490 B.C.E. in the Boarian Forum, the oldest part of the city. Pope Hadrian "transformed" the temple (as the official guidebooks say) into a church in the eighth century C.E.

The goddess's special festival, the Cerealia, was held on April 19. Rather than sit around devouring bowl after bowl of Cream of Wheat, as we might happily do in Ceres's honor today, the Romans went down to the Circus Maximus, where, as one contemporary writer tells us, they cheered as a number of wild foxes were released onto the field. The animals ran around chaotically, each with a flaming stick tied to its tail; the rite's significance escapes us today.

The energetic, comfy ambience that sets Santa Maria in Cosmedin apart from other churches is accentuated by its lack of pews. You have to keep moving, or at least standing up. Your blood circulates. The little orange, red, and white stones in the church's mosaic floor resemble scattered grains, and the warm brown shade that is used liberally throughout the church is just the color of well-baked bread. Also, a repeating motif that is painted on the wall behind the main altar but that is difficult to see looks remarkably like a basket (or vase) laden with wheat, a traditional emblem of Ceres.

Any nun with a taste for history will readily tell you how the Church of Santa Maria in Cosmedin, in its early days, used to distribute free bread to the indigent citizens of Rome. This was this church's special function, unique in the city. It was rather an unusual function for a church, but not so unusual, not strange at all, for a temple of Ceres.

Getting there: Open daily, 9:00 A.M. to noon, and 3:00 P.M. to 4:00 P.M. Admission free. On Piazza Bocca della Verità, at the end of Via Santa Maria in Cosmedin, one block east of the Tiber and the Ponte Palatino.

Rome

Cloaca Maxima and Shrine of Cloacina

Consider, if you will, the parts of a chicken. The wings and thighs are, for better or worse, absolute clichés, menu mainstays from Albany to Albania. The same goes for breasts. And everyone knows what a chicken uses its gizzard for. But the part of the chicken that is called a *cloaca* goes mostly unsung, although the chicken could not live without it.

Located conveniently just under the bird's tail, the cloaca is an opening that serves as anus and vagina, birth canal and urinary tract. It is the one and only outlet through which the hen deposits both her lowly droppings and her life-giving eggs. You might well be joyful that your own anatomy is more complex. But you have to admit that a cloaca is a very interesting and handy thing indeed.

Perhaps the early anatomists had something like that in mind when they gave the cloaca its name. In Latin, cloaca means "sewer." But to the industrious Romans, a sewer represented an architectural victory, no less worthy of respect than a bridge or a temple. As proof of this respect, the Romans had in their pantheon a goddess of sewers. Her name was Cloacina.

They built a shrine for her in the Forum, where she held her own alongside Vesta, Concordia, and the other mighty deities who resided there. But Cloacina's presence was most strongly felt in and around the Cloaca Maxima, the huge sewer that served Rome, draining the once-marshy Forum area and channeling the city's waste into the Tiber.

In most of ancient Europe, underground sewage disposal systems were unknown and undreamed of. The Roman system, in which stone-built subterranean pipes and tunnels were connected to a main channel (the Cloaca Maxima), was ages ahead of its time. After the eventual fall of the empire, the technology was virtually forgotten. The Cloaca Maxima lay abandoned, like an atrophying limb, and was never updated or reinforced, so that in many of Rome's streets, throughout the Middle Ages and the Renaissance, raw sewage ran aboveground.

Today you can still visit the gaping, brick-framed, weed-fringed maw through which the Cloaca Maxima emptied into the Tiber. Its outthrust lower lip holds a thick green pool, and out of its gelatinous depths grow ferns, nettles, wildflowers, and even fig trees. The plants' exuberance is almost obscene. This place is absurdly fecund, a cross between a cesspool and a fairy bower. It stands in wild contrast with the hot gray street above and the listless river below. It has about it the aura of a sacred spring or a holy well. And why not? It served a profound purpose. Once the anus of Rome, the Cloaca Maxima relieved the city of its filth and excess. Calmly and uncomplainingly, it went about its task of purifying, filtering, channeling, and carrying away so many things better forgotten. The Romans had the good sense to be grateful.

In the Roman Forum, you can still see the small, circular foundation of Cloacina's shrine. While originally built for Cloacina alone, the shrine later became known as that of Venus Cloacina. As often happened in the world of Roman religion, the sewer goddess had somehow merged, in the public's mind, with the love goddess, or had become an attribute of her. At one time, statues of Venus and Cloacina stood side by side in the shrine, like cohostesses at a party.

It is not really surprising, after all, to learn that Roman and Sabine soldiers visited Cloacina's shrine—this one, out of all those they could have chosen—to ritually cleanse themselves before a battle. Cloacina could be trusted, always, to carry away every impurity.

Getting there: The Cloaca Maxima is always open and freely visible. The Shrine of Cloacina is in the Forum (see the discussion later in this chapter for hours and admission price). The Cloaca Maxima is on the east bank of the Tiber, just south of the Ponte Palatino, where Lungotevere Aventino becomes Lungotevere di Pierleoni. The steps that lead down to the riverbank are on the north side of the Ponte Palatino. The shrine is the small circular stone directly in front of the Basilica Aemilia, about 100 yards to your right after you walk through the entrance to the Forum. (The shrine is not mentioned on many maps and guidebooks to the site.)

Rome

The First Depiction of the Virgin Mary

Making judgments based on the top layer of things can be misleading and dangerous, as anyone who has encountered chocolate-covered ants or a short-sheeted bed will gladly tell you. And so it is, spiritually speaking, with Rome. The city, as we see it now, is positively voluptuous with church domes. Countless crosses march across the skyline like spindly, proud soldiers. Of course, it wasn't always like this. Nor did all those churches sprout up overnight.

The predominant attitude toward religion in ancient Rome was healthy curiosity. The Romans' first gods were the ancient ones of their native Italian soil. Then, as Roman influence spread far and wide, the people were quick to adopt new and foreign deities they met along the way. Among the "Eastern" faiths that drifted into Rome in the imperial era were Judaism and Christianity. But these were not considered any more significant or interesting than Mithraism, Isis worship, or any of the other imports. If anything, Christianity was not at first well liked by the aristocracy of Rome (and thus its emperors) because its sanctification of poverty made slave revolts a palpable threat. (Thus the public torture of Christians became a popular spectator sport.) Nevertheless, Emperor Constantine was converted to Christianity in 330 C.E., and the rest, of course, is history.

During those dusk years when Christianity was just another novelty in Rome's spiritual smorgasbord, most Romans thought nothing of embracing several religions at one time. It was not at all strange to find oneself worshipping at a temple of Minerva before breakfast and then visiting shrines of Greek Athena, Egyptian Isis, and Phoenician Astarte as the day wore on. In this atmosphere, Roman converts to Christianity, then as now, were firmly exhorted to deep-six all the "pagan" divinities they had worshipped in the past. But even so, deities die hard.

Rome's catacombs, subterranean avenues that wander for cool, quiet, labyrinthine miles underneath the city, still offer the same relief that they did to the early Christians, who developed them and used them for hundreds of years. In the catacombs, they hid from hostile Roman emperors, instinctively burrowing, in their fear, into the protective body of the earth. Here they built shrines, and here they buried their dead. Today, jumbled skeletons peer from their niches at the visitors who clamber, half-blind, along the passageways.

Some of Europe's oldest Christian artworks linger on the damp walls, illuminated now by tour guides' fitful flashlights. Among these, in the Catacombs of Priscilla, small and obscure and placed high on the wall, is a painting of a woman with a child. You'd hardly notice it were it not for the tour guide, who announces solemnly that this figure, dating to the second century C.E., has been identified as the earliest known depiction of the Virgin Mary.

The woman on the wall is brown. Hers is a rich cocoa color that has withstood the centuries. Her skin, deliberately painted so much darker than that of other women painted on these walls, gives pause for thought. The first Virgin Mary is a brown Virgin Mary.

What memories, what visions influenced the person who painted this picture? Which goddesses still danced in the mind of that embryonic Christian?

Mary was a virgin like Diana, a mother like Juno, dark and a healer like Isis. For a moment Mary stood, freshly painted on a wall, one small image in a city full of images of women: women crowned, women jeweled, enthroned, armed for battle. But then that moment passed, and then 2000 years, and now all the woman-images cherished in present-day Rome are hers, Mary's. Now she alone wears the crown, the jewels.

But *anything* could have happened, and still could.

Getting there: Open Tuesday through Sunday, 8:30 A.M. to noon and 2:30 P.M. to 5:00 P.M.; closed Monday. Admission: L3000. The painting is in the Catacombs of Priscilla, which are at Via Salaria 430, on the eastern side of Villa Ada.

Rome

The Forum and the Temple of Vesta

Images of ancient Rome flicker through our minds like scenes from an epic film: toga-clad orators exhorting the rabble; sword-wielding throngs of soldiers charging into battle; sumptuous banquets in gleaming marble halls.

And if the history of Rome is a movie, then the Forum is the projector. The Temple of Vesta is the projector's bulb, and Vesta's sacred fire is the filament in the bulb, burning bright enough to shine Rome's glory over most of the Mediterranean. The Forum's Temple of Vesta was the spiritual core of the Roman world, and the Romans earnestly believed that if Vesta's eternal flame ever went out, then Rome itself would collapse.

In Rome's very earliest days, before it was even properly a city, the area now known as the Forum was a dreary marsh, frequently inundated by floods. The settlers kept to the hills surrounding the marshy valley and did business in a cattle market now called the Boarian Forum, closer to the Tiber. The marsh was used as a cemetery.

At some point the hill dwellers decided to reclaim the valley, and they built a canal to drain off the waters. Once the marsh had dried, the natives moved off the hills into the valley. As Rome grew, this centrally located area became the hub of civic life. The remaining private dwellings were cleared away, and the Forum assumed its role as the political, financial, and religious center of the new city. In the centuries that followed, Rome soared to world prominence, yet the Forum always remained its heart. The decisions made here in the Forum had ramifications in the farthest reaches of the empire.

The Forum's skyline was crowded with temples, and the most hallowed spot in this, Rome's most sacred area, was the Temple of Vesta. Paradoxically, the building was not even officially a temple, for Vesta's sanctuary was so inherently sacrosanct that to legally declare it a temple would have been redundant, even insulting, the equivalent of granting Orville Wright a pilot's license. Vesta herself was so old, so primeval, that she was actually not quite a goddess. A deity, in the later Roman conception, was something that contained or possessed *numen*, an untranslatable concept that meant something like "divine essence." Vesta did not possess *numen*; she *was* pure *numen*. Many primitive Roman deities were nonphysical, difficult to visualize, until later, under Greek and Etruscan influence, they were granted human form. Vesta was never anthropomorphized like this. Her temple had no statue and contained only a flame. Vesta was, as the poet Ovid wrote, "nothing but a living flame."

Vesta's temple was also unusual in that it was round, not rectangular. The shape was thought to preserve the outline of the primitive earth-and-straw hut that stood on this spot. This hut contained the hearth of the earliest tribal kings of Rome. The king's hearth fire, for symbolic or safety reasons, had to be kept burning constantly, and it was the responsibility of the king's daughters to make sure the fire never died.

The king's daughters eventually gave way to a class of select priestesses called the Vestal Virgins. Six in number, the Vestals' prime duty was to tend the fire at all times. If a novice were to accidentally let the fire die, she was whipped by Rome's elected chief priest, the Pontifex Maximus (who inherited the religious duties of the king). The flame would then be relit in a special ceremony, by rubbing together sticks of wood taken from a fruit-bearing tree.

The Vestal Virgins were considered the holiest people in all of Rome, and as such they enjoyed unique privileges. When their entourage proceeded through the streets, everyone they encountered—senators, fire brigades, consuls, even emperors—was obliged to back down and give them the right of way. Condemned criminals who happened to meet a Vestal in the street were immediately set free.

On the other hand, the Vestals were expected to perform an unending series of bizarre and archaic rituals and to conform to dozens of maddening restrictions in their daily behavior. They were, of course, required to remain chaste throughout their term (originally 5, but later 30 years). If they were convicted of having had sexual relations, they were walled up in a tomb and left to die. Their lovers were beaten to death.

Vestals were not allowed to drink from the city's water supply, and they had to bring water by hand from a special spring. They had to refine their own salt using primitive tools, harvest the season's first ripe wild grain on odd-numbered days between May 7 and May 14, save the blood from the head of a ritually decapitated racehorse, cut the unborn fetuses from sacrificed pregnant cows, and use all of the above in various annual rituals that, to modern sensibilities, are incomprehensible and often unpalatable.

The interior of Vesta's temple was open to worshippers only a few days out of each year during Vesta's festival, the Vestalia, from June 7 to June 15. No men were allowed inside—only women. They entered the temple barefoot and offered food to the goddess. This mirrored a ritual enacted every day in every Roman household, the offering of part of the daily meal to Vesta at her hearthside, household shrine. Vesta was not the goddess of fire in general but specifically the goddess of the hearth fire. The fire in her temple was the hearth fire of the state.

The Forum also enclosed other goddess temples and shrines. Cloacina, the goddess of the Forum's drainage canal (which later evolved into Rome's main sewer, the Cloaca Maxima), had a shrine here (see the earlier discussion). A healing spring goddess, Juturna, had a small shrine at her spring. The Romans also built temples to Concordia, goddess of harmony, and to Venus and Roma, in their role as the city's tutelary goddesses, and even to the imported Cybele, whose temple was placed on the Palatine Hill, overlooking the valley. One building in the Forum even had a shrine to the mysterious Ops Consiva, goddess of wealth and bounty, whose very name was thought to have magical properties.

Most of those temples are still visible in the forest of columns and crumbling marble that is today's Forum. The rambling ruins of the House of the Vestals sprawl next to Vesta's temple. Long rows of statues depicting Head Vestals surround the central courtyard. It was near here that a statue of Vesta, in human form, was erected during a later period of Roman history. It was kept separate from the temple and, in some reports, kept veiled. The small Temple of Vesta itself was partially reconstructed earlier this century, and the section of curved wall retains, to this day, the shape of Vesta's original hut.

For over a thousand years, the Romans entrusted their city, their state, and their empire to Vesta. They knew that if her flame were to die, then Rome itself would die. At the very end of the fourth century C.E., the flame of Vesta was extinguished by command of a Christian emperor. A few years later, Alaric the Goth descended on the city, and Rome was no more.

Getting there: Open in summer, Monday and Wednesday through Saturday, 9 A.M. to 6 P.M.; Tuesday and Sunday, 9 A.M. to 1 P.M.; in winter, Monday and Wednesday through Saturday, 9 A.M. to 3 P.M.; Tuesday and Sunday, 9 A.M. to 1 P.M. (Once you've entered, you can stay inside until 1 hour after closing time.) Admission: L5000. The entrance is on via della Salara Vecchia, just

Statues of Vestal Virgins at House of the Vestals in Rome's Forum

off via dei Fori Imperiali, about four blocks northwest of the Colosseum. Finding the temples and buildings you're looking for amid the maze of ruins is very difficult without a map; we recommend that you buy a map or guide before you enter.

Rome

Statue of Isis

From her home in Alexandria, Isis traveled, in the hearts of traders and adventurers, to far-flung settlements all over the ancient world. The Egyptian goddess with her sweet-and-sad legend of faith and resourcefulness found eager followers in such diverse places as those we now know as London, Paris, Portugal, and Hungary, not to mention Greece and Rome. Everywhere she went, Isis adapted herself to the local people's needs and cultures as gracefully and successfully as Auntie Mame.

She came to Rome in the late Republican era (100 to 31 B.C.E.) and settled in for a long and meaningful stay. (Just how meaningful can be seen in the number of Catholic Church traditions and customs that originally figured in the worship of Isis.) It is easy to see how Isis would appeal to the deity-happy Romans. None of their own goddesses—including many they had already borrowed from the Greeks, Etruscans, Gauls, and other peoples—were as majestically all-encompassing as Egyptian Isis. Among her skills and dominions were those of healer, teacher, navigator, inventor, magician, mourner, lover, mother, wife. Isis Panthea, the Romans called her, and Isis Victrix, "the Conqueror."

She was worshipped in the streets of Rome by men and—most enthusiastically—by women. The fact that a number of Roman emperors were among her devotees ensured that temples would be built here in her honor. The first of these, built by Caligula in 38 C.E., stood on the Campus Martius, near the present site of the Church of Santa Maria Sopra Minerva. Another, more elaborate temple was built by Caracalla on the Quirinal Hill in 215 C.E. (The emperor Domitian too was an initiate into Isis's mysteries.) In Isis's temples, her statues were tended by ascetic priests whose bodies were shaved from head to foot and who were forbidden to wear leather or other animal products. They sprinkled Nile water in the course of rituals, just as Catholic priests—also specially tonsured—sprinkle holy water today. Every day, the priests would unveil the statues of the goddess, so that her devotees might stand there for as long as they wished and look into her beloved, compassionate eyes.

Rome's temples to Isis are long gone. Other, older temples to other, more obscure deities remain standing, which makes it seem, at first, that Isis was never here at all, or that she was so insignificant as to vanish without a trace. But there *is* a trace, a very big one, if

Colossal statue of Isis, Rome

you know where to look for it. Thanks to the strange machinations of history in a city where thousands of years are constantly being shaken up and tossed about like the dice in a Yahtzee game, a huge statue of Isis found itself misnamed and misplaced for centuries, though it was never neglected.

It's still there, this statue, and it is still Isis, although it has been called Madame Lucrezia for as long as anyone can remember. All that remains are its head and shoulders, but even these stand over 7 feet tall. The complete original must have been colossal. The statue was discovered during the fifteenth century C.E. near the site of one of the vanished Isis temples. Its clothes and demeanor have assured historians that it once served as the temple's cult image. But when it was found, the townspeople, ever modern, immediately named the statue after a contemporary noblewoman, Madame Lucrezia, daughter of a Roman senator who served the city in 1428. Lucrezia lived in the neighborhood where the statue was discovered. Set up on a pedestal near the Church of St. Mark, the statue was from that point on cheerfully addressed as Lucrezia and garlanded with flowers every year on the first day of May, supposedly in honor of the feast day of St. Mark.

Having long outlived its human namesake, and surpassed her in popularity, the statue—of *Isis,* not of Lucrezia, despite what they call it—still stands where it was placed. She is a somewhat Romanized Isis, whose full, flowing robe, massively broad white shoulders, and powerful neck make her look amusingly different from the dark, reed-slender Isis that was known in Alexandria. Her shawl is knotted between two matronly breasts, and above that great neck is a face sadly ravaged by time. The nose and mouth are now mere holes. And the eyes are gone: Isis's famous eyes, which could understand anything, which could sympathize and forgive, are smoothed clean away, so that the marble face is a mere cipher. But the statue offers the same blessing that it always did. You come upon it on this absurd corner, deafened and blinded with traffic and glare, and she stands there as calm, as cool, as refreshing as the River Nile. She still heals.

Getting there: Always visible. Admission free. In the northwest corner of Piazza San Marcos between address numbers 49 and 50, standing against the Palazzo Venezia, across the plaza from the Vittorio Emanuele II Monument.

Rome

Temples of Fortuna and Mater Matuta

A civilization that thought itself important—that is, a civilization like ancient Rome—would understandably have some strong ideas on the subject of fortune. And so the Romans, always quick to discern the divinity inherent in every aspect of life, came to be in awe of Fortuna, goddess of destiny.

One of the oldest deities in the Roman pantheon, and possibly a pre-Roman Italian goddess, Fortuna decided people's fortunes in a deadly serious way. No mere carnival fortune-teller was she. Her name meant, simply, "she who brings," and she was responsible for everything that was to happen in everyone's future.

While the Romans firmly believed that an individual's *character* was predetermined at birth and could never be changed (a radically different idea than the Christian concept of salvation through good deeds), they knew from experience that a person's *fortune* —like a nation's—could move up and down, backward and forward. Fortuna, then, was well worth placating. Roman kings and emperors kept golden statues of Fortuna in their bedchambers, for she was their own special protectress. The statues served to remind them that a populace's fortune lay in a ruler's hands, just as their fortunes lay in the goddess's. The temple built in her honor at Praeneste (now Palestrina, discussed earlier) was one of the most ambitious goddess sanctuaries ever constructed. And the Fortuna temple whose remains can still be visited in Rome itself lies in the heart of the most ancient part of the city, the Boarian Forum, around which the rest of Rome grew up.

And grew, and grew, and withstood the slings and arrows of its own fortune, so that the temple, now flattened, stands serenely behind metal fences while all around it the traffic roars. Wary cats prowl among the stumps of columns and the smooth stone floors, aloof from the city and all its denizens, save for the cat ladies, the *mamme dei gatti,* local women who take it upon themselves to feed the feral cats that live in most of Rome's ruins.

The Fortuna temple, originally built by King Servius Tullius in 575 B.C.E. and then rebuilt later, shares this site with another ruined shrine: that of Mater Matuta, the motherly goddess whose role, in the ancient Roman view of things, was to guide people from callowness to maturity. Her function, obviously, is interwoven with Fortuna's, so it is appropriate that they should reign side by side.

This place, so pointedly still and silent in the midst of the torrent that is Rome, compels the visitor to stop short, and think, and then think some more. Fortuna worked, in her way, for the Romans who honored her with this temple. She took them up, then higher up; then down, then further down; and finally—now—back into insouciant glory. What will she do for you, if you apply to her? What will be your luck in this city? And Mater Matuta: by the time you leave Rome, will she have touched you?

Getting there: Always visible. Admission free. At the intersection of Vico Jugario and via del Teatro di Marcello, at the southern foot of the Capitoline Hill.

Rome

Temple of Minerva

You come upon this temple abruptly, maybe even accidentally, on your way to or from the Colosseum. At street level, you crane your neck, as the lower half of the temple lies far below, at the ancient ground level, while the upper part soars above your head. And so you find yourself suddenly a little bit like Minerva: poised above the world, yet still tied to it. The ruin stands tantalizingly out of reach, above and below, a reminder of the very real Rome that came before. On this very spot walked people with lives every bit as complicated as your own: self-assured, stylish people who demanded a high standard of beauty. And on this very spot worked craftspeople well able to meet that standard, as well as the standard of our modern world.

As craftspeople, they must have taken especial care in creating this particular temple, for Minerva was a goddess of handicrafts as well as of war and wisdom. In fact, she presided over the annual artisans' festival, the Quincatrus, held in late March.

Minerva was more than just a Romanized version of Athena. She had a distinctly pre-Roman pedigree and probably evolved from the Etruscan goddess Menrva, whose name meant "mind." Eventually, the Romans outfitted Minerva with so many of Athena's hand-me-downs that the two became almost indistinguishable.

Just as Athena became the favorite goddess of the ambitious Athenians, so Minerva became, along with Juno and Jupiter, a member of the Romans' leading divine trio. Both the Romans and the Athenians really needed a goddess like this, as her realm comprised the three areas that were the keys to their civilizations' success: thinking, fighting, and creative expression. She knew what mattered.

The temple's stone floor lies part in sunlight, part in shadow, while surprisingly tall fragments of stone wall, once covered in marble, rise up around it, draped with vines. A pair of slim columns rises even higher, pointing like fingers to the ruins' focal point, an intricate frieze depicting dozens of human figures, most of them female, most of them now headless, engaged in various activities. Above it all, in relief, stands the familiar, helmeted figure of Minerva. Like intellect itself she stands, thoughtfully surveying the world of human hands and minds.

Getting there: Always visible. Admission free. On via dei Fori Imperiali, just where it intersects with via Alessandrina, at the southern end of the Forum of Augustus, due north and across two streets from the entrance to the paid area of the Roman Forum.

Rome

Temple of Venus Genetrix

The Romans, by and large, were not a fanciful people. They were builders and movers rather than dreamers, fighters rather than philosophers. But soldiers and gladiators have mothers too, and Rome worshipped motherhood as much as did its contemporaries all over the ancient world. Rome, which now kneels at countless altars to the mother of Jesus, once cherished, above all, the motherly Juno, whose kind hands comforted babies, midwives, and women in labor. From the Egyptians, the Romans cheerfully adopted Isis, among whose many epithets was "Mother of God" and who was often depicted suckling her infant son, Horus. Romans thronged to the festivals of Phrygian Cybele, whom they called the Great Mother. And when they settled in Germany, they fell in love with the bounteous triple goddess whom they called, simply, the Matronae: "The Mothers." And yet, when it came to identifying their own progenitress, the mother of all Rome, the Romans looked to Venus.

Venus, of all goddesses! The goddess of love and beauty, always depicted in the nude, seems at first an unlikely mama, much less the supermama of a whole race of people. And yet she was, and here's how it happened:

In a time so remote that even the ancient Romans considered it ancient, the goddess Venus found herself attracted to a mortal, a Trojan nobleman named Priam. Lucky Priam was only too happy to return her affection, and in time Venus became pregnant. The child she bore, the half-divine Aeneas, was raised by his father and grew up to become one of Troy's leading citizens. When the Greeks won the Trojan War, Aeneas fled the burning city, carrying the now-elderly Priam on his shoulders, and embarked on a series of adventures that form the plot of Vergil's *Aeneid.* Eventually, Aeneas arrived on the shores of what is now known as Italy, and after some violent clashes with the natives, went on to found Rome. With his new wife, one of the aforementioned natives, Aeneas had children. It is from these children that aristocratic Romans, countless years hence, claimed descent. Julius Caesar and his entire clan liked to envision a direct bloodline leading back from themselves to Aeneas, and thus to Venus. And thus, they reasoned, aristocratic Romans must be inherently—if infinitesimally—divine.

Venus Genetrix, Venus the Birth Giver, was what they called the goddess in her aspect as revered ancestress. Caesar built a temple to her in the forum that bears his name. Three columns rise from the ruined temple's brick foundation, which retains the shape of a gracefully semicircular apse. Bits of the chiseled masonry that once made this temple lovely enough to be worthy of Venus now lie scattered on the ground.

It's the thought that counts. The sentiment behind the construction of this temple is every bit as interesting as the temple itself. To worship a goddess is one thing.

To worship a goddess whom you count among your blood relatives is quite another.

From your vantage point beside the temple you can watch the endless stream of modern Romans as they drive past. Almost compulsively, they preen, they check their reflections in mirrors, they smile and smirk as if constantly posing for Italian *Vogue*. This is still a nation in love with love and beauty. This is a race still, but ever so infinitesimally, descended from Venus.

Getting there: Always visible. Admission free. On via dei Fori Imperiali, on the southwest corner of its intersection with via S. Pietro in Carcere, in the Forum of Caesar but outside the paid area of the Roman Forum.

Scorano

Sanctuary of Feronia at Lucus Feroniae

The Etruscan goddess, Feronia, kept watch over the wild things—plants and animals. The beasts she loved were undoubtedly the direct ancestors of the ones that ran around Italy, many centuries later, in the company of the huntress Diana. But Feronia, unlike Diana, was no huntress. And she was certainly no Roman.

The Etruscan civilization was to Rome what the Minoan civilization was to classical Greece. Like the Minoans', the Etruscans' origins and language remain mostly a mystery to this day. But, again like the Minoans, the Etruscans left behind artworks whose free-flowing, eloquent lines depict men and women living to the hilt. Long before the development of the stolid, almost-humorless Romans, Etruscan cities flourished. And they kept on flourishing, until the ambitious Romans moved steadily in among them and assimilated their culture, not to mention their deities. The Romans deeply admired the Etruscans, and perhaps they knew that in many ways they would never catch up with the ancient culture they had so hungrily swallowed up. Artistically, for one. Socially, for another: Never would the women of Rome approach the high social status that their Etruscan foremothers had enjoyed as a birthright.

What little we know of Etruscan religion has been mostly filtered through Roman historians, who took the liberty of translating their adopted deities' original names into Latin-sounding ones. The name of the goddess Feronia bears the stamp of such tampering. She is possibly the same goddess the Etruscans called Uni: She of the Fields. (A few believe that Feronia, for whom this sanctuary was built in the place called Lucus Feroniae, was actually not Etruscan at all but a goddess of the Sabines, a local tribe with whom the Romans were always quarreling. Historians point to the fact that the site was sacred to a long succession of local tribes. Nevertheless, most hold to the Etruscan theory.)

Feronia's temple was, and is, in the fields. The land lies green and low all around it, although long gone are the woods that once heightened the site's sacred wildness. A long, stone-built avenue leads to the ruined temple with its altar, columns, neat brick stairways, and stone foundation. One side chamber features a mosaic floor whose green, black, and white tiles form an interlocking cube design worthy of M. C. Escher.

The Etruscans built this temple in the sixth century B.C.E., though this field had long been a place of worship for many who came before. Later, the temple was adopted by the Romans, to whom fell the task of rebuilding it after Hannibal, the Carthaginian general, sacked the place in 211 B.C.E. Evidence of astute Roman reconstruction is still clearly visible.

The temple occupies just a small, if prime, corner of the site. Directly below it, a few yards from its columned entrance, and also surrounded by fields, are the scrambled remains of what was once a busy marketplace. Perhaps this, after all, is what gives the temple its lasting sense of good cheer: Allowed to crouch comfortably amid forest and field, the earthy and popular goddess, Feronia, was also invited to watch over the people as they went about their work. The goddess was not held aloof. Even when life was at its most mercantile, good-natured Feronia was still close at hand.

Getting there: Open Friday through Sunday, 9:00 A.M. to 1:00 P.M.; closed Monday through Thursday. Admission free. Located 17 miles north of Rome, just a few hundred yards west of the A1, which is a major freeway. Get off at the exit for Capena, which is 3½ miles west of the town of Scorano and the site of Lucus Feroniae, both of which are very small. A few road signs show the way. About ½ mile south of the site is a Goodyear Blimp hangar, a helpful landmark. Public transportation from Rome is complicated and slow. If you want to reach the site before it closes at 1:00 P.M., you need to drive.

Selinunte, Sicily

Sanctuary of Demeter Malaphoros

At home in Greece, Demeter, stately goddess, was traditionally associated with grain, the sober staff of life. She was certainly not linked with such luxurious whimsy as *fruit*. But then Demeter came to Sicily. And like Eve in Paradise, or like anyone at all in Sicily, the goddess could not resist the island's succulent and abundant fruit. Ruby-red plum juice must have dribbled down her divine arm just as wetly as it runs down our mortal ones. Fig seeds stuck in her teeth just as they stick in ours. Did she lick the juice as guiltily and greedily as we do? Did she too delight in the infinitesimal explosions of each tiny fig seed as she ground them between her teeth?

Somehow, in Selinus, the westernmost of the Greeks' colonies in Sicily, Demeter made a bold new name for herself. Here she was worshipped as Demeter Malaphoros: Demeter the fruit bringer. Hers was the vivid, sweet harvest. Her temple, begun in 575 B.C.E., flourished in the lee of the sacred Acropolis. Then as now, the sea glittered and pounded close by the sanctuary. Then as now, the salt air whetted visitors' appetites for fresh fruit.

A jumble of rubble, scattered masonry, and skewed foundations marks the sanctuary now. High stone walls still enclose the *cella*, or inner sanctum, of Demeter's temple. Inside these pale walls you feel intimately close to the goddess, as if the two of you were a pair of friends ducking into a closet to share furtive secrets.

Visitors of old came bearing gifts. A staggering assemblage of over 5000 votive figurines, mostly terracottas and bronzes of Demeter herself, have been discovered so far in the sand drifts of the temple precinct; artifacts are still being found to this day. And perhaps Demeter herself cannot resist offering a few sweet gifts of her own: a strong fig tree is currently growing directly out of the high stone wall.

Sicilian fruits are worthy of a goddess, but some scholars nevertheless have suggested an entirely different meaning of Demeter Malaphoros. The "fruits" in question, they say, are the souls of the dead, whom she gathers, harvested, in her motherly arms. A sprawling seafront necropolis, beginning here and extending for several miles, lends credence to this theory, as does the presence, in the precinct's southeastern corner, of a small temple dedicated to Hecate Triformis, "Triple Hecate." This harrowing goddess, in all her threefold glory, was queen of the night and of the dead. Although the Greeks were careful to honor her at crossroads, which she was said to haunt, actual temples to Hecate are rare. So wherefore her friendship with Demeter Malaphoros? Are they grim reapers after all, and the salt air merely the shadow of mourners' tears?

Getting there: Open daily, 9 A.M. to 1 hour before sunset. Admission: L2000. Selinunte is on the southern coast of Sicily, 50 miles northwest of Agrigento and 6 miles south of Castelvetrano. The name of the modern resort village next to the site is Marinella. To reach the sanctuary, go west from Marinella to the entrance of the acropolis. Here you must pay to enter; continue through the acropolis, taking the one road that goes down the other side of the hill and crosses a river on a bridge. After a few hundred yards you'll pass a small house. The sanctuary is just past it on the left side of the road. The Hecate sanctuary is on the south side (toward the ocean) of the lower part of the temple.

Syracuse, Sicily

Temple of Athena

Syracuse, in the fifth century B.C.E., was a place everyone wanted to visit. Sailors steered into the harbor, guided by the golden shield of Athena which crowned the entrance to that goddess's temple in the city and flashed like a beacon in the sun. The temple's famous doors, finished with priceless gold and ivory, were a testament to the people's esteem for Athena: those doors were a lavish indicator of who, after all, was boss here.

Things change; the temple changed. The boss changed. Sometime in the seventh century C.E., the temple, like so many others, was surrounded, enclosed, and encased. A Catholic church was erected on its very foundations. The faithful of Syracuse had come to this spot for centuries, to worship. Now they would still come. But they would not enter through the same doors as they had in ancient times. Here, as in most similar cases, the traditional east-facing portals of the Greek temple were sealed up and the cathedral was reoriented, as if to show who's boss *now*. (As if the church's architect could not resist some insistent pagan impulse, the front doors are decorated with twining grapevines, as well as humanoid heads whose gaping mouths spew foliage.) Parts of the ancient temple were actually incorporated into the Christian structure's walls, so you can still see tall Doric columns both inside and outside the church, slender and tapering, like a great gray skeleton around which the vibrant flesh of the church still pulses.

Probably because the cathedral is so old—not so very far removed from the temple that preceded it—a curious back-and-forth interplay is evident throughout. Wide archways, running the length of the nave, suggest the open, airy atmosphere of an ancient temple, and their light color echoes that of the Doric columns which stand just behind them. Some of the columns now frame the cathedral's side chapels, many of which are stuffed with tributes to female saints whose meek martyrdom would surely make Athena want to gag. One can't help but think that the columns, thus placed, are humiliated,

Temple columns incorporated into cathedral walls, Syracuse

that the Christian imagery mocks them. Or are the columns, rather, like old and patient parents whose offspring scurry and tumble around their ankles? The columns, after all, still feel the touch of the pious, and have done so for 2500 years. The columns, despite everything, are still here.

Getting there: Open daily, 7:00 A.M. to 1:00 P.M., 4:30 to 7:00 P.M., approximately. Admission free. The Temple of Athena is incorporated into the cathedral (Duomo) on Piazza Duomo, in the Ortygia section of town, which is an island at the southernmost part of the city, connected by a short bridge to the mainland.

Goddesses in Captivity: Museums

Naples: National Archaeology Museum (Museo Nazionale Archeologico) Among the many representations of goddesses on display here, you can see the beautiful "Sinuous" Aphrodite, which, despite the absence of arms and head, still seems to move and breathe. Here also is one of the best known goddess statues ever made, the alabaster and bronze Artemis of Ephesus, who has a profusion of breasts; flawless dark bronze face, feet, and hands; a dress patterned with magical animals and deities; and a castlelike crown. Elsewhere in the museum are all the outstanding finds from Pompeii and from the sibyl's cave at Cuma.

Getting there: Open Tuesday through Saturday, 9:00 A.M. to 2:00 P.M. (in July and August, 9:00 A.M. to 7:30 P.M.); Sundays, 9:00 A.M. to 1:00 P.M.; closed Mondays. Admission: L4000. On Piazza Museo Nazionale, next to Piazza Cavour. (Take the Metro to the Piazza Cavour station.)

Rome: National Museum of Rome (Museo Nazionale Romano, or Museo delle Terme) This museum, semiofficially nicknamed after the baths (*terme*) of Diocletian in which it is housed, is a virtual forest of statuary, much of which is goddess-related. The most remarkable piece is the so-called Ludovisi Throne (named after the villa in which it was found), also known as The Birth of the Goddess. This pure white marble relief of a goddess rising from the waves probably represents Aphrodite Ericena, whose temple in Erice, Sicily, it was probably made to adorn. Also here is a perfect Venus Genetrix; larger-than-life votives of Demeter and Kore; a hunting Diana; and a cloister lined with innumerable soft-shouldered Venuses, portentious Fortunas, and other goddesses—most of which, regrettably, have no labels identifying them.

Getting there: Open Tuesday through Sunday, 9:00 A.M. to 2:00 P.M.; closed Mondays. Admission: L1000. The entrance is at Viale E. de Nicola 79, facing onto Piazza dei Cinquecento, which is just in front of the Termini train station.

Malta

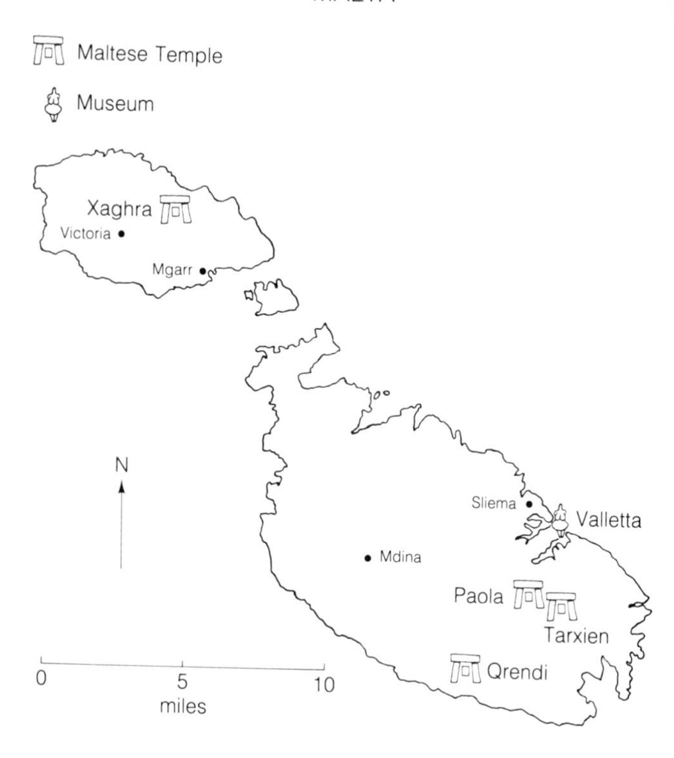

Malta is a dry little sesame-seed biscuit of an island, of which some of your friends have undoubtedly never heard. You can't blame them, really. Malta doesn't often make the headlines.

But if goddesses were a required academic subject, then Malta's name would linger on everyone's lips. And so, although not without difficulty, would linger the names of the Maltese temples where a big goddess was worshipped amid stone spirals and sea breezes: names like Tarxien, Ggigantija, Hagar Qim, and Mnajdra.

Malta's ancient temple builders, whose creative and spiritual pinnacle lasted from about 3600 to 2200 B.C.E., roughly contemporary with the builders of the early pyramids of Egypt, had arrived on the island long before that, in boats. But from where? No one knows. Using only the most primitive of tools, they fashioned mighty structures whose consummate balance of delicacy and power mirrored that of the goddess herself. Then, mysteriously, these people withdrew. No one knows why. Perhaps they had overworked their lands, or perhaps their goddess told them to go. In any case, their shadows on Malta were overlaid by an endless succession of others, so that the modern Maltese are a genetic macédoine of Italian, Arab, British, and other bloodlines. Yet the island, and its people who are only tenuously related to those ancient temple builders, still radiate a nurturing warmth that can only be a legacy of that serene hulk of a goddess. Under the unbroken cobalt peace of an island sky, this is a place where you want to walk slowly. Your friends have never heard of Malta. That you have found it, and are here at all, is a gift from the goddess, a secret troth between you.

Paola

Hal-Saflieni Prehistoric Hypogeum

It served as a tomb for as many as 7000 bodies, as a temple to a goddess of death and of the underworld. It may also have been an oracular center, and many other things besides. When building the Hypogeum—whatever it was—the ancient Maltese (whoever they were) pulled out all the stops.

Hewn out of solid stone and extending deep underground, the Hypogeum, whose dull archaeological name means merely "cavity below the ground," comprises three separate levels and dozens of assorted chambers. The chambers lead, one to another, through halls and snug passageways. You feel, groping your way along moist walls in semidarkness, that you are exploring inside some vast human body.

Like bodily organs, too, all these chambers—no two alike—are enticingly round and oval in shape. Doors, stairsteps, niches, and shelves form sharp right angles that, against the curved walls, provide a sense of balance.

Working some 5000 years ago, the Hypogeum's builders used nothing more sophisticated than deer antlers and horns to open the earth and split the rock. They took advantage of natural faults and shapes to define floors and walls. Then they added a wealth of detail in the form of stone-cut doorways, pillars, and ornaments, creating an overall effect whose stylized refinement intimidates architects to this day. Then they embellished their work with spirals, dots, and other designs. You can still see traces of the red ochre that once made these walls fairly glow with the traditional color of death and blood.

They worked seemingly beyond the limits of their own technology, driven by reverence for their dead and for the goddess who guarded the dead. Besides the many cubbyholes that once were filled with human bones, jewelry, and funerary offerings, archaeologists have identified many rooms in the Hypogeum as having served ritual and religious purposes. The antechambered "Holy of Holies," as it is now called, strongly resembles an aboveground temple, with a fancy facade, apse, corbeled roof, altar niches, and lashings of red paint. Aboveground, these features would be built by laying stone upon stone; down here, they were painstakingly carved out of solid rock.

An echo chamber whose remarkable acoustic properties can still be tested may once have been used in oracular rituals. Another room contains a 4-foot-deep pit that may or may not have been used for keeping live snakes. The pit's concave shape and its templelike pillars have suggested that use to some, and it's an exciting idea, to anyone who associates snakes with earth or mother goddesses. However, Maltese archaeologists are quick to point out the lack of proof.

They are quick, but wistful. It is difficult to prove anything at all about the Hypogeum. After it was uncovered accidentally, in 1902, by a group of workers digging cisterns for a new housing development, the developer deliberately hushed up the discovery; he wanted his houses built quickly, without interference. A great deal of the Hypogeum must have been destroyed as the homes went up, especially on the two upper levels. Eventually, a priest was given the task of "clearing" the Hypogeum's chambers, but his work was neither precise nor thorough. A full 3 years went by before sensitive archaeologists had a chance to take up the project.

Still, among the pottery and painted spirals, one tantalizing clue remains. It is a stone carving, just a few inches long, of a big woman asleep on a raised divan. She looks natural and comfortable, her little head pillowed on one vast bolsterlike arm, massive hips in repose under a demure skirt. You can practically see the rhythm of her breathing. Found in the Hypogeum and now in the National Museum of Archaeology (discussed at the end of this chapter), this so-called Sleeping Lady might represent the goddess whose somnolent presence rendered safe and holy the world of the dead. Then again, she might represent a female pilgrim, who hopes to meet her goddess in a dream.

Getting there: Open June 16 through September 30, daily, 8:30 A.M. to 1:45 P.M.; October 1 through June 15, Monday to Saturday, 8:30 A.M. to 4:45 P.M.; Sunday, 8:30 A.M. to 8:15 P.M. The Hypogeum opens and closes at 45-minute intervals throughout the day. If you arrive while it is closed, you must wait until the next open period before entering. Admission: 25¢. The Hypogeum is on Burials Street (*Triq Ic-Cimiterju* in Maltese) in Paola, which is 2½ miles south of Valletta. Take bus 11 from the depot in Valletta; tell the driver you want to go to the Hypogeum, and he'll drop you off at the nearest stop, just two blocks from the entrance. Signs point the way. A map at the Hypogeum shows the route to the Tarxien temples, just a 5-minute walk away.

Qrendi

Temple of Hagar Qim

In the illustrious family of Maltese temples, Hagar Qim is the "difficult" sister. Compared with the others, Hagar Qim is neither architecturally neat nor even sensible. From above, it resembles a thumbless hand with four stubby fingers and is often dismissed as an architectural jumble. Also, Hagar Qim's pattern of tall upright megaliths differs slightly from that of the others, leading at least one author to suggest that this was the island's one "masculine" temple. Built, unlike the others, of soft globigerina limestone, Hagar Qim is, unlike the others, badly weatherbeaten.

And yet among this temple's battered, misunderstood remains were found no fewer than seven female figurines. Goddesses or priestesses, these carvings share the generous figures that have led archaeologists to call them, along with other prehistoric Maltese figurines, "fat lady" statuettes. Their restful, almost hypnotically peaceful poses tell you that fear, intimidation, and violence could not have been part of ancient Maltese religion. Also found here was another figurine, more naturalistic in style. Now headless and footless, the so-called "Venus of Malta" has expansive, soft-looking breasts, an orderly little navel, and a broad back whose gentle dimpling reveals the artisan's appreciation of the female body.

On the temple's outside wall, you can just make out, in relief, the shapes of two pairs of female legs, part, probably, of a once-complete goddess or priestess scene, which either decorated this very wall or perhaps an older one, from which masonry was reused to build Hagar Qim.

Inside the temple, among the other architectural details, is an oval opening behind an altar, which suggests that oracular activity was part of the religous rituals that went on here. A pilgrim would have listened at the opening for utterances from divine beings, channeled through a priest or priestess who sat in an adjoining room. Unique on Malta is Hagar Qim's pair of free-standing "mushroom" altars, named for their shape, as well as another free-standing altar (now in the National Museum), of which all four faces bear the carved image of a graceful potted plant.

Some "jumble," huh?

Getting there: Open Monday through Saturday, 8:30 A.M. to 4:45 P.M.; Sunday, 8:30 A.M. to 4 P.M. Admission: 15¢. Qrendi is 7 miles southwest of Valletta. To reach the temple, take bus 35 from the depot at Valletta to Qrendi; from there, you must walk about 1 mile west to the

Courtyard of Temple of Hagar Qim, Qrendi

temple. Ask the bus driver or passersby for directions as the route is rather confusing and directional signposts are few.

Qrendi

Temples of Mnajdra

It's impossible to look at Mnajdra without thinking, "Maltese Stonehenge." Mnajdra's venerable powder-white megaliths stand like patient, ageless ancestors in a field of green.

Yet with their carved passageways and decorated stones, Mnajdra's triple temples are prettier than Stonehenge. Best of all, Mnajdra overlooks the sea, and there's no sea like the moody, cloud-canopied sea surrounding an island.

Like Stonehenge, and unlike its sister temples on Malta and Gozo, Mnajdra seems to have been built with the cosmos in mind. Its southern part is perfectly aligned with the rising sun at the spring and autumn equinoxes. But even so, archaeologists will not definitively agree that this placement was deliberate.

Temple niche in Mnajdra complex, Qrendi

Everyone does agree, however, that this was a very sacred place. Its many chambers are liberally studded with altars: broad platform slabs as well as narrow, inset altar niches. Tiny chambers separated from larger ones by tight passageways may, according to some, have served an oracular purpose. A priest or priestess may have crouched in the small recess, channeling advice and blessings from the deities and passing it out to the worshippers who stood in the adjacent larger chamber.

But no one knows for sure. The passions and labors of 5500 years ago, so beautiful, leave us baffled, wandering bereft from empty altar to empty altar.

But look at an aerial view, even a diagram, of Mnajdra. Like the temple of Ggantija, discussed shortly, its blueprint mirrors the generous body of the Maltese goddess herself: the wide oval of hips, surmounted by the smaller oval of shoulders and breasts; between them a waist; on top, a head, small and delicate.

Getting there: Always open. Admission free. To reach Mnajdra, follow the directions to Hagar Qim (see above). From there, Mnajdra is just ¼ mile downhill toward the sea, on a paved pathway that starts right next to Hagar Qim.

Tarxien

Prehistoric Temples

Tarxien is the undisputed queen of temples—in Malta and perhaps in the entire Mediterranean. It is exotic, built by ancient Maltese whose origins remain, to this day, an absolute cipher. It is washed in mystery, for we still don't know how, or whom, these ancients worshipped, although the clues are delicious. Tarxien is supremely well built, huge stone upon huge stone, with a skill that belies its creators' simple technology. Decorated throughout by a talented hand, it's downright hard to remember that Tarxien is prehistoric. *And* its door is guarded by a goddess in a pleated skirt. Who could ask for anything more?

The crowning achievement of Malta's Temple Age, this four-temple complex was enlarged and embellished over many years—perhaps a thousand—and enjoyed the role of "island cathedral" before it was finally abandoned around 2300 B.C.E.

The complex was probably once much larger than it is today. There may have been more decorative carvings than the ones you can see today. We'll never know, and the reasons for this lie not in ancient times but in modern ones. The field on which Tarxien lies had become, by the dawn of the twentieth century, privately owned farmland. After years of breaking up and clearing away the pesky stone blocks that interfered with his plow, the exhausted farmer finally complained to authorities. In 1915, archaeologists moved in and spent the next 3 years alternately tearing their hair over the farmer's destruction and marveling at the richness of what was left intact.

As you wander the monumental halls and chambers of Tarxien today, remember that each of the huge paving stones was placed by hand. These and the wall stones, which fit so precisely together, were hewn and assembled by people who had no knowledge of metal tools. So too with mere horn and flint blades they carved the long chains of double spirals that meander across altars and slabs in the temple. Spirals were goddess symbols in many ancient cultures. Double spirals like these have been said to represent the ever-watchful and protective eyes of the goddess herself.

The spirals are the most abstract of the carved designs adorning Tarxien today, some of which appear in their original form and others of which are copies, the originals having been removed to the National Museum. Animals were important here, as evidenced by the art: two narrow friezes depict long rows of sheep, goats, pigs, and other beasts, virile and fertile. Some say these animals stand waiting to be sacrificed. That animal sacrifices were indeed practiced at this temple was proven by the discovery of a flint-bladed ritual knife, a goat horn, and other animal remains within an altar niche. Elsewhere is a relief depicting a bull and a sow—potent motherly mascot—busily suckling her 13 piglets.

And all in honor of the goddess in the pleated skirt. Though we save her for last, like dessert, she is really the first: the first in importance, probably in all of ancient Malta, and the first to greet you as you enter the gates of Tarxien.

We can only guess at how she looked when she was all there. Pickaxe-wielding local farmers had their way with her; all that remains are the skirt-draped hips, the legs, and the feet of a once-colossal figure which stood about 7 feet tall. Like the many small stone figurines that have been found in other Maltese temples, this one has a robust figure, with almost spherical calves tapering down to tiny delicate feet whose long, sensitive toes look very human indeed. While scholars will not definitively agree that the smaller figurines actually depict a goddess, about Tarxien's massive statue they are all quite sure. Her position and size clinch it, they say.

We don't know what this goddess stood for. But something about the perky fall of her full skirt, those roundly

Chiseled spirals decorate the temples at Tarxien

sturdy legs, makes you want to throw your arms around one big stone hip, lay your cheek against its cool smoothness, and never, ever let go.

Getting there: Open June 16 through September 30, daily, 8:30 A.M. to 5 P.M.; October 1 through June 15, daily, 8 A.M. to 2 P.M. Admission: 15¢. The site is on Temples Street in Tarxien, which is 2½ miles south of Valletta. Take bus 11 from the depot in Valletta, and tell the driver you'd like to go to the Tarxien temples. He'll drop you off at the nearest stop, four blocks from the entrance. Signs point the way. A map at Tarxien shows the route to the Hypogeum, just a 5-minute walk away.

Xaghra, Gozo

Temples of Ggantija

A giantess, they say, once dwelt on this tiny island. Towering she was; ingenious, loving. With a child suckling at her breast, she carried enormous stone blocks on her head, and piled them upon the earth until she had built a monument so striking that later mortals, dazzled, named it The Giant's Tower. Now, the area is simply called Ggantija, Maltese for "giantess," in honor of the legendary woman herself.

The giantess of this allegorical myth is none other than the goddess of the early Maltese. The baby represents the people who worshipped her, and her buildings were the temples. Just as the pious describe certain churches as having been "built by the hand of God," so the Maltese still like to say that these ancient temples were built by a "giantess."

Legends of goddesses on Gozo don't stop there. Just a couple of miles north of Ggantija is the cave where, according to Homer, the immortal nymph Calypso held Odysseus captive for 7 years. A few miles to the west is the Basilica of Ta'Pinu, built on the spot where the Virgin Mary allegedly spoke to a local peasant woman. Each culture, it seems, identifies the divine female presence of Gozo according to its own terms.

The temples at Ggantija are the oldest in Malta. And they are more than that. A recent recalculation of the true age of the temples at Ggantija has shown that they were begun as early as 3600 B.C.E., which makes them older than Stonehenge, older than the pyramids of Egypt—in fact, not only the oldest of all temples but actually the most ancient permanent buildings of any kind on earth.

The stones of Ggantija are rough-hewn, imposing, raw; a far cry from the carefully chiseled stones that were used to build later temples in Malta. The design and plan of Ggantija are also much more direct and obvious in their intent. Seen from above, both temples here are shaped like the Maltese goddess herself, as she has been depicted in figurines found nearby. The rounded walls mirror her abundant breasts, hips, and thighs. So to enter Ggantija is to enter the Goddess herself. Her walls surround you, enclose you. You are safe, inside.

Getting there: Open daily, 8:45 A.M. to 3:15 P.M. Admission: 15¢. Xaghra is on the island of Gozo, 3 miles northwest of the port of Mgarr, and 2 miles east of the capital, Victoria. Ggantija is ½ mile east of Xhagra. To reach the temples, take a ferry from near Valletta or Cirkewwa on Malta to Mgarr on Gozo; buses from Mgarr will take you to Xaghra and the temples.

Goddesses in Captivity: Museum

Valletta: National Museum of Archaeology
All the images of the goddess found on Malta have been brought here. Seeing them displayed all together like this would convince even the most determined skeptic that the prehistoric Maltese not only worshipped goddesses but a single great goddess and that they worshipped her unchangingly for thousands of years. Whatever the medium, whatever the era, her representations are consistent: corpulent thighs, broad hips, full breasts. Often as not, like other prehistoric goddess figurines, her head is either tiny or left off entirely.

The museum's pride and joy is the small but exquisite "Sleeping Lady," a perfectly crafted votive figurine found in the Hypogeum (discussed at the beginning of this chapter). The museum also houses most of the architectural decorations found at the temples; the ones you see at Tarxien and elsewhere are usually reproductions.

Getting there: Open June 16 through September 30, Monday to Saturday, 9 A.M. to 2 P.M.; Sunday, 8:15 A.M. to 4 P.M. Admission: 15¢. The museum is on Republic Street, near Melita Street, in the center of Valletta.

The Netherlands

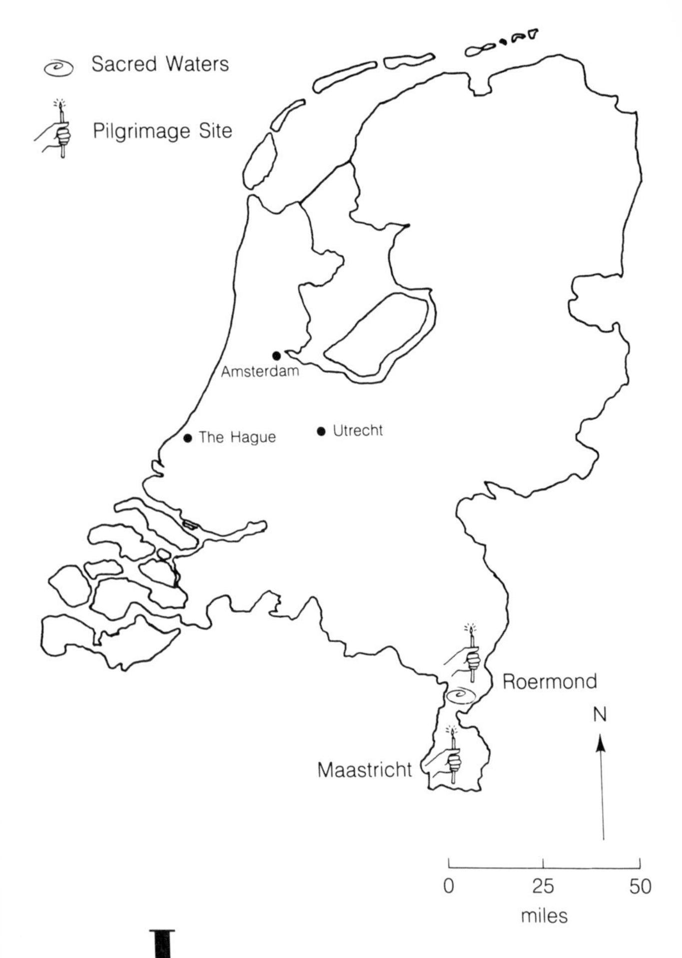

In the Netherlands, you find yourself wanting to rhythmically bang your coffee cup on the table like a perturbed prisoner during an uprising, and shout, "Where's the goddess? Where's the goddess? Where's the goddess?" In the Netherlands you want to keep peeking under napkins and under the lids of sugar bowls to see if she might be hiding there.

But that's just it. *Look* at that coffee cup, those snowy napkins. Could a country that makes such good breakfasts really be devoid of goddesses? Shame on you for even thinking such a thing. It was from Holland that the Stone Age "Beaker People" traveled to England, where they built the dazzling goddess sanctuary at Avebury (see the Avebury discussion in the Great Britain chapter). (The Netherlands has its own share of prehistoric tombs and earthworks, but none matches the emigrants' masterwork.)

The Roman army, under Julius Caesar, arrived circa 60 B.C.E. to find Celtic tribes populating these lowlands. Roman as well as Celtic goddesses romped and then ebbed and had vanished long before Pieter Breughel the Younger was even a twinkle in Pieter Breughel the Elder's eye. In 1647, while the Netherlands was basking in artistic, political, and navigational glory, the seashore near Domburg shifted to reveal the ancient remains of a temple of Nehalennia, a Celtic goddess who once, aboard a long boat and attended by hounds, prevailed over this watery region. (Another shrine in her honor was later found nearby at Colijnsplaat.) It was as if the goddess, with mighty arms, had moved the very shoreline and risen from the sea. Perhaps one day, as you spread jam on your breakfast toast, it will happen again.

Maastricht

Stella Maris and Relics of Mary

If you confronted an ancient Egyptian or Roman with a flash card imprinted with the words "Stella Maris," she'd respond, without a moment's hesitation, "Isis, of course." For that nickname, which means "Star of the Sea," belonged to Isis long before Mary was born. The latter inherited it from Isis, along with the burning of frankincense, the sprinkling of holy water by tonsured priests, the offering of ex-votos, and many other powerful traditions.

The Romans settled for a while in this fertile, riverfed region. But ever since the Middle Ages it has been Mary and not Isis who is venerated here, whose altar seems to vibrate in the heat and glow of hundreds of votive candles. Legends say that this statue came to Maastricht in the hold of a sailing ship, where it lay, undignified, a mere lump of ballast. When his business in town was completed, the impious captain hoisted anchor, but his ship refused to budge. Finally, on an impulse, the captain gathered the statue of Mary in his arms and carried it into the first church that he saw. After this, his ship became obedient again and he sailed gratefully away. The statue began its thousand-year career of veneration.

Today, clad in the gold and royal blue of a sun-spangled sea, Stella Maris—*Sterre der Zee*—presides over a glassed-in chapel, surrounded by offerings. A museum in the basilica's treasury displays relics purported to be Mary's own: a scrap of her belt, a twist of her hair, a thread of her veil, and an ancient copy of her wedding ring. It deepens the sensation, so European, of eons overlapping, of centuries melting.

Getting there: Open daily, normal church hours (generally around 8 A.M. to 8 P.M.). The treasury is open Monday through Saturday, 10:30 A.M. to 5 P.M. and Sunday, 1 to 5 P.M. Admission free to basilica; to treasury f2. Maastricht is at the very southern tip of the Netherlands, near Liège, Belgium. Onze Lieve Vrouwebasiliek, which houses the statue, is on Onze Lieve Vrouweplein, a few blocks south of the tourist office. The statue of Stella Maris is in the side chapel on the left side of the church. The treasury has its entrance inside the church, near the back on the left wall.

Roermond

Our Lady in the Sand

Holland is a country riven by waterways. Through its flatlands wind nourishing, slow rivers. Through its cities march glassy canals. Around the edges, the sea presses in, forever threatening while it beckons and promises. In this country, this lacework of land and water, sand is a special element, representing the gateway between water and land and thus perhaps all other transitions as well.

One of the Netherlands' best-loved shrines celebrates the sand. The madonna who dwells here, Our Lady in the Sand, is as brown as Dutch cocoa. The carved pedestal beneath her feet ripples and rolls like water. Satin smooth and serene, she cradles a bowl in her large hands. She is said to have been found buried in the sandy banks of a spring.

Wendelin, a medieval Polish nobleman, having abandoned his glamorous life in search of simplicity, wandered Europe until he finally settled down as a shepherd along Limburg's Roer river. According to the legend, Wendelin's sheep led him to a spring. While the animals drank from it, Wendelin meditated, peering into its cool depths. He began praying beside the spring every day. One day, as his fingers idly sifted the sand at the water's edge, Wendelin found the statue. By 1417, a chapel was built on the site. By 1578, Roermond's town chronicles related that the chapel and statue were "well known for their miracles."

The story of Wendelin is pretty enough, but something—or *someone*—is missing. A goddess called Rura was once worshipped here. Hers was the river now known as the Roer. An altar dedicated to Rura was recently fished up from the bottom of the river. Historians speculate about a temple that may once have graced the riverbank.

In the *Kapel in 't Zand* ("chapel in the sand"), an 1895 replacement of the original building, which was bombed during a war, lives the dark madonna and her spring. Shiny spigots offer healing water to drink on the spot and to take home in bottles. The spring shimmers several feet below the floor, visible under a sheet of glass.

Ex-voto tiles, covering the walls from floor to ceiling, show that Our Lady in the Sand is as high an achiever as the Dutch people she serves. The faithful thank her for healings, for averting financial disasters, for fending off Nazis. Many people have given more than tiles. One wall, also protected behind glass, sports floor-to-ceiling gold jewelry, plaques, and watches.

So Roermond is still guarded by a miraculous, watery woman. This guardianship, under whatever name, has never ebbed. It has survived, if you will, in a long continuous stream.

Getting there: Open daily, normal church hours (generally around 8 A.M. to 6 P.M.). Admission free. Roermond is in the southern part of the Netherlands, 28 miles northeast of Maastricht, 30 miles southeast of Eindhoven. From the town center of Roermond, head south until you come to Kapellerlaan; continue south down Kapellerlaan across the railroad tracks about ½ mile. The Kapel in 't Zand is on the right side of Kapellerlaan, where it intersects Parklaan. The statue of Our Lady in the Sand is on the top of the high altar. The holy well and faucets are in a side hallway on the right side of the nave, accessible either through the church itself or by a separate outside door to the right of the door leading into the church.

Poland

POLAND

Like a wounded giantess, Poland sits in her corner, broad back against the wall. Not quite mortally wounded, she tries bravely to smile, and she cheers herself by cutting pastel tissue paper into the silhouettes of birds and fruit trees and hearts and by decorating eggs, symbols of hope and renewal.

She wasn't always infirm. Ancient Poland was the home of rural Slavonic peoples, who recognized tantalizing divinity in the sun, water, the forest, the soil, the hearth, love, animals, the morning and evening stars, thunder, blackness and whiteness. The draw of these forces was strong, so much so that Poland was not Christianized until as late as 952 C.E. In the centuries following the Renaissance, a series of wars, invasions, attacks, and seizures rained on Poland like ax blows. Finally, with one-fifth of its entire population wiped out, Poland suffered bitterly in the aftermath of World War II. The giantess reeled, numb with pain and loss.

Through it all, Poland's folk spirit has persevered. This is the spirit that can look beyond factory walls and see the Lady in the evening star. Though devoutly Catholic, Poland is the home of a vibrant folk art tradition, whose life-affirming animal and plant imagery, its elaborate "Easter" eggs, tell of a lasting faith in the earth, in Poland's broad, strong, eternal back.

Czestochowa

Pilgrimage Site

Few countries resonate to motherhood as strongly as Poland does. The tongue-clucking, wool-stockinged, aproned matriarch has *not* permanently receded into the fairy-tale books. She's here, in Poland, where every woman over a certain age seems to fix you with a compassionate gaze as if she'd like to pile high your plate with kasha, noodles, and blintzes.

The Great Mother of Poland, on the other hand, looks almost too exotic to fill her role. Squinty-eyed and swarthy, with a piratical scar streaking across one gaunt cheek, Our Lady of Czestochowa (pronounced "khen-sto-khova") would look right at home in some souk or casbah, were it not for the ostentatious halo that radiates like a golden dinner plate from her head. (The child in her lap has one too.) She'd probably never cook a blintz. And yet, Our Lady of Czestochowa is the spiritual mother of all Polish mothers, and of all their children.

Her shrine, among whose many features is a small chapel dedicated to concentration camp victims, is the goal of every religious Eastern European, many of whom save up for years to make the trip. The shrine's walls, every bit as fascinating as the icon they frame, are jammed with gifts befitting a mother—in this case, a mother of millions. Every inch of available space is hung with pilgrims' donations: necklaces, bracelets, rosaries of all sizes, gold rings, plastic pearls, matchbooks, ban-

Spire of the church housing Czestochowa's black madonna

ners, and rusted crutches: the precious and homely gifts of a poor people who believe in miracles.

The icon, its charcoal gray face veiled in silver some of the time, veiled in mystery all of the time, was brought here "from the East," presumably the Holy Land, in 1384. But the legends like to say it was painted in Jerusalem long, long before that date. One rumor suggests that the picture was painted from life. But even an art history freshman can spot the icon's Byzantine trademarks: the impossibly long nose, the gold halos, the robe with its fleur-de-lis pattern. But whatever its actual age, the icon has been here long enough to have seen Poland through times bright and dismal. Surely there were times, many and not so long ago, when hers was the only ear in which Poles dared whisper their secret hopes and fears. Through it all, her dark sorrowful face has been a constant.

That face has worn its grievous scar since 1430, when rampaging Hussites slashed the picture with a sword, as it represented the mother-worshipping religion they loathed. Tales are still told of how the icon bled on that day. Afterward, church officials decided to leave the slash unmended, as a sad reminder. It is said that the swordsmen who damaged the icon were supernaturally punished almost immediately after their misdeed.

Truly, the scar gives her character. Poland is a scarred country, and it makes some kind of sense that its beloved mother also has a scar that doesn't heal. People flock to see her, now more jubilantly than ever. On any given day, even a rainy one, the smallish church is hot with fervent human bodies. All kneel and press unabashedly; there is no room on the floor, just as there is none on those crowded walls. Who ever said Poland was gray and colorless? Who ever said it was leached of emotion? The outpouring of love in this dark place is so thick and real that it sticks in your throat. It clouds around your head like a wool scarf. It feels medieval.

Getting there: Open daily, generally during daylight hours. During a pilgrimage, there might be a long wait to get into the church. Admission free. Czestochowa is in south-central Poland, 70 miles south of Lodz, and 70 miles northwest of Krakow. The monastery of Jasna Gora is at the western end of town and can be clearly seen at the end of the city's main thoroughfare, Al. Najswietszej Marii Panny (usually shortened to Al. NMP). The monastery's church's towering spire on the top of the hill makes it impossible to miss. The black madonna is not in the main church but is in the side chapel adjoining the main church on the north side. To reach the black madonna chapel, enter through the gate to the left of the main church entrance; go straight about 100 yards, and then go through the door on your right. You can also reach the chapel by entering the main church and exiting through the connecting door on the back left side. The icon is not always visible but is revealed several times daily during ceremonies.

Portugal

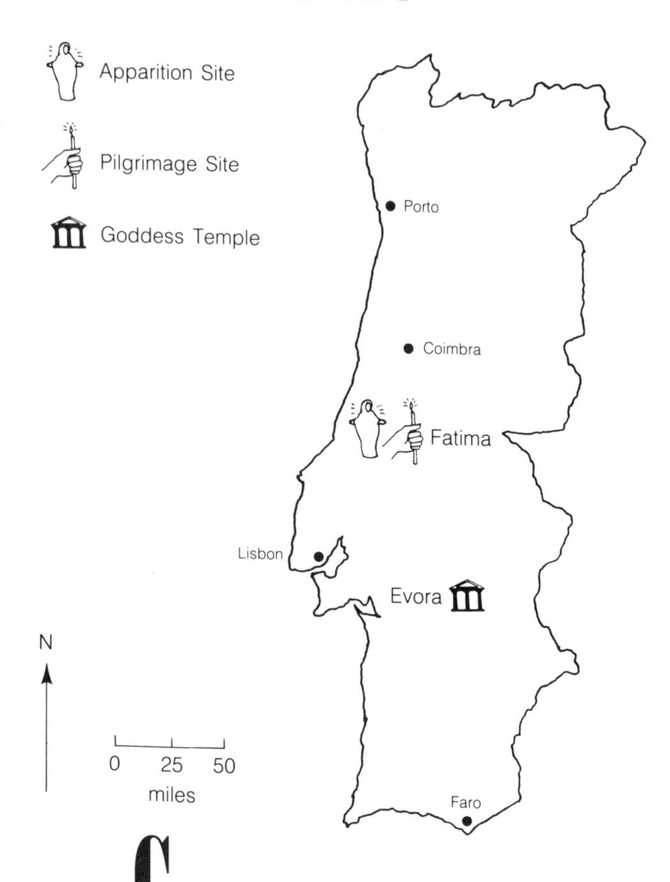

Cursed with one of the poorest economies in Europe, and blessedly undeveloped, Portugal lives, of necessity, in close harmony with nature. Life is simple under the Portuguese sun and the big Portuguese moon that is as cool as the silver filigree pendants the mountain women wear. Under this sun and moon thrive plum, tomato, Port wine grape, and clam.

Portugal's prehistoric inhabitants, flourishing as early as 8000 B.C.E., gave way to Stone Age and Iron Age cultures. Waves of Celtic tribes arrived from northern Europe around 700 B.C.E. They built fortified villages where the familiar Celtic goddesses were safely ensconced. In the green northeast, the Celtic *verracos* people venerated granite sculptures of sows, motherly beasts that have been linked with many goddesses, including such far-flung ones as Demeter and Astarte.

Today's golden-skinned, jade-eyed Portuguese people don't look pure Latin, and they're not. In addition to the strong Celtic strain, they also represent the ancient intermixing of Phoenicians, Carthaginians, and Romans, and, later on, still other cultures. The fifteenth and sixteenth centuries were Portugal's heyday. Sailing away from the southwestern spur they called "the End of the World," Portuguese explorers roamed the globe and discovered whole new continents. Then all fell silent, at rest, like a wavelet retreating down a beach. Here at the end of the twentieth century, Portugal lives, still, by its sun and moon.

Evora

Temple of Diana

Animals, real and imaginary, romp and play across the heart of Portugal. Because this is a rural nation, because it depends on nature's goodness, animals loom large and vivid, as anyone knows who has seen the phalanxes of trademark black ceramic roosters crowding the shelves of every Portuguese gift shop. Or the bloody, sensual frenzy of a Portuguese fish market; the light reverent hand with which fish are cooked and eaten. Animals for work and pleasure: animals are no mere luxury.

It's no surprise, then, that the country's most striking archaeological monument is a temple of Diana, Roman lady of the beasts.

Built of local marble in the second century C.E., the temple rose light and willowy above a rugged plain. Its presence not only honored the goddess but also proclaimed the importance of Liberalitus Julia, the Roman walled city that was a bright spot of the colony, just as its descendant, Evora, is still a regional capital today. Aside from the temple, no trace of the 400-year Roman occupation remains. It is a white stucco, Moorish-flavored skyline that Evora offers the tourist now.

With the departure of the Romans came waves of invaders, who left in their wake a mosque, a university, a royal residence, monasteries, and Manueline mansions. The temple of Diana became just another old building in a city of old buildings. For many years, until 1870, the temple was used as a slaughterhouse. Thus were countless animal sacrifices unwittingly performed in Diana's hallowed halls. Toward the end of the last century, when archaeology became all the rage in southern Europe, Evora's temple was brushed off and finally given its due as an important monument. Today, its Corinthian columns shimmer in the summer heat, making a strange and stunning backdrop for the religious processions that wind past it on holy days.

The temple builders are long gone. But, in the region around Evora, the need for Diana's graces is still as strong as ever. The arid plain, baked hard by an oven-like summer sun, still echoes with the stamp and clatter of hooves. Bulls and horses are raised here, an economic staple to offset the valiant attempts at agriculture that nevertheless leave so many people in this region hungry and jobless.

Diana, put in a good word for them, won't you?

Getting there: Always open and visible. Admission free. Evora is in the Alentejo region of central Portugal, 90 miles east of Lisbon, from which there are frequent trains. The temple is in the center of town, on the Praca do Giraldo, just north of the cathedral and the Museu de Evora.

Fatima

Pilgrimage Site

Perhaps she was looking for the beach, like every other savvy tourist in Portugal. Perhaps she made a wrong turn. And finding herself just a bit too far inland, and maybe liking it anyway, she simply changed her plans.

All we know is that on May 13, 1917, three shepherd children were tending their flocks in an open field at Cova da Iria, near Fatima. Suddenly they saw the sky blaze with light, and the youngsters' startled eyes came to rest on a young woman who had appeared out of nowhere and was now standing, of all places, in the branches of a nearby oak tree. They recognized her as the Virgin Mary. Thus was born one of the world's most popular Marian shrines, where in recent times 1 million visitors have been known to gather in a single day.

Rather than ask the children for directions to Estoril or Nazaré, the stranger asked them to pray for world peace. She returned a month later, again on the thirteenth, and then she came back the next month, and the next, and the next. Always she appeared in the tree, and always her doleful message was the same.

More and more believers gathered at Cova da Iria as the months passed, although none but the children could see or hear the visitor. She must have sympathized with their frustrating plight, for on October 13, which proved to be her final visit, she pulled off a feat that came to be known as "the Miracle of the Sun." Precisely at noon, 70,000 pilgrims watched as the rain ceased abruptly, like a faucet shutting off. Then the sun began to revolve crazily in the sky, twirling and sparkling like a giant mirror-studded disco ball. Finally, the enraptured crowd gasped as the orb blazed earthward.

This story, and other tales of Cova da Iria's sacredness, spread far and wide. Pilgrims promptly erected a crude wooden archway over the site and then replaced it with a cozy chapel, which fell victim to a mysterious dynamite blast in 1922. Six years later, a grand new basilica was underway. The cult of Our Lady of Fatima had not yet received official church approval, and two of the little shepherds, Francisco and Jacinta Marto, were already dead, victims of a massive influenza epidemic.

Shepherds, innocent children, and oak trees are features that recur with astounding frequency in stories of Virgin Mary apparitions and hidden Mary statue discoveries. It is nearly always a young herder who sees Mary first. Sometimes it is even the animals themselves. Mary shares her predilection for oaks with the Celtic Druids, who worshipped the oak above all other trees. The classical Greeks believed oaks to be inhabited by special spirits called dryads. And the Roman goddess Diana, she of the sacred grove, was associated with oaks.

Today's Fatima, with its armies of tiny plastic shepherds, its maudlin wax museum, and its teeming plaza, is a far cry from the pasture in which the children first saw the Virgin in 1917. The basilica's crown jewel is exactly that: a 7-ton bronze crown supporting a huge crystal cross. You can't help but wonder whether Mary really likes it like this. After all, didn't she choose Portugal for its pastoral, quiet self? Or did she choose it precisely because she saw its great potential for development?

Getting there: Always open. Admission free. Fatima is 75 miles north of Lisbon and 15 miles west of Tomar. Buses run frequently to Fatima. The basilica dominates the town. The Chapel of the Apparitions and the replacement of the oak tree in which the apparitions occurred are on the side of the plaza in front of the basilica.

Spain

Spain is as dainty as a lace *mantilla*, as brashly erotic as black satin matador pants, as elusive and haunting as saffron, and as poignantly mysterious as all three.

And so was Tanit, the goddess who came to Spain in the sleek ships of the Phoenicians and then stayed on. Her sanctuaries, in Ibiza's Es Cuieram cave and elsewhere in Spain, reveal a people in awe of her dark beauty, her moon power, her sea power, her sex power. Again and again they sculpted images of her jeweled bust.

Phoenicians colonized Iberia from the eighth century B.C.E. onward. Their eastern style, savvy, and spirituality were an incalculable gift to the native tribes, whose indigenous ancestors were among Europe's first artists, adorning cave walls some 30,000 years ago. Along with

Tanit, the Iberians worshipped a complicated pantheon. To full-scale temples as well as barely marked nature shrines, they brought their gifts of bread, pots of oil, and thousands upon thousands of tiny metal figurines.

Into this Iberian Eden came the Romans, whose conquest in 200 B.C.E. is still remembered as *la Baja Epoca*, "the low time." Later, the Moslems and finally the Christians made Spain their own. Now those jeweled busts sulk in museums; the people bring gifts to churches. But Tanit's moon still shimmers on Tanit's sea, and behind every bit of passion that erupts in still-romantic Spain, Tanit smiles a randy smile.

Montserrat

Black Madonna Pilgrimage Site

One look at the fleshlike folds of Montserrat, the "serrated mountain," tells you this place could not fail, once glimpsed, to inspire hermits and holy ramblers. And one look at Our Lady of Montserrat tells you that she *must* live here and nowhere else. Mountain and madonna deserve each other. Dark and hard, they are kin. Inseparable, they are the spiritual jewel of Catalonia, a lodestone in whose honor hundreds of churches have been founded, both in the Old World and the New.

Our Lady of Montserrat, adored all over Spain but also as far away as Chile and Peru, not to mention Italy, is represented by a wooden statue with a black face. Darker even than the mountain itself, she must be the color of the mountain's heart.

According to legend, she was not born here but was brought here, by no less a personage than St. Peter. His colleague, St. Luke, carved the statue in Palestine during Mary's lifetime, the legend goes. Peter carried it to Europe 50 years after the crucifixion and left it among the crags on Montserrat, where it stayed for several centuries. During this time, another legend has it, the knight Parsifal found the Holy Grail on this very mountain.

During the eighth century, Christians hid the statue—again, among the crags—to safeguard it from invading Moslems. Once the danger was past, however, no one could find the statue, so for yet another century it languished amid the elements.

In 880 the statue was found, or let itself be found, in a cave partway up Montserrat. Bedazzled animals led their keepers to the cave; the air filled with strange music. The statue, grasped by a bishop, refused to budge, so a shrine was erected on that very spot. Other miracles followed, and Our Lady of Montserrat developed a reputation.

Today a replica of the original statue dwells in the bedecked Santa Cova ("holy cave"), where it enjoys colorful popular devotion. The original, which bears a much stronger resemblance to twelfth-century Romanesque art than to first-century Palestinian art, now lives indoors in the hilltop basilica. In a shadowy chamber it sits, enthroned, behind a plexiglass shield. One slender hand, cupping a wooden globe, emerges from the shield to be stroked, even kissed, by the pilgrims who file past in a constant, conveyor belt-like queue: They are unable to back up, turn around, or linger more than a split second before the Santa Imagen ("sacred image") that they have come so far to see.

They rode on a harrowing, shuddering aerial cable car to reach this place, rising like angels past the beetling cliffs and crags. The air is thin, mountain-narcotic. Fleetingly the pilgrims can meet Our Lady's eyes and bask in the half-smile that plays across her black lips. Some say she is dark because Mary, a Semite, was dark, and Luke carved her from life, as the legend says. Others attribute her color to candlesmoke. Still others, including many Catalonian historians, maintain that statues of Isis, in which the goddess suckles the infant Horus, were brought to Catalonia by Egyptian sailors during the Roman era. These figurines circulated throughout the region and were eagerly adopted by rural people who had long worshipped dark, earthy mother goddesses of their own. Enthroned, the mountain mother smiles. Kiss her quick.

Getting there: Open daily, 9 A.M. to 10:30 A.M., noon to 1:30 P.M., and 3 P.M. to 6:30 P.M. (These hours refer to the times the statue is open to the public.) Admission free. Montserrat is 25 miles northwest of Barcelona. There are trains from Barcelona to a station at the foot

Rock formations, Montserrat

of the mountain from which there is an aerial tramway to the monastery. The basilica housing the black madonna is a 5-minute walk from where the tramway lets you off. Enter the basilica through the right-hand door; signs point the way to the stairs that lead to the statue. The funicular to Santa Cova leaves from the plaza in front of the monastery. It is also possible to walk to Santa Cova along the signposted pathway. Make sure you don't miss the last tram back to the station (usually at 6:45 P.M.).

Women's Day Festivals

Look into the eyes of a flamenco dancer, if you dare. Look into the face of the black-clad crone who sells tomatoes in the marketplace from dawn to dusk. In a continent blessed with kind Irish women, sensual

French women, and unbreakable Polish women, the Spanish woman is markedly, gorgeously proud. Refusing to simper, refusing to bow, she flaunts the mixed blood that makes hers a striking silhouette against the stark and hungry Spanish landscape. She refuses to relinquish her morsel of inherited power. She lives in one of the most sexist countries in Europe. She can see that behind every Ferdinand is, for better or for worse, an Isabella. Behind every macho man is a mama, a madonna.

In certain Spanish villages, every year on February 5 the social order topples, and for that brief day, women rule—and men run scared.

The women, taking their power, do not slay bulls or swig red wine. Instead, they dress up like fine ladies and make up laws.

February 5 is the feast day of St. Agatha. The festival is supposed to honor her. Agatha, a Sicilian virgin martyr, has been linked with various goddesses, and in fact she could often be found pinch-hitting for them when the early church, with its flair for presto-chango tricks, decided to "rededicate" those few goddess temples that it had not destroyed. As a virgin, and a noble virgin at that, Agatha calls to mind the classical virgin goddesses. But there's more. Before killing her, Agatha's torturers tore off her breasts. Forever afterward, she has been depicted in Christian artworks carrying the severed glands on a platter. Their shape suggested bells and loaves of bread, so Agatha eventually became the patron saint of bakers and bell makers as well, of course, as nursing mothers. The image of a woman carrying her own breasts has an irresistible power that strikes deep. Breasts held aloft, Agatha thrust her foot in the door left open by departing goddesses.

No one can trace the actual origins of Spain's Women's Day festivals. But they are clearly remnants of a time when a goddess, not a martyr, held this land in thrall, a time when women, in the goddess's image, enjoyed a higher status. Like any rite of sisterhood, it brings to mind gatherings of priestesses.

Each participating village has its own slant on the festival. In Escatron, 40 miles southeast of Zaragoza, the women carry bread in a "sacred loaves" procession and then take over the town. In Miranda del Castañar, 45 miles southwest of Salamanca, the churchwardens' wives act as mayoresses for a day. In Sotosalbos, 12 miles northeast of Segovia, one woman is elected mayoress and is aided throughout the day by a team of female counselors. The village women also participate in a program of female-only events. In Zamarramala, 4 miles northwest of Segovia, all men are confined to their homes, where they are required to perform more or less unfamiliar tasks such as changing diapers and dishwashing. Lest they venture out of doors, the men face chastisement by the women, who are led in majesty by a pair of matrons whose traditional red and black costumes are heavy with silver ornaments.

Our Lady in Captivity: Museum

Barcelona: Museum of Catalonian Art Independent, separatist Catalonia is home to a remarkable concentration of dark madonnas. Black-faced Our Lady of Montserrat is the queen of them all; her unfamous dusky sisters—echoes, it is said, of ancient goddesses—are venerated in crags, caves, and other remote sites all over the region.

The Museum of Catalonian Art houses what is said to be the world's largest collection of black madonna statues. Yanked from the aeries where they once held sway, they now line the glass cases, shoulder to shoulder, in good and noble company but still looking puzzled, if not actually disgruntled, to find themselves here instead of in church. Having them right here behind glass, well lighted, lets you examine close up and at your leisure their carved wooden faces, the velvety reds and yellows of their painted gowns, and other details you might never notice otherwise.

Getting there: Open Tuesday through Sunday, 9 A.M. to 2 P.M. Admission: 400 ptas; students free. The museum is in the Palau Nacional, on Montjuic, west of the center of town. Take the Metro to the Espanya stop and walk south up Av. Reina M. Cristina; climb the stairs to the palace. The museum is right through the front doors. Most of the madonnas are in rooms 13, 19, 20, and 22.

Switzerland

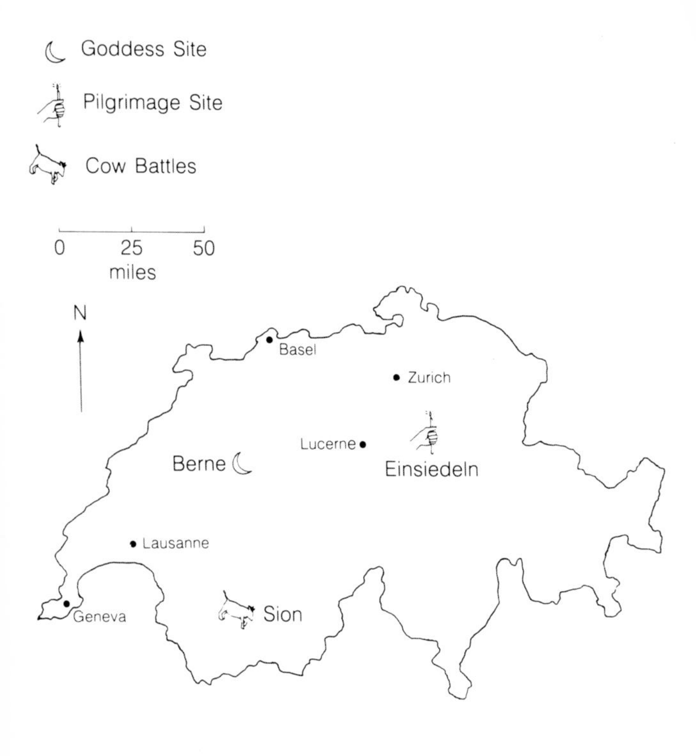

Despite its sworn neutrality and strict noninvolvement policies, Switzerland goes down in history as the epicenter, or at least the namesake, of a movement that shook Europe from top to bottom, from east to west. Named for a rich archaeological find in Switzerland, La Tène became the name for an entire phase of Celtic culture that spanned the final four centuries B.C.E. and beyond and that thrived all over Gaul, the Rhineland, Britain, and even Scandinavia. La Tène art, still hailed as one of the wonders of ancient Europe, depicts a magical world of goggle-eyed, shape-shifting beasts, humans and deities, sinuous plants, hypnotic spirals, and triple-horned whorls.

There is evidence that prehistoric Swiss worshipped goddesses, long before La Tène. Now, although Christianity—Calvinism, yet—has come to stay, Switzerland still revels in the customs, celebrations, and pagan joys of a rural, half-wild land. And rightly so. The Matterhorn will not crawl away disheartened just because times are changing. Lake Geneva will not vanish underground. Swiss winters are still as fierce and lovely as the goddesses who once rode these bitter winds. So the twentieth-century Swiss show no signs that they will ever stop burning Winter in effigy and crowning big black cows Queen of the Mountains.

Berne

Berne's Bear Goddess

Many cities adopt animals as mascots. The custom, a form of totemism, stems from an irresistible attraction to wild things, and the beast appears in the cities' coats of arms, local legends, lore, and festivals.

Few cities cleave to their animal mascots as loyally as does Berne to its chosen beast, the bear. The very name of the city means "bear," but it goes far beyond that. For centuries, bruins have been depicted on Bernese coins, flags, and shop signs. And bears still romp through the city's real and imaginary landscapes. (In fact, one of the funniest travel posters ever produced depicts a crowd of people dressed in shabby bear suits, lumbering around one of Berne's many fountains.)

Bears are everywhere in Berne. Celtic tribes who lived in this region several thousand years ago worshipped a lovely goddess called Artio, who had as her constant companion that powerhouse of the forest, that creature both fierce and familial, the bear. Little is known of Artio, as the people who worshipped her left neither written descriptions nor temples. Like most Celtic deities, she was undoubtedly of a highly localized nature, her powers and her worship specific to this small region. A single statuette has been found near Berne, which shows the goddess seated beside a bear. Her pose reflects the blissful relaxation of true friendship.

But no one speaks of Artio today. Even in Berne, with its phalanxes of bears depicted everywhere, the goddess is unknown, unremembered. It is a different story they

Statuette of Artio, the bear goddess, found near Berne

tell today to explain the city's kinship with bruins: a brutal and strangely masculine story. It is said that a certain Duke Berchtold V, a local nobleman, was given the task of naming the city. Berchtold set out on a hunt, vowing that he would name the town after the first animal that he killed. That unlucky first animal turned out to be a bear. The city was duly named Berne, and the Bernese have since taken the kinship to heart. (We are probably not the first to come along and wonder what would have happened if that bear had killed Berchtold.)

Today, bears still appear in local companies' trademarks. Several of the city's famous fountains depict bears. Bears dance, albeit clumsily, with cherubs in the metalwork of the cathedral bell. An army of mechanical bears marches across the city's clocktower (*Zytglugge*), as adorable as only toy bears can be, despite the fact that they carry weapons slung over their hairy shoulders.

Most interestingly of all, Berne is possibly the only city in the world that maintains its own bear pit. Families of bears are raised and kept in the sunken pit near the Nydeggbrucke, following a tradition that officially goes back as far as the eighteenth century and is probably much older on an unofficial level. The live bears, who will consent to perform tricks for spectators (granted, in a rather desultory fashion), constitute Berne's leading tourist attraction, especially in the springtime when the young are born. Berne's bears are fed a wholly vegetarian diet: carrots and figs and such, which seems a bizarre footnote to a tale that begins (or so they say) with a bloody *hunt.*

Are Berne's bears here as mere symbols of Duke Berchtold's ramble in the woods? Or are they here because of some older tradition, lost in the mists of time, of keeping live bears in Artio's honor? We do not know. Perhaps the bears know.

Getting there: All the sites mentioned here are always visible and free to visit. The bear pits are just east of the old town, next to where the Nydeggbrucke bridge crosses the Aare river and intersects Grosser Muristalden. The various fountains that depict bears, and the clocktower, are all on Berne's main street, which changes names every block, running down the center of the old town. The Musketeer Fountain is on Marktgasse; the Ogre Fountain is on Kornhausplatz where Marktgasse ends. The Zahringen Fountain is on Kramgasse, and the clocktower is at the intersection where Marktgasse becomes Kramgasse.

Einsiedeln

The Black Madonna of Einsiedeln

All that is neat and orderly reaches sublime heights in Switzerland. You really *can* set your watch by the Swiss national train system; Swiss landscapes look like retouched photographs; the meadows look manicured; the cows seem made of china. And yet of all the central European countries, Switzerland is in many ways the wildest and most natural. Nature roars and raves well beyond the control of any order-bent hand. Switzerland is the place whose mountains can and do devour climbers for breakfast.

The madonna that has been loved above all others in Switzerland for centuries has a face as black as a forest by night. She receives half a million visitors a year, and many healings and other wonders have been attributed to her. Our Lady of Einsiedeln personifies the unruly realm of boar and bear and bramble, which every Swiss person knows is the country's true heritage, multinational banks notwithstanding. An official church brochure recounts that every Swiss Catholic's most vivid childhood memory is of his or her first visit to Einsiedeln where, standing before the black marble altar, they "held their mother's hand, gazing up half in fear, half in love, at the other, greater mother."

She lives in a church. Her face peers out from a cumbersome swath of stiff brocade, walled in on all sides from wilderness and the brisk mountain air. Yet the legend of how her shrine came to be here is a story in which the forces of nature triumph over evil.

St. Meinrad, a Swabian priest, retired to this densely wooded spot in 835. He set up his hermitage just beside a fountain that, according to folklore, had once provided refreshment to Jesus himself during his supposed travels through Europe. According to historians, the spring was probably already a sacred site for the Germanic tribes who lived here in pre-Christian times. Meinrad gave his fellow humans a wide berth, but he enjoyed the company of his two pet ravens, who actually brought him his meals every day. All went well until January 21, 861, when a pair of robbers sneaked up on the hermit and clubbed him to death. But justice would be served. The ravens followed the fleeing murderers all the way to Zurich, a distance of 30 miles, where they cawed loudly over the killers' heads until local lawmen questioned and then arrested the men. Meinrad's head, preserved, was thereafter exhibited on holidays in the monastic abbey that was erected on the site of his hermitage some 70 years after his murder. The head still resides at the Einsiedeln abbey, but now it rests under the feet of the black madonna, whose own legends and popularity and supposed miracles have far surpassed those of the martyr.

The statue, 4 feet tall, was carved in 1466. Local tradition has it that the statue went into foreign exile from 1798 to 1803, during which time its face was darkened by excessive candlesmoke "and has been black ever since." But the madonna's calm, sober face with its precise features and sharp chin seems too uniformly black to have become that way by accident.

Ever since the Middle Ages, mass pilgrimages have enhanced and increased the statue's fame. Handmade ex-votos (including paintings and charming embroideries) attest to the healings attributed to prayers at this shrine. On any given day, the racks provided for votive candles will be blazingly full, as dozens of tiny flames, leaping behind red and gold glass, are a vibrant counterpoint to the black stillness of the face they celebrate.

So regally erect and steady, the statue makes you want to approach in solitude and ask all those questions you've been saving up. Our Lady of Einsiedeln, separated by thick church walls from the woods and from the fountain in whose low murmurings the ancient people divined the words of an "other, greater mother" of their own, is herself a window into all that is dark and wild in Switzerland and beyond.

Getting there: Open daily, 6:00 A.M. to 7:00 P.M. Admission free. Einsiedeln is 22 miles southeast of Zurich. The black madonna is in the so-called Lady Chapel in the center of the monastery that dominates the north side of Einsiedeln, facing the Klosterplatz. The fountain is directly in front of the monastery.

Sion

Cow Battles

Wander around any self-respecting souvenir shop in Switzerland. What do you see? Watches, army knives, and . . . cowbells. Ranging all the way from walnut-sized to football-sized, often painted with bright wildflower designs, the bells are as rough and homely as the watches and knives are sleek and practical. They represent a pastoral, ancient way of life that is still very much alive in Switzerland. In dozens of villages, many of them high and remote, the old ways persist, uninterrupted, and the dissonant murmur of cowbells rings across hills and valleys, keeping farmers ever alert to their herds' rocinations.

The meaning of cowbells, the reason for their popularity as eternal symbols of Switzerland, goes deeper than that. In a country so perfectly suited to dairy farming, where milk and cheese are a delight as well as a livelihood, it's no wonder that cows are afforded such heavy symbolism. The cow is the warm, generous mother of Switzerland, her countless generations pouring forth that livelihood and that delight.

In the Alpine region that is called Valais by the French-speaking Swiss and Wallis by the German-speaking ones, a curious annual ritual is enacted: cow battles. It is one of the most striking in a yearly calendar of festivals that reveal Switzerland as a land still in awe of the changing seasons.

In macho Spain, men spar with bulls. But as spring arrives in gentle, dairy-rich Valais, thousands gather to watch as milk cows fight each other, hurling their massive bodies into earth-pounding, head-butting, horn-locking, udder-shuddering battle. After a series of tournaments, a winner emerges. Her horns are garlanded with flowers, and she is proclaimed Queen of the Mountains. A special breed takes part in this ritual: the satiny-black Herens (also known as Erringer) is especially strong and large, with short legs and stout horns, and is well suited to both dairy production and fighting. Ten thousand of them live and work in Valais. It is said that competitive battling is a natural hierarchical instinct among this breed, who use this method to determine which among them is most fit to lead the herds up to the summer grazing lands, high in the mountains. Even in the wild, we are assured, they would fly at each other. Nevertheless, their human keepers have turned this into a spectator sport, arranging "battles" in villages all over the region. As the torn grass flies, so do the bets.

In cultures as far afield as Egypt, Greece, India, and Scandinavia, cows have been identified with goddesses, perhaps more so than any other animal. Among Hera's nicknames was "the cow-eyed one"; Isis's graceful cow horns are as noble as any crown. Milk is the elixir of life; those who give it give life and are powerful. So in Switzerland, which more than most nations owes great homage to the cow, the awe and the worship continue, albeit in a form which some might disdain. The bestial, instinct-born violence, the flower garlands, the crowning of a queen among cows, all hint at ancient pagan rituals of yore.

Getting there: Cow battles take place every year in April and early May and September and early October. Admission prices vary. The organized battles take place in various towns throughout Valais canton. The exact locations change from year to year, but they are generally held in certain towns around the cities of Sion and Martigny, including Aproz, Chippis, Sembrancher, Veysonnaz, and Verbier.

Yugoslavia

YUGOSLAVIA

If you could just see every ancient goddess image, every priestess statue and woman statue that has ever been unearthed in Yugoslavia, all arranged neatly, side by side, we guarantee you'd fall instantly to your knees, weep tears of reverence, and then storm the UN demanding that Yugoslavia be made Queen of Nations.

Surely this country, with its great goddess heritage, deserves the honor. Archaeological paradises like Lepenski Vir, along the Danube, with its goddess-centered water shrines, and Vinca in Serbia, which gave its name to an entire fifth-millennium culture, yielded a wealth of female-oriented artifacts. There were many other such settlements as well, and many statues.

The Greeks settled here, the Romans, the Slavs, and other peoples as well. Each group brought its own deities and forms of worship, all the while snuggling into the comfortable embrace of those older goddesses who knew no other home but this one. Even modern Christianity takes on surprising twists in Yugoslavia. What of the shining lady who rode in on a cloud in 1981, speaking fluent Serbo-Croatian, wringing her hands over the future of the world? Who, pray tell, is she?

Medjugorje

Contemporary Apparition Site

Visions of the Virgin Mary, with all their references to a radiant white-gowned woman, perched in earnest in a tree or on a hill, seem so naive, so cunningly low-tech and nature-oriented as to be the stuff of medieval legend. And yet the most famous madonna visions of all, those of Fatima and Lourdes, were startlingly recent events. Perhaps it is, after all, a phenomenon ideally suited to these high-tension modern times: The Virgin, or whoever she is, usually implores her visionaries to pray for world peace and international understanding. Often she vouchsafes secret messages about upcoming international affairs. Whoever she is, she is clearly resorting to desperate measures.

On June 24, 1981, when other young people were discovering spandex and Michael Jackson and refusing to register for the draft, six Yugoslavian youngsters began a long series of tête-à-têtes with the Virgin Mary. Two of the youngsters were walking casually across a field when they spotted her. The Virgin, floating on a cloud, beckoned to them. "Look, Mirjana!" one girl blurted. "There's Our Lady!" Then, as teenagers anywhere might do, they went and got their friends.

When they returned, the Virgin had moved from her cloud to a hillside. Black-haired, blue-eyed, and ruddy-cheeked, like a peasant woman from their own village, the visitor spoke tenderly to them in flawless Serbo-Croatian. (Bernadette Soubirous's Virgin, in Lourdes, fluently spoke the obscure Pyrenees dialect.) Devout, but modern enough to be inquisitive, one of them demanded to know why she had chosen them. Because you are ordinary, she replied. "I never choose the best."

She told them she was the Virgin Mary. She had secrets to share about the future of the world. She cried bitter tears for "unbelievers," and warned that these visits, the ones here at Medjugorje, would be her last appearances "in this era."

She has appeared to the youngsters every night since then. There have been some changes. She has moved from the hillside to a small room in the village church. (The village priest was hounded by the government and eventually imprisoned for his support of the young visionaries, whose adventure met with initial hostility from authorities.) She no longer appears to all of the original six; only two. Every night, crowds gather to watch as Maria and Jakov, no longer teenagers, kneel before the altar of the Virgin, eyes alight. Over the years, the pair has been subjected to countless scientific tests, all of which conclude that, yes, theirs is a genuine state of ecstasy. After each session, the pair report on the Virgin's message for that evening, which usually include such admonitions as "Pray with your whole heart" and "Make your life a good life."

Outside, pilgrims wander on the hill where she appeared that first day. The hill is now studded with crosses. Tour buses roar in over the mountains, swelling and overwhelming this once-remote hamlet. Over 9 million visitors have come to Medjugorje by this time, and hundreds of books have been written on the phenomenon. People talk of miraculous healings. Vicka, one of the original six visionaries, was recently cured of a brain tumor.

The government has finally decided to cease its persecutions of Medjugorje. The tourist revenues are enormous. No one knows how much longer the Virgin will keep appearing here. Any day could be her last.

In Marian circles, in all circles that welcome visits from mysterious, miraculous ladies, this is one red-hot topic.

Getting there: Always open and visible. Admission free. Medjugorje is 15 miles southwest of Mostar, in the region of Bosnia and Hercegovina. From Mostar, go southwest 11 miles to the city of Citluk; from there, take the narrow road 4 miles south to Medjugorje.

Suggested Reading

Ashe, Geoffrey

The Virgin. London: Routledge and Paul, 1976

Begg, Ean

The Cult of the Black Virgin. London: Arkana, 1985

Bolen, Jean Shinoda

Goddesses in Everywoman. New York: Harper & Row, 1984

Bryher, Winifred

The Gate to the Sea. New York: Pantheon, 1958

Geldard, Richard G.

The Traveler's Key to Ancient Greece. New York: Alfred A. Knopf, 1989

Gimbutas, Marija

The Goddesses and Gods of Old Europe. London: Thames and Hudson, 1982

Gimbutas, Marija

The Language of the Goddess. San Francisco: Harper & Row, 1989

Harding, M.E.

Woman's Mysteries. New York: Putnam, 1971

Monaghan, Patricia

The Book of Goddesses and Heroines. New York: E.P. Dutton, 1981

Sandars, N.K.

Prehistoric Art in Europe. New York: Penguin, 1985

Stone, Merlin

When God Was a Woman. New York: Dial, 1976

Walker, Barbara G.
The Woman's Dictionary of Symbols & Sacred Objects. San Francisco: Harper & Row, 1988

Witt, Reginald E.
Isis in the Graeco-Roman World. Ithaca: Cornell University Press, 1971

Index of Goddesses

Page numbers in **boldface** *indicate sacred sites dedicated to that particular goddess.*

Index of Places

Names and page numbers in **boldface** *indicate in-depth entries.*

General Index